Raymond B. Maurstad

SOS

KOREA
1950
Illustrated

They Were There Then...
& Write About It Now.
Eyewitness Accounts of
Americans in South Korea
when the North Attacked

Beaver's Pond Press, Inc.
Edina　Minnesota

SOS KOREA 1950 © copyright 2003 by Raymond B. Maurstad.
All rights reserved.

ISBN 1-931646-91-0

Library of Congress Catalog Number: 2002115486

Printed in the United States of America

First Printing: November 2002

06 05 04 03 02   6 5 4 3 2 1

Beaver's Pond Press, Inc.

7104 Ohms Lane Suite 216
Edina, MN 55439-1465
(952) 829-8818
www.beaverspondpress.com

So many years…
Too many tears.

This book is dedicated to the many thousands
who sacrificed their lives so that others
may live in freedom.

Contents

Contents

Epilogue 293

List of Illustrations

Insert

Foreword

Americans living in South Korea when North Korea invaded have maintained a relative silence for more than fifty years. Several of them have collaborated with the author to tell interesting, humorous and frequently exciting stories about their lives in the poverty-stricken land just before and after June 25, 1950, including encounters with a culture that was strange and new to them.

Acknowledgments

My daughter Deborah for assisting in computer development of this book. The following contributors for their patience and understanding while I made seemingly unreasonable demands. I would not have undertaken this writing without their input.

David De La Cruz

James DeWan

Mary Logan Greenwood

Joe & Dorothy Kelly

Tom King

Professor Deok-Su Lee

Desmond and Ethyl Mann

Maryknoll Sisters

Milton Nottingham Jr.

Professor Jin-Soo Park

Mary Roth

Robert Rudolph

Bob Simmons

Robert and Ruth Slaven

Frank and Josselyn Winslow

Tom Ziglinski

Author Larry Zellers for his advice and encouragement.

Andrew Gosling, Chief Librarian at the National Library of Australia for his assistance on Korean history.

Alex Grundhoffer for his early encouragement and assistance when this book was only a thought.

Finally, my wife Marion, who kept everything else going.

Introduction

By Lt. Francis J. Winslow

The 1950 to 1953 war in Korea is well documented but not so the history of U.S. actions in Korea during the preceding five years. The period begins with the surrender of Japan on 14 August 1945 and ends with the return in July 1950 of U.S. Forces to assist the Republic of (south) Korea in repelling the attack by the communist Democratic People's Republic of (north) Korea.

Inadequately covered are the U.S. and Soviet armies occupying the former colonies of Japan that for the U.S. began on 8 September 1945 with the arrival of US troops at Inchon and for the Soviets that began 28 days earlier on 10 August 1945 with the Soviet Army's arrival in Japan's former colony in Manchuria (Manchukuo) and in northern Korea (Chosen).

General MacArthur's Far East Command relinquished all responsibility for Korea on 30 June 1949, except for the responsibility to evacuate Americans, if the need should arise, and it did. What we want to record in this modest book is some of the accomplishments of the U.S. Department of State and our experiences during the period 1 July 1949 to 27 June 1950. The period ended for most Department of State people when General MacArthur's Far East Command once again took charge of U.S. interests in Korea, only this time to fight a war.

This record is focused primarily upon the year immediately prior to the war by a very few people who were in Korea as U.S. advisors, civilian and military, to elements of Republic of Korea government. Some 12 of us who were then age 20 to 30 are contributors to this effort to share experiences—while we are still able. In the intervening 52 or more years, those older than 30 have since died or are unable to contribute.

Contributors to this book had neither the inclination nor resources to research records of the U.S. Department of State and Department of Defense agencies or Republic of Korea sources to fill voids in published accounts, should such data exist for the prewar period. They choose instead to rely upon their own memories and sources. The task to fill the any voids is left to professional historical researchers. One such professional, Stanley Sandler has in his 1999 book *The Korean War: No Victors, No Vanquished* compiled what is probably the most extensive bibliography on Korea. This contributor regrets not having the time to review many of Sandler's references. Most valuable to my contribution is the well documented *Military Advisors in Korea: KMAG in Peace and War* 1962 by Major Robert K. Sawyer of Department of Army's Office of Chief of Military History. It focuses on the period between September 1945 to June 1950 and filled in many voids in my memory of over two years with KMAG, or I should say, the United States Military Advisory Group to the Republic of Korea. A mouthful; hence the short title KMAG. There never existed a Korean Military Advisory Group, contrary to what many authors say.

Prologue

By Francis J. "Frank" Winslow

(In 1949 a 23 year old Army Signal Corps Lieutenant) Beginning History of Korea to Liberation Day in 1945

Much of this data came from General Hodge's comprehensive 220-page book published by the Troop Information and Education Section of his XXIV Corps headquarters, undated but probably published May 1947. I have seen no reference to Hodge's book in any of the bibliography's texts. It presents an excellent source of data on the history of Korea and of the first 18 months of military government. Hodge's book was "issued" to me upon arrival in Korea in early October 1948. The unit to which I was assigned, the 123rd Signal Service Detachment was credited with the book's photography. Another source that supplemented my spotty personal recollection of my two years with KMAG was Sawyer's well-documented Military Advisors in Korea.

Koreans marked the passage of time (at least in 1946) in two systems: one in Gregorian years and one in Korean years. Koreans began their count of years in the year 2333 BC. Thus, 2002 AD is the Korean year 4335. The dual system of accounting for time was manifested by four yellowing sheets of very coarse paper in the files of my wife's mother, Dorothy Bennett. They were pages from a 1946 Korean wall calendar. Written on the reverse blank sides was an essay in English on the poet Wordsworth by one of her young Korean students in 1949. This academic exercise generated three thoughts: Korea has a view of history in which Christ's birth year has no significance in counting years; writing paper was a scarce item in Korea; and young Koreans valued a classical education in English literature.

Liberation Day for Koreans is the day when the hated Empire of Japan ceased its forty-year rule of Korea by Japan's defeat in World War II. The long awaited Day of Liberation meant realization of self-determination free of subjugation and exploitation by foreign nations. For Koreans liberation meant freedom and opportunity to build their first truly sovereign and democratic state.

Over the centuries Korea, as a genetically distinct people occupying their peninsula has benefited by having a single unifying culture and by having invented 600 years ago a Korean alphabet (Hangul). It has borders defined by the Yellow Sea on the west, the Sea of Japan on the east, and the Straits of Korea and Tsushima on the south. Its northern border is defined by the Yalu and Tumen rivers across which lies Manchuria (China). In the far northeast corner, Korea shares about 18 miles of border with the Russian Far East. The map of Korea in use in 1949-1951 omits the northeastern portion of Korea above 42 degrees North latitude, probably because of unreliable map data, or perhaps by the thought that no American map user would ever want to know what existed north of 42 degrees. The 1966 issue of this map extending coverage to 43 degrees probably reflects expanded geopolitical interests and use of mapping photography by USAF RB-17s based at Clark Air Base in the Philippines.

The mythical and mysterious father of Korea, Tangoon, in the twenty-fourth century BC founded the first civilization of primitive tribes of northern Korea and Manchuria with his capital near Pyongyang. He named his country Chosen, "Land of the Morning Freshness." In 1122 BC, a Chinese refugee, Kija, with 5000 followers, brought much of Chinese civilization with him to Korea. His dynasty lasted for almost a thousand years. The Kingdom of Chosen extended north of the Han River and Seoul to Mukden in Manchuria. Deserters from the Great Wall of China construction work in 225 BC fled to the area south of the Han River to join with other tribes, the Chinhan, who later became known as the Silla.

The Palhae - Unified Silla or Shilla Dynasty with its capital at Kyongju (57 BC to 935 AD)[The Shilla is a fine hotel in today's Seoul] also known as the North—South Kingdoms, marks the end of Korea's Ancient History. The Koryo Dynasty (935-1392 AD) had its capital at Kaesong northwest of Seoul on the 38th parallel, the site of the first truce talk in 1951.

The weakness and antiquity of the Chosen Dynasty, better known as the Yi Dynasty, with its capitol in Seoul, (1392-1910) made the Korean peninsula at the beginning of the 20th century ripe for the taking, e.g., as a protectorate, colony or annexation. The Japanese in 1910 named its new Korean colony *Chosen* after the *Chosen Dynasty*. Korea was dubbed the Hermit Kingdom because it was closed to the world trade until 1876. Another popular and descriptive name for Korea is the *Land of the Morning Calm.*

In the colonial period of world powers, China, Russia and Japan vied with one another for control of Korea. China and Korea had a long and mutually beneficial association and shared Confucianism, a code of morals which has shaped Korean life for over 500 years. It is not a religion in the sense of worship of a divine power. Under Confucian doctrine, China acted as the older brother to the younger brother, Korea. International news in Korean newspapers was written in Chinese. Japan broke China's close association with Korea by a nine-month war (1894-5). When Russia challenged Japan for control of Korea, a weakened China deferred to the winner of the Russo-Japanese War (1904-5). This war, fought in Manchuria, the Yellow Sea and in the Straits of Tsushima, earned for Japan the respect of western colonial powers. The first major naval battle of the 20th Century occurred in these straits in May 1905 (Pleshakov-Bibliography). The Russian warship *Aurora* survived the battle and was, when I walked its decks in 1977, moored near the Hermitage in Leningrad, now once again St. Petersburg. Russia's ignominious defeat by the upstart Japan was a factor in the revolt that ousted the Czar and brought the Soviets to power.

In 1905, Japan prevailed in the Russo Japan war and took control of Korea. Japan held a protectorate over Korea from 1905 to 1910 with support and endorsement of western powers, some of whom were also colonial powers, such as the United States and Great Britain. The Empire of Japan formally annexed Korea in 1910, and appointed a succession of governors general who exercised absolute power.

For the next 35 years, Japan tried to transform Koreans into Japanese. Japan did this by acculturation, destruction of Korean identity, and assimilation into the Japanese mainstream. Shintoism, worship of the Japanese emperor as a direct descendent of the sun-goddess, was mandated by the Japanese upon the Koreans. Christian missionaries in Korea acquiesced to avoid being deported.

Japan suppressed use of the Korean language and required use of Japanese. This practice was evidenced in a 1945 U.S. Army map of

3

Korea which contains Japanese Romanizations for many Korean cities. Particularly onerous was the requirement that family names be converted to Japanese names. Korean children needed a Japanese name to attend school. None of these measures was successful; they only served to deepen the Koreans' animosity toward their oppressors.

Japan developed its new colony's water sources into hydroelectric power in the Yalu River and in Korea's central mountains. A wide variety of minerals was extracted in the north. Japan managed the agricultural south to feed not only its colony but also the Japanese home islands. They built networks of highways, railroads, seaports, a postal system and telephone and telegraph lines to support the colony's development to benefit the empire. Highways were well engineered except in larger cities where they were narrow and unpaved and often lined with shade trees [some of which were felled during the 1950 war to expose targets for USAF aircraft].

The Empire of Japan must be credited for bringing its colony of Chosen into the 20th Century. The well engineered roads; bridges and extensive railroad system served well the US/UN forces during the 1945 to 1953 period. The ubiquitous, standard, well-designed housing built for the Japanese bureaucracy that managed the colony was sought out by American advisors as they moved about with their ROK Army units. The standard design school buildings made desirable headquarters for ROK army units during the fighting. Before the war, it seemed that all buildings of modern construction were Japanese built. The community bathhouses, however, could not survive their misuse by their western customers who arrived in July 1950. These newcomers never got the message that before one got into the community hot tub one had to be well scrubbed and squeaky clean out of consideration of those who came later. The Americans' notion of ever-lasting hot running water came to grief in Korea.

The Japanese, being excellent builders of railroads, concentrated their effort on this form of transportation. A main trunk line, almost completely doubled tracked, extended from Pusan through Seoul to Sinuiju at the mouth of the Yalu River. Another line from Pusan to Seoul ran east of the double track line. At Sinuiju, a traveler could transfer to the Trans-Asiatic Railway to connect in one direction with the

Eastern China Railway or the other way to connect with the Trans-Siberian Railway at Vladivostok to Moscow and thence to Western Europe. Another main line in 1914 crossed the peninsula from Seoul to Wonsan. In 1928, the line was extended up the east coast to connect with a line through Manchuria and Russia to Vladivostok. The first line built by American interests in 1896 ran between Seoul and Inchon. In 1908, Japanese interests built the line between Seoul and Pusan and a branch line from Pusan to Masan. The Taejon to Mokpo line was completed in 1914. Other lines served agricultural and commercial regions of Korea. This infrastructure facilitated Japan's attack on Manchuria in 1931 to create another new Japanese colony (named Manchukuo) formed from five Manchurian provinces. In 1937, Japan used its well-developed land route through Korea and Manchukuo to launch its attack on China and Southeast Asia.

Japan sent promising young Koreans such as Paik Sun Yup, who eventually became a Republic of Korea (ROK) Army Chief of Staff, to the Japanese Military Academy in Mukden (Shen Yang), Manchuria. Japan brought other Korean men into its military forces to include Chae Byong Duk, ROK Army's first Chief of Staff, a former Japanese Army major. The Korean advisor to the US Military Government director of Internal Security had been a colonel in the Japanese army. In the 1920's, the Japanese allowed some Koreans to attend college in the US. The Korean Army deputy Chief Signal officer had a degree unrelated to communications from Indiana University. Several Koreans in supervisory positions of the colonial railroad system (an exception to the Japanese only policy) were sent to acquire civil engineering degrees from Ohio State in the 1930's.

Noteworthy was the Empire of Japan's installation of a buried communications cable running from Mukden (Shen-Yang), Manchuria down the length of Korea and undersea to Kyushu. This reliable communications backbone not only served Japan's expansionist aims but also the aims of those who succeeded the Japanese Empire in governing Korea.

Many prominent Japanese built structures in Seoul have been replaced since the war to erase memories of Japan's brutal forty-year rule. Other reasons may have been for modernization or restoring antiq-

A stream of Protesters in the street at the Banto Hotel & U.S. Embassy. Photo by F. J. Winslow

uity, as in Seoul's Kyong Bok palace grounds where in 1925 Japan built the capitol building (recently razed).

Also gone is the ten-story Banto hotel/office building which in 1949 was the tallest structure in Seoul. The Banto backed on an interior park with stone drums and ancient temple shared by the Chosen Hotel, a majestic old railroad hotel (which is now replaced by a very tall hotel devoid of charm). Senior officials who worked at the Banto resided and dined at the Chosen. They walked to and from work through the most serene and beautiful of oriental settings. Today, the setting remains but no one walks to work through it on the way between buildings. It is accessible only to those who know it still exists, such as photographers who use it as a background for bride and groom photos, and to those determined after 50 years to once again enjoy its beauty. Officers senior enough to be billeted in the Chosen Hotel in 1948, 1949 and 1950 came to refer to their hotel as the "Frozen Chosen" as heat was unreliable and electricity in '48 and '49 went to the street car transportation and other high priority services. "Frozen Chosen" became the soldier's name for wintertime Korea.

Leaders of the Allied Powers met during World War II to coordinate their goals and far-reaching actions. Disposition of Japan's colonies in Korea and Manchuria were discussed. As the USSR was not at war with Japan, Stalin did not participate in conferences concerning the Pacific Theater. At the Cairo and Yalta meetings the conclusion was that "Korea would be free and independent" not immediately or without delay, but "in due course." It would appear that Churchill and Roosevelt, and Truman after the death of Roosevelt on 12 April 1945, were not convinced that Korea, after forty years of Japanese subjugation, would be ready for nationhood for some time. In any discussion of Japan and Korea in 1945 the competition between China, Russia, and Japan just fifty years earlier for control of Korea and Manchuria must have been discussed, particularly that the Russians might expect that they were next in line to "own" Korea. It seems that Roosevelt and Churchill were not listening. The geographic significance of the Korean peninsula had not changed in the forty years that Japan had control of it. Japan used their colonies as an overland route to attack China. If the Korean peninsula came into Soviet hands in 1945, or in 1950, it would pose a direct threat to Japan and to China, just as the Czar had done when he tried to control the peninsula in 1905.

Chiang Kai-shek representing China at the 1943 Cairo conference may have spoken, as Korea's Confucian big brother, on behalf of Korea to his fellow world leaders. Chiang was fighting the Chinese Communists and knew first hand the aggressiveness of international communism. Stalin endorsed the Potsdam agreement when the Soviets declared war on Japan on 8 August 1945; he had promised at Yalta in February 1945 to do so after the war was over in Europe. Japan surrendered on 14 August 1945 having been at war with the Soviets for six days. Koreans who were oppressed by Japan for 40 years were in no mood to wait for independence "in due course." One historian commented that "in due course" could not be translated into the Korean language. Had the leaders of the Allied Powers been more sensitive to USSR's goals, they may have frustrated the USSR's attainment of at least some of their objectives.

Requiring two Armies of Occupation, one for the U.S. zone and one for the Soviet zone to "receive the surrender of the Japanese army", was a formalistic and needless contrivance for a newly liberated Korea. The USSR had not fought the Japanese having been "at war" with them for only six days. But for the US, it was in keeping with misapplied military tradition. An occupation army is appropriate for a defeated enemy country. Korea was not a defeated enemy when the Empire of Japan was defeated and Japan gave up its colonies. Several U.S. Army Military Police and Transportation battalions could have (and perhaps did) move the Japanese colonials and troops back to Japan in short order. The US planners' notion that Japanese could not be cleared from Korea without the help of the Soviet Army and imposing on the peninsula, two separate Armies of Occupation were self-inflicted wounds resulting from a failure to act prudently in dealing with the USSR. What Korea needed in place of two Armies of Occupation was an internal security (police) force and a transitional government to fill the void left by the departed Japanese colonialists. This was the purpose of the Trusteeship proposal blocked by the Soviets and the Korean Nationalist who demanded immediate self-government.

One wonders whether the Allied Powers ever proposed to limit USSR to the surrender and repatriation of the Japanese in Manchukuo, reserving to US and its allies in the Pacific those functions in Korea. It seems unlikely. The surrender of Japanese Armed Forces in Korea and in Manchukuo to the Allied Powers could have been done in a brief ceremony in each colony. The repatriation of Japanese colonials in South Korea was mostly complete by November and was probably even faster in North Korea. Instead of a simple and fast removal of the Japanese from the mainland of Asia, we allowed the Army of Occupation process to be a tool for Soviet maneuverings.

The Soviets readily accepted the U.S. proposal to take responsibility for the area north of the 38th parallel with the U.S. being responsible for the area south of that arbitrary line on the map. Partition of the Korean peninsula into two roughly equal land areas was, superficially, the work of credulous and trusting U.S. decision makers who seemed intent upon devising a temporary expedient to facilitate return of the Japanese military and civilian bureaucracy to Japan. To the Soviets, it was an easy incremental and permanent step towards their goal of extending their communist system not just into North Korea but eventually to the entire Korean peninsula.

Actually, the division of Korea at the 38th parallel was a means by the US to contain the USSR to half of the country. US leadership was facing the reality that it was powerless to keep Stalin from taking over all of Korea and handing control of it to the band of Koreans he had been indoctrinating in Moscow for many years.

The timing of the positioning of Soviet armed forces in the Far East combined with Soviet resoluteness of purpose enabled the USSR to set the parameters for the United States and the South Korea from 8 August 1945 to 27 June 1950.

An example of the foregoing is the indication that US staff officers dealing with the Soviets were under orders to accede to their demands to avoid causing the Soviets from feeling displeased with the US in any way.

North Korea and the USSR

The US and Soviet commanders arrived in their respective halves of Korea with entirely different instructions from their governments.

The Soviets were an Army of Occupation in North Korea only to the extent of the common mission with the US of moving Japanese colonials back to Japan after the surrender of the Japanese Armed Forces— a mission completed in two months.

Unlike the US Army of Occupation, the Soviets had no peacekeeping mission. Indeed, the Soviets had just the opposite. The North Koreans were aided by the USSR in establishing a military force to attain the longstanding Soviet objective of a Communistic Korean Peninsula indirectly controlled by the USSR.

The Soviet nation-building mission (to a dictatorship standard) had been mostly completed by August 1945, having begun in Moscow in the 1930s with Kim Il Sung and his comrades. By contrast, the US commander had a nation-building mission (to a democratic free enterprise standard) in a fractious state that had yearnings for, but no experience in creating, a representative government for a free society and economy.

The Soviets placed their protégé, Soviet-trained communist leader Kim Il Sung, in charge of the northern half of Korea. Kim ruled with absolute authority from 1945 to 1985 and his son, Kim Jong Il, the "Beloved Leader Comrade" continues that rule today.

Russia bided its time for the forty years Japan controlled Korea. The USSR would do what the Czar of Russia failed to do in 1905: make Korea, with its ice free ports, a part of the Soviet Far East.

In the 1930s the USSR recruited Koreans who were living in Korea and who actively opposed Japanese colonials for extensive training in the USSR. These Koreans proved themselves worthy of training by serving in Korea as guerrillas against the Japanese colony or by service with the Mao's Chinese Communist Army. In 1930, at age 18, Kim Il Sung, the North Korea leader to be, fought a guerrilla war in Korea against the Empire of Japan. Captured by the Japanese, Kim survived a concentration camp and escaped to the Soviet Far East. Thirty-three other members of Kim's government were dedicated communists also trained by the Soviets. In the eyes of their fellow (north) Koreans, members of this cadre were true patriots because they fought as guerrillas against Japan colonial government and against Japan in its 1937 attack on China. They later joined with communist China against Nationalist China until the Nationalist Army retreated to Formosa (Taiwan) in 1949. These Soviet-trained Koreans became the communist leadership cadre that moved into northern Korea with the USSR forces a few days after the Japan's surrender and 30 days prior to the U.S. Forces arrival in Korea on 8 Sep 1945.

The Soviets ignored their agreement to enter the War against Japan at the end of the war in Europe. They used the three months between the end of the war in Europe and their declaration of war on Japan to shift armed forces to the Soviet Far East. The USSR waited while USAF bombers fire bombed Japanese cities and dropped the first atom bomb on 6 August. USSR declared war on 8 August. On 9 August, the second atom bomb was dropped on Nagasaki. On 10 August, USSR invaded Manchuria; they entered North Korea on 12 August when General Hodge and his XXIV Corps were still 600 miles away on Okinawa. On 14 August 1945, Japan surrendered.

The Communist North had no need to go through the South's US Military Government phase of selecting and training Koreans to manage its new government. This training had mostly been done earlier and over an extended period in the USSR. The communist-trained units arrived in Korea with their Soviet patrons shortly after the Soviets declared war on Japan; they were ready to govern not only north part of Korea but the South as well. Because of the Soviet, planning the void caused by the return of the Japanese managers to Japan apparently did not have the impact in the north that it had in the south.

The Soviet trained North Koreans who formed the government easily dispensed with North Korean nationalists. Many like-minded Korean nationalists in the south, such as Kim Ku Sic, wanted a single Korean government free of alignment with both the US and the Soviets, but they were unsuccessful too.

Communist North Korea formally established the Democratic People's Republic of Korea on 9 September 1948, three weeks after the Republic of Korea was established on 15 August 1948. Both governments asserted sovereignty over all of Korea.

After thwarting the United Nations supervised election throughout Korea in 1948, the North Koreans failed in their 25 June 1950 attack across the 38th parallel to unify Korea under the banner of International Communism and failed to drive a wedge between South Korea and the US and its UN allies.

To get a flavor of North Korea's xenophobia, nationalism and isolation visit its internet site at **http://korea-np.co.jp** (cancel download, click on English)

South Korea & US Military Government

As a consequence of being in Okinawa and closest to Korea, Lt. Gen. John R. Hodge and his U.S. XXIV Corps was given the following mission by the Supreme Commander of the Allied Powers and Joint Chiefs of Staff:

1. Take the Japanese surrender, disarm the Japanese armed forces, enforce the terms of the surrender and remove Japanese imperialism from Korea.

2. Maintain order, establish an effective government along democratic lines to replace the Japanese government in Korea, and rebuild a sound economy as a basis for Korean Independence.

3. Train Koreans in handling their own affairs and prepare Korea to govern itself as a free and independent nation."

The first mission was done with ease and dispatch by the US Military.

The second and third missions were what today our political leaders call *peacekeeping* and *nation building*. The task was monumental and the US support given to its accomplishment ranged from token to half-hearted to superficial. This disinterest was more clearly expressed by the Department of State's pronouncement in January 1950 that Korea was excluded from the US Security Zone in the Far East.

In 1945 in a country of 30 million people, 18 million Koreans lived below the 38th parallel. The XXIV Corps shipped almost 200,000 Japanese military and 701,644 civilian colonialists to Japan. Most of the Japanese were gone by November with a few specialists retained until December 1946.

During that time, 1,913,693 Koreans living abroad had been repatriated to South Korea from Japan, China, Manchuria, and other places along the Pacific Rim. A retired university professor I know tells me that he was a Navy seaman aboard an LST carrying Koreans home from ports on the South China Sea.

The Japanese departure created a huge void in Koreans trained and experienced to do the work the Japanese did in all aspects of society for forty years. Japanese policy excluded Koreans from essentially all managerial and operating positions in government and business. Koreans who were appointed by the Japanese to responsible positions were treated as quislings and banished. The adverse effects of near total exclusion of Koreans from the management of their country were evident to the US Military Government for its three-year duration and the lack of management expertise continued to be a detriment after the Republic of Korea was established on 15 August 1948.

Americans sent to Korea to perform a wide range of military government and military advisor functions arrived with little or no knowledge of Korean history and customs. I was one of them. Being informed should not have been optional. Rather, it should have been mandatory, as was the military's Race Relations Seminar in 1973. I read General Hodges' excellent book (see bibliography) 54 years after it was issued to me. My poor excuse could be that the Quartermaster candles issued every evening did not put out enough light for me to read.

The US Department of State indoctrinates its Foreign Service employees for the country of assignment and so should the Department of Defense if the US is to engage in nation building.

The first military governor belatedly learned what history should have taught: Koreans had amassed abiding hatred for their Japanese masters over forty years. His decision to retain Japanese officials in their positions because of a lack of qualified Koreans generated a harmful uproar from Koreans.

By contrast, his successor Maj. Gen. Lerch, in September 1946 showed his sensitivity to the Koreans having to submit to more years (as it happened, two more years) of military government. He directed that all U.S. Military Government department heads step down, find a Korean to run the department and become an advisor to the new department head he selected.

This Confucius-like directive was in today's lingo a win-win situation: Koreans "made the decision" and Americans who had experience in the matter were (hopefully) available to advise in an atmosphere that did not recall the authoritative rule of the Japanese. On 15 August 1948 when the Republic of Korea was established all Military Government personnel except Brig. Gen. Roberts and those in PMAG went on to other assignments. Advisors to the other parts of ROK government were not to appear for nearly a year when the ECA programs became operational under the Ambassador.

Internal security was the main concern of US Military Government. Its first action was removal of the Japanese chief of National Police. In Japan's Korean colony, internal security was a Japanese police function and the Japanese Army performed the national defense function. Only 30 percent of the police were Korean - with most in lowest ranks.

Koreans' hatred for this force made it prudent for internal security to be performed by Koreans in an organization without "Police" in its title. Private armies that arose had to be carefully contended with. In January 1946, a Korean Constabulary was established to perform both police and military functions with backup by U.S. Army of Occupation soldiers.

Korean "policemen/soldiers" and a handful of U.S. Army officers in the Constabulary performed both police and military functions. The termination of US Military Government and creation of the Republic of Korea (ROK) on 15 August 1948 was followed by formation on 15 December 1948 of Republic of Korea Army (ROKA). On this day, the Korean Constabulary was replaced by ROK National Police.

US Military Government's mission in Korea was routinely impeded by the US national impetus to disengage from foreign commitments and to withdraw within itself. This was reflected in a continuing shortage of personnel, particularly in 1946, to fill the ranks of US Military Government in Korea. Military duty in the Army of Occupation was deemed as most undesirable as was duty in KMAG. Demobilization of combat troops and deactivation of units and rotation of career personnel who had completed their tours of duty reduced the capability of military government.

The US had drastically demobilized its mighty Second World War military force. It had all it could do to focus the public on the spread of Soviet Communism in Europe. The US declared it had no vital national interest in Korea, or Formosa. Its interests were limited to Japan, Okinawa and the Philippines. If the US commitment to Korea had been taken seriously and military were not available, civilians who were experienced to perform military government functions could have been hired.

A Provisional Military Advisory Group (PMAG) was organized on 15 August 1948; the day the ROK government was established. Brig. Gen. William L Roberts who had been the US Military Government's last Director of Internal Security was assigned as Chief. PMAG advised the ROK Constabulary and successively the ROK Army, Coast Guard, and National Police on internal security and national defense matters. Advisors were located wherever the ROK element to which they were assigned was located. PMAG became the US Military Advisory Group to the Republic of Korea (KMAG) on 1 July 1949. (Refer to KMAG under the heading of AMIK.) Sawyer (see bibliography) provides an excellent account of the early days of US Military Government, PMAG and KMAG and is a major source of my summarized data.

When the Soviets refused to join the U.S. in holding elections throughout the country in spring of 1948, the reality of Soviet intent to take over the entire country became evident. This forced the US military to focus on the creation of a government for the Koreans living south of the 38th Parallel.

The proposal and notion of a single government for Korea faded away due to Soviet intransigence. The Soviet-American Joint Commission and the Soviet's four power, five-year trusteeship proposal disappeared.

Three years of U.S. Military Government of South Korea (8 September 1945 to 15 August 1948) was too long a time for many South Koreans who expected, and then demanded, immediate self-rule. It was an especially long time, when compared with the alacrity of the Soviet trained cadre of North Koreans who quickly established a dictatorial government; they were not impeded by the democratic and inefficient processes of a free society.

The nationalists in both parts of Korea who expected that liberation from forty years of Japanese rule would produce instant self–rule had unreal expectations. The abrupt departure of the autocratic colonial government that dictated policy in all aspects of life had to be filled by Military Government. Many groups clamored for recognition to have their views implemented by the military government. But they could not offer candidates for jobs who were both qualified and acceptable to other groups. Representative government processes to determine policy did not yet exist. Nor did a government administration to implement such policy exist. Bringing both into existence was the task of US Military Government.

Someone described Koreans as the Irish of the Orient. Factionalism among the voices claiming to speak for the Koreans was a major issue for US Military Government. Horace Bristol (1908-1996) in his 1948 photographic book of Korea depicted five political leaders who reflected a range of political viewpoints. All of them opposed Japanese colonial rule. They were:

- **Kim Ku Sic**, educated in US, highly regarded by Bristol as a true friend of democracy;

- **Kim Koo**, Freedom fighter, fought annexation in 1910, fled to China after his part in the 1919 independence movement, in Shanghai he founded a Korean Provisional Government in Exile, returned to Korea to work with Rhee to form ROK government, opposition leader in Rhee's government, assassinated by ROK army officer 26 June 1949.

- **Rhee Syngman**, Princeton PhD in exile for 36 years, Austrian wife, at age 75 first President ROK on 15 August 1948, resigned 27 April 1960 after riots against his regime.

- **Lyn Woon Hiyung**, Liberal intellectual, Korean Laboring People's Party, commended by Gen. Hodge for attempting to bring together extremes of right and left, assassinated in 1947 after nine unsuccessful attempts on his life.

- **Rhee Ji Kungo** PhD., (Berlin University) jailed by the Japanese because of the content of his Korean dictionary.

Left to right: Syngman Rhee, Dr. Kim Koo and General Hodge. Dr. Kim Koo, President of the Provisional Government of Korea in exile, during a meeting in 1945. U.S. Army Photo

The two patriots Kim Koo and Rhee Syngman (family name comes first in Korea, but US press often converts Korean form to western form) pressed their divergent views. Kim wanted a united Korea above all other considerations; whereas Rhee would split Korea into a communist north and free democratic south rather than risk a subsequent Soviet takeover of a unified Korea. Given the USSR's resoluteness to unite Korea as a communist nation and the US lack of it, it was fortunate that Rhee's position prevailed.

I watched Kim Koo's majestic funeral procession as it passed through Seoul and around the South Gate. It exhibited the high esteem Koreans held for Kim Koo. We in KMAG were prohibited from photographing the ceremony. Some 100 men carried a bier constructed of array of long poles with interlaced shoulder straps. The heavy weight of the coffin and bier on the warm June day caused the bearers to halt frequently. Professional mourners in their traditional stiff brown sackcloth accompanied the bier—a fascinating sight for western eyes and memories, but regretfully no photographs.

A 6 Sep 2001 Pacific Stars and Stripes (Osan) story told of the ROKA officer found guilty of assassinating Kim Koo on 26 June 1949; he was reported to be a former agent of the US Counter Intelligence Corps (forerunner of CIA). The story originated with the National Institute of Korean History whose researcher found a document in the US National Archives by a US Army Major who served as a CIC officer in 1948. The Stripes story said the assassin was sentenced to life but had been released in less than a year. The Stripes story said that Kim's assassin was killed in October 1996 by a bus driver who said he was avenging Kim's death. This is ironic because Bristol said Kim Koo facetiously referred to himself as a "retired assassin" and the press referred to him as an "old assassin."

Two-thirds of all electrical power consumed in South Korea came from North Korea. On 14 May 1948, the Russians cut off all power to the South leaving much of the country in permanent blackout conditions. This forced our photo unit to use its gasoline generator to operate our lab. In time, our generator needed parts, which the supply system was unable to produce. In Korea, we learned to do without. Our photo lab scheduled work hours became 2 to 5 A.M. because it was then we might have voltage to print photos using long exposures. The power was coming from either the power barge at Inchon or the coal fired plant at Yongwol. I do not know when the two power generating barges at Inchon and at Pusan (described by Chapter 22) went on line relative to 14 May 1948. We had no power during the day because it all went to power Seoul's streetcar system and some other essential services. Being without electricity all over town at night made for a romantic setting. Merchants had very dim yellow flame carbide lamps on their sidewalk tables to cast some illumination to conduct business. You might be able, if you could see it, to buy back the item that had been stolen while you slept the night or two before. By contrast, on the few occasions when we flew from Korea to Japan we were dazzled by the bright lights of Japanese cities.

American Mission in Korea (AMIK)
July 1949 to June 1950

The US Department of State in the person of U. S. Ambassador to the Republic of Korea, John J. Muccio, took control of US interests in the Republic of Korea on 1 July 1949. The control ended at Tuesday afternoon on 27 June 1950 when General MacArthur's Far East Command reassumed control from Department of State to fight a three year long war. As of 1 July Far East Command's only responsibility for Korea was to evacuate AMIK staff to safety from Korea should the need arise. The only element of the Far East Command based in Korea was a detachment of the US Air Force Far East, who was served by KMAG's photo lab.

AMIK consisted of four elements, most of which were located in the Banto Hotel, a ten floor building in the center of downtown Seoul that housed a succession of commanding generals of US forces in Korea (and probably Japanese Governor-Generals of the colonial period). The four elements were:

1. The *US Embassy* provided diplomatic and consular functions, military attaché and Marine Corps guards.

2. *Joint Administrative Services (JAS)* Provided administrative and logistic support of AMIK. JAS operated all facilities in the Banto Hotel including the Communications Center with the

Washington switchboard and cryptographic section, Armed Forces Radio broadcast station, and hotel rooms for AMIK transients. Away from the Banto, JAS operated a motor pool, a supply facility and a number of billets including the "Frozen" Chosen Hotel for senior officials and the Traymore Hotel where I lived. I appreciated State Department's policy, unlike the Army's, which allowed men and women to be billeted in the same facility. JAS also operated facilities in Pusan and perhaps elsewhere. Directly across the street from the Banto was the two-story Mitsui building that housed JAS and KMAG support facilities including the Army Post Exchange, the postal facility, the RCA telegraph office and my KMAG photo facility. Upon transferring to KMAG from the 67th Signal Service Battalion, I shifted to JAS all responsibility for 16mm motion picture projectors used to show Armed Forces entertainment films.

3. *Economic Cooperation Administration program (ECA).* Director Edgar A.J. Johnson PhD. Established on April 3 1948 by Act of Congress; Economic Cooperation Act of 1948. Also, known as Foreign Assistance Act of 1948, this program funded economic aid to the Republic of Korea in the form of advice to ROK officials in certain essential economic services; it also funded certain economic projects. The program consisted of a variety of economic specialty groups, two of which are represented in this book, i.e., Maritime services and Railroad services. Other ECA activity in Korea was described by Enzo de Chetelat (see bibliography). Further information of the accomplishments of the Department of State U.S. aid programs to the Republic of Korea beyond the cited National Geographic and these pages must be sought from Department of State's historical files.

ECA advisors to Republic of Korea's Railway System.

Korea's Japanese built and operated railway system was divided into two parts by the 38th parallel. Most of the biggest engines were in the North. Railway equipment was badly overloaded. Wartime austerity in Japan caused maintenance on Korean rail equipment to be deferred. To keep the trains running all resources went to overdue maintenance. The shortage of railroad managers and supervisors added to the problems facing the rail transportation office of the US Military Government. From 15 August 1948, when the Republic of Korea was established to 1 July 1949 when ECA program began, the Korean Railway system operated without US assistance. As railroads were the primary freight and people mover, the US Department of State's Economic Cooperation Assistance program hired US railway company officials, some who also had railroad experience with the US Army in Europe.

Harold Bennett of the Baltimore and Ohio Railroad was among several US railroaders who arrived by air on 1 July 1949 for a tour of two years. His wife and daughter arrived two weeks later on an Army troop ship. As the only AMIK transportation advisor with a family in Seoul, he was assigned a house in the walled ROK Minister of Transportation compound guarded by National Police. It was directly across the street from Seoul Railway Station (where now stands the very tall Daewoo Building, recently acquired by General Motors).

The only account of his work with the ECA's Ministry of Transportation is from the viewpoint of his wife Dorothy, and his daughter, Josselyn. (See their papers in Chapter 6B and the Epilogue.)

ECA Advisors to Republic of Korea's Maritime System (Chapters 2, 3)

4. US Military Assistance Group to the Republic of Korea
    (KMAG) The three years of "Korean Army-building" by US
    Military Government's Directorate of Internal Security ended
    on 15 August 1948. A ten-month period of Korean
    Army–building by the US Army of Occupation's Provisional
    Military Advisory Group (PMAG) followed that, terminating
    on 30 June 1949 with the end of the US Army of Occupation.
    On 1 July 1949, KMAG (under Department of State) contin-
    ued the Korean Army-building. The attack by North Korea on
    25 June 1950 caused control of KMAG to be moved back
    from the Department of State to Far East Command on 27
    June 1950. During that year KMAG was under Department
    of State, KMAG reported on Army matters directly to the
    Pentagon's Department of the Army.

KMAG and PMAG did not have a commanding officer but rather the senior officer was designated Chief. KMAG had an advisory mission; it was not a combat unit as some historians presume. Its organization was that of the ROK organizations it advised. KMAG consisted mostly of military specialists (182 officers, 1 warrant officer, 9 civilians and 288 enlisted. KMAG advised the ROK Ministry of National Defense to include Army, Coast Guard (which employed 9 civilians who were former members of the U.S. Coast Guard) and National Police on internal security and national defense matters.

KMAG was located with the ROK Ministry of National Defense and ROK Army (ROKA) Headquarters in Seoul's Sobingo area in the southern part of Seoul between Nam Sam Mountain and the Han River. Advisors were located wherever the ROK element to which they were

The KMAG shoulder patch

assigned was located. The objective was for U.S. Army lieutenant colonels to advise ROKA infantry division commanders, majors to advise regimental commanders and company grade officers to advise ROKA battalion commanders. Technical service branches followed the same pattern. Some Korean officers objected to the lower rank of their advisor but they learned to live with it.

A "Korean Military Advisory (or Assistance) Group" never existed, as many writers mistakenly deduce from the short title KMAG. The Provisional Military Advisory Group created by the senior officer in Pusan during the confusion of 25 June to 2 July 1950 period was an appropriate local initiative with an inappropriate title that had no recognition beyond Pusan.

Brig. Gen. William L. Roberts served two years shaping the most basic of security forces of Korea with the most inadequate support for

Brig.Gen.Roberts, Defense Minister Shin Sung Mo
(in background), U.S Ambassador Muccio, President Syngman Rhee
and Secretary of the Army Kenneth G. Royall strolling the grounds of
Ambassador Muccio's residence. U.S.Army Photo

his successive missions. In May 1948 he became Director of Internal Security in US Military Government overseeing the constabulary formed by Military Government some two years earlier. On 15 Aug 1948, he became Chief, PMAG and for a while was the commander of all US forces in Korea. On 1 July 1949, he became Chief, U.S. Military Advisory Group to the Republic of Korea (short title: KMAG) and reported to the US Ambassador. He departed Korea in May 1950 at the conclusion of his two-year tour about 30 days before North Korea attack and before arrival of his replacement, a major general who decided to retire rather than to replace Roberts.

During his two year tour of duty Roberts was the chief trainer of an army of riflemen, non-commissioned and commissioned officers. He was the chief advocate for equipment to make the armed forces of South Korea more than an army of riflemen—a paper tiger confronting a

USSR equipped North Korean army standing 30 miles to the north with its T-34 tanks and heavy firepower.

Brig. Gen. Roberts was badly treated by historian Stanley Sandler on page 43 his book (see Bibliography). He accused Roberts of "mounting a publicity campaign portraying that army as a truly formidable military arm." Sandler said, "Roberts asserted in Time Magazine of 5 June 1950 that the ROK Army was the "best doggone shooting Army outside the United States." While some readers would accept this statement by a professional historian as true, I did not because Sandler's charge against Roberts had the earmarks of tabloid journalism. The cited 5 June 1950 issue of Time Magazine contains no such quote by Roberts. Frank Gibney wrote the Progress Report on Korea in the Foreign News Section. Gibney's only mention of Roberts was that he was head of the U.S. military advisors.

The cited Gibney report was an across-the-spectrum report on Korean affairs. It reported that KMAG's interest area was in much better shape than ECA's (those who keep tabs on Korea's economy) and better than the political development area. I am sure that Gibney would say his report was not the place to do an intelligence assessment on the likelihood of an attack from the North, nor on the ability of the South to react to such an attack. Gibney was not the sort of journalist to induce KMAG advisors or Chief KMAG to sound off to the press about matters contained in official reports. Sandler listed six consistently gloomy official intelligence reports, by Ambassador Muccio, by USAF Far East, by G-2 FEC, by the CIA, and two by KMAG. What motivated Sandler to charge Roberts with "making a statement that he would never live down"—especially when the statement was not where he said it was? I am certain Gibney would take offence at Sandler's charge that Roberts used his report to conduct a publicity campaign.

But let us assume that Roberts did make the quoted statement at some other time to some other audience, perhaps a farewell talk with the Koreans he worked with before his departure. And let us assume that it is the basis for Sandler's charge that "KMAG's right hand did not seem to know the doings of its left hand." Knowing both the fatherly Roberts and the troop commander Roberts, he might have said what Sandler put in quotes. Fathers and commanders when talking publicly to or about their sons or troops who are struggling to live up to others high expectations will always, if they are wise, tell the world that they are the best—even though in a private talk with an errant soldier or son he might tell them they were not doing their best.

I conclude that Sandler has no leadership experience and is, therefore unable to distinguish between a context requiring an official statement on a policy issue and an informal family or leadership context that conveys confidence, trust, respect, and even affection, for example, for Korean soldiers that Roberts had been training to be the best for two years.

Col. W.H. Sterling Wright was the Acting Chief KMAG from the May departure of Roberts to retirement and arrival of Brig. Gen. Francis Farrell in July. Col. Wright demonstrated his leadership and deservedly retired as a Lt. General in 1965.

US national authorities used their fear that President Rhee would send a well-equipped South Korean Army off to attack North Korea as the reason for not providing ROK Armed Forces with resources to defend itself. The consequent collapse of ROKA within the first week after the North Korean attack was the subject of much derision of the ROK Army but little if any was directed to the US policy makers who refused to adequately equip it. Just a couple of the items found in an Infantry division were in the ROKA inventory. I fired every type weapon in a US infantry division during my six months at Fort Riley's Ground General Officer Candidate School (1947- 1948). ROKA was essentially an army of riflemen who just a few months or weeks earlier had been rice farmers.

My job was not such as to acquaint me with all weaponry provided to ROK, but I do recall this much: Jap 99 rifles from weapons stocks surrendered by the Japanese in September 1945 were the principle weapon. I saw the equivalent of the Colt 45 being manufactured in a Korean shop. When the war got underway in the Pusan Perimeter, the US cal.30 carbine became the individual weapon. Only one of 16 ROKA's tank substitutes, the M-8 Armored Car (2.5 ton truck chassis) existed on 11 Oct 1950. It was in Wonsan with the 3rd ROKA division. Major Sorensen's Horse Cavalry was no more. I did see 105mm howitzers and pack 75 howitzers (breaks down to mule size loads). I was not

24

aware of many mortars or automatic weapons (BAR, 30 and 50 cal. machine guns). Antitank rocket launchers 3.5 were not issued until August 1950. ROKA had no recoilless rifles, but they had some 37 and 57mm tripod mounted guns. They had a few L-4 and T-6 aircraft being used by ROKA for observation and targeting for close air support. Signal had some SCR 300 radios but few batteries. WD-1 field wire was always in short supply.

In July 1950 ROKA was essentially a 30 caliber carbine equipped army, clad in rubber shoes whose primary field ration was a big ball of rice wrapped in leaves. I kept my interpreter supplied with salt from my field rations. Also in short supply were the company grade officers and NCOs that General Roberts often said take such a long time to produce.

I have an artillery story and color slides to support it: It demonstrates what a well-trained ROKA howitzer battery can do. North Korean tanks came up behind the battery at night with a load of infantry. These indirect fire weapons were reversed and put into 100 yard direct fire mode and fired both high explosive anti-tank and white phosphorus rounds. Burnt bodies on the tanks and next to the treads indicated complete surprise. No survivors. An artist's painting of this event was in a large format book at ROKA HQ in Seoul in June 2000.

KMAG seems to have grown considerably in size in the final two years of the war. Three years of combat experience by the ROK Armed Forces made a U.S. military advisory group redundant. I presumed KMAG was eliminated shortly after the war's conclusion. In three years of combat ROKA had evidently developed to the point that Brig. Gen. Roberts sought: the redundancy of KMAG. The ROK and US had a joint command structure working in 2000.

President Truman's Change of Policy on 27 June 1950

President (1945 to 1953) Truman's decision to use United States Armed Forces to defend the Republic of (South) Korea against the Communists' attack from the north had these momentous consequences:

It reversed US foreign policy announced by the US Secretary of State in January 1950 that had the effect of abandoning Republic of

(South) Korea to any aggressor force desiring to attack it without fear of intervention by the United States. The wording of the Department of State policy (reflecting Congressional mood) placed Korea outside of a delineated Far East Security Zone. That policy was taken as an invitation for the North Koreans to attack South Korea on 25 June 1950.

The decision terminated de facto US policy in effect since the early days of US Military Government in Korea (8 September 1945 to 15 August 1948) that severely limited the types of military equipment sent to the South Korea's constabulary and subsequently to the armed forces of the Republic of Korea (reflecting Congressional mood).

It terminated the Far East Command evacuation plan for removal of US Department of State personnel and military advisors when less than 100 remained in Korea. The decision was delivered by HF radio message from General MacArthur to Colonel Wright of KMAG and Ambassador Muccio on Tuesday 27 June 1950 at 1355 hours Tokyo-Seoul Time.

Had President Truman failed to act to oppose the North Korean aggression, the entire landmass of East Asia would have fallen into the hands of Communists. A hostile communist neighbor in Japan's backyard would destabilize the Far East.

His decision frustrated the Soviet's forty-year intent to bring all of Korea into the Soviet Far East.

The thriving Republic of Korea in 2002 is testimony to his wise decision.

Lieutenant Slaven by his jeep "I had to tell my commanding officer that some of his boys would not be coming back" Photo by Lt. Slaven

U.S. Occupation Forces in South Korea
The Train Wreck

1948/1949

During the winter of 1948/49, 1st Lieutenant Robert K. Slaven, age 34, was assigned to the 76th Signal Service Battalion with Headquarters in Seoul. In that organization, his principle duty was "Officer in Charge" of the Tenth Corps Radio Receiving Station located at Kosa. This had been a former Japanese installation on a small hill surrounded by rice paddies and about 10 miles from Seoul over almost impossible roads. Bob would make it into headquarters once a month for a haircut, PX supplies, etc. They had no running water at the station, only a privy, very little heat from stoves and power units for electricity to run the receivers. A kind of primitive living. The battalion also had a transmitting station, of course, and wire teams, telephone people and all the other duties of a signal service battalion. Since the landline phone communications between Seoul and Pusan were unreliable at best, they also provided radio links between the two towns.

The equipment they used was highly directional, portable and multi-channel radio with limited range up to approximately fifty miles. Therefore, it was necessary to set up and operate some 4 or 5 mountaintop stations along the spine of mountains the length of the peninsula. This provided "line-of-sight" communications through relays between Seoul and Pusan; some 250 miles as the crow flies.

Korean porters had lugged the equipment up the mountains and the stations were manned by a crew of 4 or 5 who were supplied by airdrop, weather permitting. The radio equipment was boxed in coffin-size containers and the power supplies were air-cooled motor-generators weighing about 150 pounds each. Prior to the war, the South Korean occupation military had war-weary equipment and no funds were available for special operations like the mountaintop installations. It was therefore necessary to pay for any Korean labor with cigarettes. The non-smokers, or light-smokers among the battalion officers, (cigarettes were rationed) pitched in their unused packs or cartons to pay for the Korean labor.

In September of 1948, station #3 unaccountably went off the air. The Battalion Commander, a Lt. Colonel, called on Bob to go down by rail and find out what was wrong with station #3. He was given a team of six men, some of whom had been to station #3 on past duty. They loaded their packs with everything they could think of to fix what might have gone wrong and they took along two generators. The train took all day to cover the 100 miles to the town at the foot of the mountain below station #3.

After the Japanese left Korea, the rail system deteriorated and the north-south railroad was mostly single-tracked except for a few passing tracks. The mountain was about 4500 feet high and Bob's team had only about one hour left of daylight when they arrived. They took all their gear to the local police station and using "Pidgin English", they found they could not hire any porters to carry the generators at that late hour. Bob left most of the GIs (non-commission) at the police station to guard the equipment and to break down the generators into small packages. He gave them three cartons of cigarettes to hire porters first thing in the morning. Then Bob took three of the men and started up the mountain. In his own pack, Bob had one carton of cigarettes, personal gear, radio spare parts and food (K-rations). He carried a canteen of water and a side arm on his belt. The trail up the mountain was mostly in a dry streambed strewn with boulders and Bob's pack got heavier with every step. They met some Koreans who lived on the mountain about two-thirds of the way up and for most of the remaining cigarettes they agreed to lug the packs up the hill. Bob's porter turned out to be a little old woman about five feet tall and he had trouble keeping up with her!

After the Koreans peeled off into their town, Bob crawled up the last few hundred feet on his hands and knees in total darkness. As they arrived at the station without food to go around, the lads on duty were pretty upset. They had been short of food because heavy cloud cover had precluded airdrops. An upper level storm of rain, hail and high winds had blown down the tents and saturated all of the equipment including the power units. They had used the packing cases for sidewalls for the tents but even these had blown all over the place. They had partially dug the tents and walls into the slope of the hill so they had some protection.

Bob slept on the wet ground that night and when he got up in the morning he noticed that they were above the clouds! Because of the lack

of food, he sent the men who had come up with him back down immediately. When the non-commissions showed up around noon with the
porters carrying generators and spares he sent them back down too,
keeping only one of the radiomen, a corporal, with him. The two of
them stayed there for three days helping the station crew put the equipment back on the air and by that time they were down to one can each
of K-rations of cheese. The mountaintop crew was due for an airdrop so
Bob and the Corporal left early the next morning to catch the daily
northbound train due at the town at the foot of the hill at noon. They
stopped at a stream on the way to wash, shave and fill their canteens.
They got to the station before noon. Then they waited, waited and waited. The train finally showed up by late afternoon. It was a long train,
about six or eight of the cars packed with Koreans and the last four cars
were marked "Transportation Corps-U.S. Army" and manned by military police (MPs). The fourth car from the rear was a baggage car. The
next two coaches were filled with GIs and the last car was reserved for
officers and mostly American Civilians, known as DACs (Department
of Army Civilians). There were only a handful of DACs and a few officers. They included one medical officer and a Master Sergeant who were
doing some kind of paperwork. There were about 15 in total in that
coach and Bob took the Corporal in there with him.

It was obvious that the train was in some kind of trouble, running
very slowly, and along about sundown it stopped completely. Bob had
eaten his K-ration of cheese and he drank all of the water in his canteen.
The train had stopped near the small town of Napnin where there were
double tracks for a mile or so. On the near left were rice-paddies; the
passing tracks and the town were on the right. Most of the Americans
got out on the right side to stretch their legs and gripe about the slow-
ness of the train. However, the train jerked ahead a few times so everyone hastened to climb back aboard even though it really never got under
way. Bob was the last one to get aboard the last car and a sergeant who
was just ahead of him on the steps looked aft and said, "Jeese, isn't that
train on our track?" Bob looked back too and in the gathering darkness,
he could see a train way back down the track, maybe a quarter of a mile
and coming fast. Bob said, "Maybe it will be switched onto the passing
track," and he jumped down to get a better look. It was getting quite dark
by this time and Bob couldn't really tell which track it was on so he got

into the coach-car and looked down the length of it, the rear door being open, and it surely was on their track and not slowing down. Bob's first instinct was to get the hell out of there but instead he started yelling, "Get out! Everybody get out! There's going to be a collision!" Everyone looked at Bob as if he had lost his mind but then he was able to put enough urgency into his voice, shouting his warning over again and pointing to the rear. Finally, they started piling out. They all piled out of the front entrance where Bob was and they were milling around on the passing track. One civilian ran out the rear door and down the tracks toward the oncoming train waving a flashlight, but to no avail. Bob was convinced that the cars would "jack-knife" and pile up, so he didn't want to go out the right side where all the people were. At this point a big MP Sergeant brushed by Bob and went into the car ahead saying, "I'll see if I can get the fellers out of that car." Bob never saw him again. Bob went to the other side of the car and jumped. While he was in mid-air, he looked backed and saw the engine of the coming train only a few feet away and sparks were flying from under the wheels. The Engineer apparently had awakened to the danger in the last seconds and locked the wheels. Bob hit the water of the rice-paddy at the same instant of the collision and in a panic he crawled and ran through the muck fully expecting to have the train roll over on him. When he finally stopped and looked back, and it was fully dark now; he could see the outlines of the trains against the horizon and they were still on the tracks. The engine of the rear train had penetrated into the rear of the coach-car and knocked it off its wheels. Then there was an empty space of about a car-length and Bob could make out the outline of his train stretching out ahead. He thought the collision had uncoupled his car and knocked his train ahead a hundred feet or so and he thought, "How lucky we were". He waded back and joined the people of his car. The Corporal said, "I thought you were a goner" then some of them climbed into the coach which was a complete mess. They found their packs and baggage and then found a young MP whose head was injured and badly cut-up by glass. They got him out, handed out the baggage and asked a female DAC to guard it. Two of the civilians said they would walk to the town and see if they could get a message out by phone about the accident. Bob said he would walk up to the two troop cars and see how they made out. As he approached the cars, he was impressed by the silence. Just before the crash, the troops had been singing "Across the Alley from the Alamo" and Bob fully expected to hear the Sergeant saying, "Alright fellers, let's fall out and see if anyone is hurt or missing." But instead, there was dead silence. As Bob walked alongside the car, something brushed across his head. Bob was bareheaded, having lost his cap in the rice-paddy. Bob reached up and felt a human hand. He crouched down low against the car, looked up against the star-lit sky and he could see the silhouette of a man hanging upside down, caught by one foot. Now Bob backed away from the car and could see that it was higher than the car ahead. He ran around behind the car and could see that the sides were angled out and only then did he realize that the cars were telescoped. The second car from the rear was inside the third car and both were jammed up against the baggage car. He went back to the non-commissions and said, "We've got trouble up ahead fellers, the troop cars have telescoped."

Some of the men climbed up into the upper car through the rear door. It was impossible to get into the lower car and in almost total darkness; they felt their way to the front. The entire contents of the car; men, seats, baggage, rifles, etc. were jammed together in a few square feet at the front end of the car. It appeared to Bob that what might have happened was that as the car was thrust forward by the collision, everything piled up in the rear. Then, when it stopped suddenly against the baggage car everything cascaded forward and all of this in a split second. The men felt around for warm limbs and dragged bodies to the rear of the car. Somebody remembered that that there were blankets in the baggage car and eventually when things got organized, a slide of blankets was devised and bodies were lowered down the slide to the medical officer who determined if they were dead or alive. Crews wrapped them in blankets and put the dead on the tracks between the trains and the injured on the passing tracks. A sort of sling made of blankets was devised to take the weight off the ankle of the hanging man. He had apparently been thrust out of a window.

Bob didn't last long in the upper car. He was wet, shivering and sick to his stomach. He got down out of the car and did what he could to help matters on the ground. Soon a Korean team from the local village showed up with a cart full of tools. They had torches to supply some light and manpower to help. During the whole night, not a single railroad man showed up. Sometime in the early hours, they uncoupled the

36 Killed In Train Wreck

SEOUL, Sept. 16
Thirty-five Americans and one Korean died Tuesday night, when a speeding Korean train crashed into the rear of a stalled troop train 80 miles south of Seoul, an Army spokesman announced.

The official casualty toll showed 80 Americans injured, 35 of them seriously. Korean casualties included four seriously injured and 41 slightly injured.

It was the worst disaster to strike American Occupation Forces since they landed in Korea. One eyewitness said the crash was caused by inefficiency and lack of proper safety measures.

The last three coaches of the front train, in which American cocupation personnel were traveling from Pusan to Seoul, were telescoped by the impact.

The Americans' train developed engine trouble and stopped at the town of Napnin for repairs after delays that caused it to be more than four hours behind schedule.

One of the passengers, Melborn Penry, Military Government employe, said the casualty toll would have been higher except that a number of men left the train to stretch their legs.

Penry said he saw no evidence of sabotage. "In my opinion, there was no particular person to blame for the accident—only the system."

Names of the victims were expected be released early tomorrow, following notification of next of kin.

UP & The Stars & Stripes

train from the baggage car and steamed off to the north. No one appeared to get off the train behind them but it was reported later that there were also casualties there due to the quick stop of the collision. After all the bodies, dead or alive, had been evacuated from the upper car, some moans could be heard coming from the front end of the lower car. The seats and other materials were thrown out of the windows in their attempts to reach the injured. All of the seats and gear had been pushed and jammed into the front of that car and jammed against the rear of the baggage car. There was no way of getting in there. Someone suggested that by using the tools in the Korean cart that an opening could be cut in the side of the car near the front. A pyramid of men was formed to hold up a man with hammer and chisel and two vertical cuts were made in the side of the car. When an attempt was made to cut horizontally, they ran into a steel frame. All that labor had gone for naught. At least the doctor was able to reach through an aperture and stick a needle of morphine into any body that he could reach. Injured men on the passing track were also treated as long as the morphine lasted. Men regaining consciousness asked if they had been bombed. Bob's count of 20 dead and 40 injured was before the bodies and injured were recovered much later from the lower car. In the very early morning a hospital train came up from Taegu and Bob and the

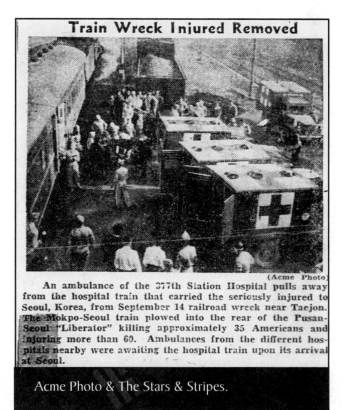

Train Wreck Injured Removed

(Acme Photo)

An ambulance of the 377th Station Hospital pulls away from the hospital train that carried the seriously injured to Seoul, Korea, from September 14 railroad wreck near Taejon. The Mokpo-Seoul train plowed into the rear of the Pusan-Seoul "Liberator" killing approximately 35 Americans and injuring more than 60. Ambulances from the different hospitals nearby were awaiting the hospital train upon its arrival at Seoul.

Acme Photo & The Stars & Stripes.

rest helped load the injured aboard. Then at dawn, a train came down from Seoul and took the survivors back to the capitol. Bob was run through the hospital even though he didn't want to be, but he was covered with mud and blood. All he wanted to do was to get up to battalion headquarters and get something to drink and eat. He had to tell his company commander that some of his boys would not be coming back.

The last of the U.S. Occupation troops were withdrawn from South Korea June 29, 1949.

Lt. Slaven was subsequently promoted to Captain and assigned to the 71st Signal Service Battalion in Tokyo. From that position, he would play a major role in the evacuation of civilians from South Korea in 1950. (See chapter 14)

The author Ray as a Radio Officer.

New York to Yokahama

June 8, 1949

President Truman recommended that Congress appropriate $150,000,000 for aid to the South Korean Republic. REJECTED; it was later approved in the amount of $60,000,000...

—The Encyclopedia Americana 1960 Edition page 528d

August 1949

New York City was one of the busiest shipping ports in the world in 1949. The North River piers on the west side of Manhattan were alive around the clock loading and unloading the great ocean liners. The R.M.S. *Queen Elizabeth*, the R.M.S. *Queen Mary*, the R.M.S. *Mauretania*, the S.S. *America* and others kept the piers buzzing with the sounds of thousands of passengers embarking and disembarking to and from their foreign voyages. Automobiles, letter and package mail and passenger luggage filled the limited freight spaces. These leviathans dwarfed my ship, the S.S. *Marine Marlin* under the command of Captain William Barr. The *Marlin* was originally launched as a cargo vessel but had been converted to a passenger liner to transport displaced persons from Europe to North and South America. The United States government leased the *Marlin* to United States Lines on a "cost-plus five percent" (no limit on expenditures) contract, which meant that the more money U.S. Lines could spend on the vessel, the more they could profit. Consequently, the ship was supplied with luxurious and costly items such as silverware, the best linens, crystal, fine draperies, oriental carpeting and collector art. The food fare often included giant shrimp and lobster, steaks, and delicious foreign cuisine prepared by a few of the best chefs in the world and at high salaries. The recreation room had a piano, Ping-Pong table, jukebox and refrigerator.

I had been one of three radio officers on board the *Marlin* since October 1948. The *Marlin* carried 800 passengers and a crew of 200. I made three more voyages after the government refused to renew the contract and took over operation of the ship from United States Lines.

Effective April 1, 1949 the vessel was turned over to the U.S. Army Transportation Service to continue the relocation of displaced person's at a more reasonable cost. The ship's new name prefix became USAT for United States Army Transport. Thereafter the passengers had to work their way across the Atlantic. In stark contrast to being served like royalty they were issued work uniforms, brooms, mops, scrub-buckets, and tools and put to work chipping rusted paint and keeping all decks clean. On May 10, the second day after departing Germany enroute to New York, a group of Jewish people, perhaps twenty-five of them, sent a delegate to the chief officer and informed him that they would not work until they were provided with kosher food. The chief officer informed them that there was no kosher food on board and that they would just have to go without eating. Whether they ate or not, they arrived in New York in good health.

Marion and I had married in Minnesota in June 1948. To be closer to a busy shipping port, in May 1949, we moved to an apartment in upper Manhattan. I opted for a vacation and left the *Marlin* on August 20, 1949. When I was ready to return to the *Marlin* in early September I was told that my job had been filled by a radio officer with seniority in the union. I relieved a Radio Officer on a Tidewater oil tanker, the M.V. *Tydol Bayonne*, for one month carrying crude oil from Texas ports to the refinery at Bayonne, New Jersey. Shipping was very slow and I had difficulty finding another berth. I took a job as office manager for a local antique shop owned and operated by Lanny and Ginger Grey. They were the couple that wrote and sang the "Adam Hat Jingle" on broadcast radio. They also owned and operated Ginger Grey Cosmetics.

In November 1949, I received a call from the Marine Division of the Economic Cooperation Administration (ECA) in Washington, D.C. offering me a position in Korea as radio instructor. Marion could join me after I found suitable living accommodations. We debated our options for a couple days. Her argument for accepting the offer was that we would be together for a change. The offer sounded exciting, and we decided to throw caution to the winds and go.

Marion flew home to Minnesota and I flew to San Francisco to rendezvous with the sixteen other members of the American Mission to South Korea. Pacific Far East Lines in San Francisco was the agent for the ECA American Mission in Korea. We received our indoctrination in their offices.

The primary objective of the mission was to assist South Korea in establishing a productive and profitable merchant marine fleet. We were to move five ships from the Yokohama shipyards in Japan, where they were being overhauled, to Pusan, South Korea. Six shipmasters, six marine engineers, three radio officers, a project leader and his male secretary staffed our mission. We would crew the ships with Japanese from Yokohama and exchange for Korean crews in Pusan. Thereafter, we were to train Koreans to operate the ships while steaming the ships between South Korean ports in the general cargo trade and between South Korea and Japan, trading Korean rice and coal for Japanese chemical fertilizer. The ultimate goal was to establish a merchant marine academy in Pusan fashioned after the U.S. Merchant Marine Academy at Kings Point, New York. We signed a one-year contract with the option to renew if we were still needed.

We flew from San Francisco to Seattle on the modern-day Strato-Cruiser, the first aircraft with two decks. The lower deck was a bar-lounge. At Seattle, we changed planes, and then flew to Anchorage, Alaska and on to the Aleutian island of Shemya for fuel. The landing at Shemya was difficult, on instruments and in a whiteout blizzard. We were taken by bus to a quonset hut at the edge of the field while the plane was refueled. There we tasted what had to be the worst coffee ever brewed.

The take-off a couple of hours later was as precarious as the landing. It seemed that the aircraft went down the runway sideways. An otherwise uneventful trip led to an easy landing in Tokyo. The trip had taken about 27 hours including our waiting time at Anchorage and Shemya.

I was assigned to the S.S. *William Lester*, a 250-foot, 2500-ton Baltic Coaster, then in dry-dock. The other ships, the S.S. *Charles Winsor*, S.S. *John Whidden*, S.S. *Nat Brown* and S.S. *Elisha Whitney* were the same type vessels and were also in dry-dock and being refitted.

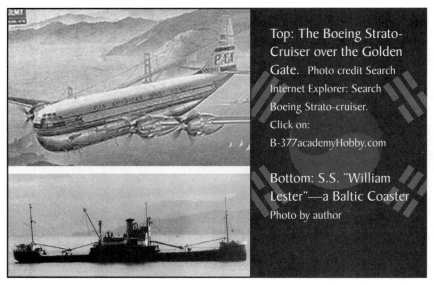

Top: The Boeing Strato-Cruiser over the Golden Gate. Photo credit Search Internet Explorer: Search Boeing Strato-cruiser. Click on: B-377academyHobby.com

Bottom: S.S. "William Lester"—a Baltic Coaster Photo by author

These ships, originally built for the Great Lakes trade, had large winches and booms on their decks for self-loading and discharging cargo. They were ideal for training the Korean crews and starting a shipping industry. They had already been in South Korea on a similar program run by the U.S. Army, but that effort had failed for one reason or another.

After one night in the comparative luxury of a hotel, I was told that the ship would be my quarters until it was fitted and launched for the trip to Korea. I spent a considerable amount of time over the next few weeks cleaning up the radio room, checking emergency batteries and restoring them to a charged condition, checking the radio receivers, testing the vacuum tubes, and burnishing contacts. The transmitters, both main and emergency, checked out okay on a dummy load substituting for an antenna since all the antenna wires were laying on deck and would not be raised until sailing time. The only thing left to do was to make sure we had the required documents in the radio room. These documents, issued by the International Telecommunications Union in Geneva, Switzerland, include the List of Call Signs and Numerical Identities, List of Ship Stations by ship name, and List of Coast Stations, all of which are mandatory items to be on board before a ship can venture to sea. Operating and servicing manuals for each radio unit were also required.

Because the ship had no self-generated power, we had only dim lighting provided by a shore-plugged power line. The ship was very cold, and a small portable heater warmed my quarters. All meals were taken ashore. I slept fully clothed for warmth and changed in the mornings. I busied myself each morning by painting the radio room and wheelhouse bulkheads. December 1949 in Japan was very cold. I spent much time over the next few weeks at the American Club where I met many other Americans who were on various assignments in Japan.

I could take a hot shower at the club, change clothes in comfort in contrast to the cold quarters on the ship. There is nothing as unfriendly as a ship that is idle.

During the New Year's Eve celebration at the club, I called Marion, and she announced that she was pregnant. I let out a big "Yahoo", slammed my beer bottle to my mouth and broke off half of a tooth. It did not even occur to me at the time that with a baby on the way I should try to back out of the contract and return home. In the next week, a Japanese dentist pegged the tooth with a false extension.

One snowy evening, while walking back to the ship, I was attracted by the warmth of lantern light from a canvas and wooden shack. I was treated to one of the most unusual but enjoyable dining experiences I have ever had. An old woman motioned to me and called out in broken English, "Good food . . . good food." I decided to go in. A younger woman came from behind a curtain with dishes of vegetables and meat and placed them near the hibachi occupying the center of the large round table. I sat on a pillow on the floor, and when I put my feet under the table, they dropped into a pit of welcome warmth. Someone under the shack was stoking a fire. They served me a great beef teriyaki dinner that came to about one or two dollars. I remember that I left a very generous tip, and they ushered me out bowing repeatedly as I resumed my walk back to the ship.

1/12/50—**Dean Acheson** in a major speech before the National Press Club—"In Korea we have taken great steps which have ended our military occupation, and in cooperation with the United Nations we have established an independent and sovereign country recognized by all the rest of the world. We have given that nation great help in getting itself established. We are asking the congress to continue that help until it is firmly established and that legislation is now pending before the congress. The idea that we ought to scrap all of that, that we should stop half way through the achievement of the establishment of this country seems to me to be the most utter defeatism and utter madness in our interest in Asia."

After ten weeks in Japan, the S.S. *Nat Brown*, with Jim Scanlin as captain, Des Mann as chief engineer and Frank Crosby as radio officer, departed Yokohama and was the first of our ships to arrive in South Korea. During the next week, the other four ships were removed from the dry-docks and crewed with Japanese officers and seamen. After the ships were loaded with their cargos of fertilizer, we set our first course for Pusan, South Korea.

At the American Club (L-R) Author, Acquaintance, Alex Roth.
Photo by Alex Roth

This was an exciting time for me. I eagerly anticipated my first radio contact with a Japanese radio station. As we departed, I fired up the ship's transmitter, tuned in the Yokohama marine radio station, plugged in the telegraph key and tapped out the departure time and destination of the S.S. *William Lester*, call letters AOFA. (The ships retained the Army radio call signs that had been assigned to them in previous years.) The Japanese radio operator responded, acknowledged my departure announcement and wished us a bon voyage. I felt ownership and pride.

The Maritime Advisors

Maritime Group on hatch of S.S. "William Lester" in Yokohama (Left to right): Frank Crosby, Capt. Woods, Milo Atkinson, Jim Scanlin, John Connolly, Alex Roth, Capt. Peterson, (Front row kneeling): Joe Kelly and Ray Maurstad (author). Photo by author

Our Maritime Group numbered seventeen men. Nine of then posed for this photo on the deck of the S.S. *William Lester* in Yokohama before the ship left for Korea.

> *Project Manager:*   Forrest K. Peterson
>
> *Project Secretary:*   Joseph T. Kelly
>
> *Six Ship Captains:*   James Scanlin
>   Jay Kressen
>   F.J. "Tom" Kitts
>   E.B. Nelson
>   William Woods
>   Alexander Roth Jr.

Six Marine Engineers: Desmond Mann
John Connolly
John Murphy
Harold D. Stevens
Milo Atkinson
Herbert C. Basford

Three Radio Officers: Francis X. Crosby
Frank Compton
Raymond B. Maurstad

Forrest K. Peterson

Forrest K. Peterson was Project Manager for the Maritime Division of the American Mission in Korea. We referred to him as "Captain Pete" or, just "Pete". A large man in his mid forties, he was usually very quiet but spoke with authority and confidence when the subject matter was the project. We learned over the ensuing months that he was a career government man and had spent some years in China. He was no stranger to the customs and culture of the Orient and he was an experienced leader. His hat and pipe were permanent parts of his make-up. Always in a tweed suit with baggy pants, he smiled easily. Captain Pete was married and his wife would join him in Korea with their two sons, Johnny age 10 and Richard age 1. As advisors, all 16 of us reported directly to Captain Peterson when ashore. At sea, however, the American Chief Engineer Advisors and Radio Officer Advisors reported directly to the American Captain advisor on their respective vessels.

Joseph Kelly

Administrative Assistant to the Maritime project. Age 23, ex navy, congenial, easygoing. Joe's wife Dorothy would join him in Korea. He was an important and pivotal man in the project, the focal point for administrative matters. Captain Pete and Joe were the only two in the Marine Group who had offices ashore. They would occasionally visit the ships to assist with paperwork and more often than not, they would bring some kind of treat for our private refrigerators.

James Scanlin (Ship Captain) "Jim"

Age 31, from New York, a graduate of King's Point Merchant Marine Academy. Jim married a New York model, "Ada", who would join him in Korea in April with their two young daughters. Neither Jim nor Ada had ever had a driver's license. Real New Yorkers, they always used rail, bus and taxi transportation. Jim was an excellent Ship Master. Raised during the depression of the thirties, he was in the Civilian Construction Corps (CCC) before his graduation from King's point and his career as a ship captain.

Jay Kressen (Ship Captain)

Jay was forty and an ex-tennis pro of some repute. He was a large and jovial fellow and resembled the actor, Robert Mitchum. His wife Jane and their 8-year-old daughter joined him in Korea in April. Jay and Joe Kelly kept the dust from settling on the Hialeah tennis court.

Thomas Kitts (Ship Captain) Ship Captain "Kitts"

Kitts was a short man, in his early forties, slender and sinewy. A "James Cagney" type, he walked with the typical sailor's swagger. His wife joined Kitts in Korea in April.

E.B. Nelson (Ship Captain)

"Nelson", the oldest of the group, perhaps 65. Nelson's wife joined him in April. She was a classy dresser. Her hats were brimmed as large as umbrellas. She wore a lot of make-up and loved a lot of attention. They were an interesting and entertaining couple. She brought her appliances from home and they did not work on 50-cycle power so they had to be stored for the duration. Nelson was a licensed amateur radio operator. His call letters were HLICF.

William Woods (Ship Captain)

"Woods" Another one of the "older guys", Woods was an impeccable dresser, usually in a suit and tie. He knew he was comical and would pose outlandishly when being photographed. Proud and dignified, while entertaining, he was the object of many jokes. When he posed on the bridge of a ship you knew that he was in command. His marital status was unknown.

Alexander J. Roth (Ship Captain)

"Alex" Alex was very engrossed in the project and worked at it around the clock. A handsome man of about 30 years he kept his walrus moustache meticulously trimmed. Alex's wife, Mary, petite and demure, with a young daughter named Susan, joined Alex in Korea in April.

Desmond Mann (Chief Engineer)

"Des" From New Jersey, age 25, a graduate of Kings Point Merchant Marine Academy, polite, serious and very much a gentleman. Married to Ethyl with one young son, Billy, they joined Des in Korea.

John Connelly

Connolly was the 3rd oldster. He seemed often pre-occupied with his thoughts (memories?). He was recalled and went back to the U.S. in mid-May "to address some union problem". We thought his leaving so early was mysterious, that he perhaps knew something we didn't know.

John Murphy (Chief Engineer)

"Murph" A smiling and jovial Irish American, Murphy had "the glint" in his eyes. Always good company and ready with a joke. His wife Margaret joined him in Korea.

Harold Stevens (Chief Engineer)

"Stevens" Harold's wife Grace arrived in South Korea a day or two before the North attacked.

Milo Atkinson (Chief Engineer)

"The Commander" We called him "Commander" because he was always in the full dress uniform of the U.S. Maritime Service with the bright yellow "scrambled eggs" of a commander on the bill of his cap. We believed that at times he even wore that uniform and gold braid in the greasy engine-room while on duty.

Herbert Basford (Chief Engineer)

"Basford" An older man, he was difficult to know. His alcoholism kept him isolated. He would quietly venture in and out of the clubhouse to replenish the bar at his house.

Francis X. Crosby (Radio Officer)

"Crosby" Frank was a thin young man in his late twenties. He always wore a suit and a hat. The canvas bag he carried was full of cameras and accessories. His first hobby was photography, his second was ham radio. His final, but perhaps his last interest was his wife and their marriage. Frank married Doris in Lima, Peru and she would join him in April. When she arrived, she was in her eighth month of pregnancy. A World War II shipmate wrote, "Frank was quite a character. Our ship was ferrying troops around the Pacific in 1945/46 and at one port, Balikpapan, he picked up a beat up Army Harley Davidson. The engine room crew helped him fix it up and the Captain allowed him to carry it on deck so we had transportation in the islands. At one time, we went ashore with four guys on that bike! It was a very big bike that had been used by the Military Police. Frank was an inspiration to me. After that trip I went back to school and got my radio license and sailed for several years on tankers as Radio Officer".

 **Frank Compton** (Radio Officer)

"Compton" Frank Compton was in his forties, from California and a very well mannered gentleman. I do not remember seeing Frank more than once. When he was at sea, I was in port and vice-versa.

Raymond Maurstad (Radio Officer)

"Ray" (the author). Ray's wife Marion, age 21, joined Ray in Korea in April. She was pregnant with their first child.

All seventeen of us, with the exception of Joe Kelly, were professional merchant seamen hired by the U.S. Government as Maritime instructors to train South Korean merchant seamen in the operation of five American-built vessels. Out ultimate goal was to develop a merchant marine academy for South Korea.

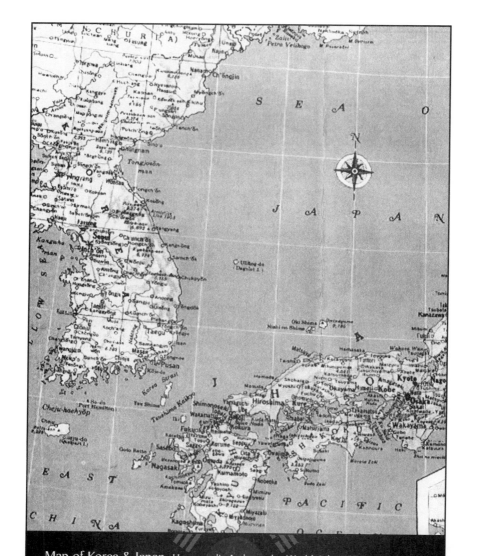

Map of Korea & Japan   Hammond's Ambassador World Atlas-1954

3

The Crossing & Crew Change

January 1950

The ships steamed westward along the coast of Japan and entered the Bungo Suido between Shikoku and Kyushu on the third day.

We cleared the straits without incident and crossed the Sea of Japan. On the fourth evening, we sighted the navigation light and antenna towers on the peak of Cho-Do Island. The ships eased into anchorage locations about a mile off the Pusan harbor entrance.

The hatred that Koreans felt for the Japanese played an important part in the logistics of turning the ships over to the Korea Shipping Corporation. The Japanese had occupied Korea (Chosen) for 36 years before the end of World War II and many events during that occupation enraged the Korean populace. It was therefore essential that the change of crew be carried out in such a way that the Japanese and Korean crewmembers would not have to face each other. More than one of the Japanese crew informed us that they were afraid of the Koreans and wanted assurance that they would not have to go ashore. They said they could be beaten and jailed or even murdered.

A Japanese ship had followed our three Baltic Coasters to Pusan and was standing by at anchor while the Japanese crews were transferred to her decks. The ship then departed without delay, returning her human cargo to Japan. When there were no longer any Japanese on the four vessels, the Korean crewmembers were transported from shore to the ships to become the proud operators of their "own" ships. The Korean flags went up the halyards.

Pusan is at latitude 35 degrees North, the same latitude as southern North Carolina. The climate is pleasant the year round but the winter season can bring very cold weather to the northern part of South Korea. The atmosphere is dry and the skies are usually clear. The morning sun warmed our decks and the sea around us was calm with a light swell. A dozen fishing boats were riding the swells and the fishermen were busy bringing in Mackerel and Pollock. A few of the boats were very close to our vessel and we enjoyed watching them cut up fish, add the raw pieces to a large community bowl of rice, and scoop the mixture to their mouths. We would learn that the fishing industry in Korea was very big with dozens of different kinds of fish caught off its shores. Sardines made up about 25% of a catch value. Fish were in abundance and included Alaska Pollock, Mackerel, Herring and Shrimp. The divers' targets were a variety of Shellfish, Clams, Oysters, Sponges, Scallops, Abalone and Irish Moss. Whaling was an important part of the industry furnishing oil, fertilizer and especially food in years of a poor land harvest. I made a mental note to fish with them one day. Fishing was one of my favorite pastimes in Minnesota.

The American instructors introduced the Korean crews to their on board duties. Each ship in turn soon had boarding parties from shore including harbor pilots who guided the ships into the harbor. Among a few good Korean ports, Pusan provided excellent, protected anchorage for 3,000-ton ships. Tugboats met the vessels and assisted them in tying up to Pier One. The crossing and crew change were complete.

The S.S. *Nat Brown* had arrived ahead of the rest of the ships and, before the Japanese crew left the vessel, the Japanese Chief Engineer, Y. Orito, handed Chief Engineer Desmond Mann the following note:

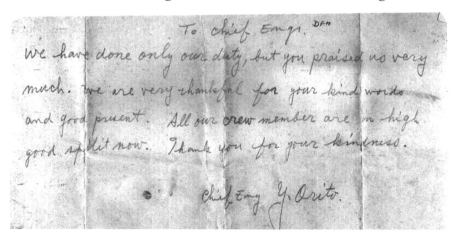

A note to Des Mann from the Japanese Chief Engineer

4

Pier One

The "Charles Winsor" docked at Pier One
Photo by author

Pier One was a strong, narrow, concrete structure about 900 feet long. It was the heart of the port shipping activities.

A 2-story brick building at the head of the pier housed the offices of the Korea Shipping Corporation. One of those offices was that of Port Captain Milton J. Nottingham. Nottingham was a young, tall version of John Wayne. He was a career officer out of Washington D.C. Part of his assignment as port captain was to guide the activities of the Korea Shipping Company. He assisted the company in accepting the turnover of the vessels. One of the assignments of his position was to follow the development of the company into a successful South Korean shipping industry.

On the south side of the pier, a small isolated wooden shack housed the port's marine radio station, call letters HLP. This radio station and three others on the south and west coasts of South Korea would be the only points of contact between our ships and our home port of Pusan. The presence of the ships drew a large curious crowd and crewmembers were posted at the gangways to keep visitors from coming on board the ships.

A World War I battleship dominated the north shore of the harbor. Milton Nottingham offered a short explanation. The battleship had no propellers and was permanently docked there to provide power to the city of Pusan.

The American Captains, Chief Engineers and Radio Officers left their ships and proceeded to the office building. We were surprised to learn that there were no customs or immigration authorities to approve our landing in Korea. These agencies existed but I suspect Nottingham had arranged for us to land without showing our documents. We entered Captain Nottingham's office where we were introduced to his assistants. We received an interesting indoctrination on the objectives of the mission and what was expected of us. The emphasis was on assisting the South Koreans in recovering their economy and becoming as self sufficient as possible, especially in the way of foreign trade. The indoctrination matched the one we received in San Francisco at the offices of Pacific Far East Lines.

The harbor was excellent for deep-draft vessels. Ships from all over the world frequently visited Pusan, which was the major shipping port for South Korea. The future maritime academy would be built here near the harbor. We were excited about our task of training Korean seamen and officers.

Pier One was fitted with rails and cranes and was well equipped to handle heavy cargo loads. Our ships had steam-driven cargo winches adding to the lift-out and lift-in capabilities. Warehousing nearby allowed for short trips of the small trucks receiving the cargo. Overloaded bicycles and oxen-pulled wooden wagons carried their share to local storage. Heavier Japanese-built trucks moved cargo to more distant locations.

Our ships had carried general cargo and much-needed bulk chemical fertilizer from Japan. We off-loaded the general cargo in Pusan over the next few days. Most of the fertilizer would remain in the holds until we carried it to Korean ports on the south and west coasts of South Korea.

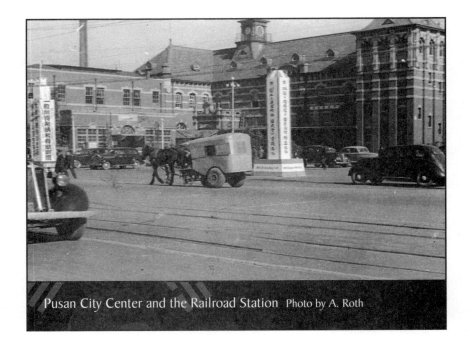

Pusan City Center and the Railroad Station   Photo by A. Roth

The City of Pusan

The Americans were transported from Pier 1 to "Hialeah Compound" in an old Japanese military motorbus. The slow trip through the city gave the group their first glimpse of Pusan and revealed an unexpected primitiveness and poverty. The level of economics and living conditions in South Korea had not been given much attention in our indoctrination back in San Francisco. Motor-less buses were over-loaded and pulled by a single horse.

Our motorbus had to stop for a large crowd in the road. A bus-pulling horse had dropped dead and the crowd was beating the animal with paddles, poles, pieces of pipe and other weapons. The horse was being butchered where it lay and the beaters reaped the reward of the meat they could cut off and carry. We were told the beating was necessary to tenderize the meat. The scene was very bloody.

Small children had slits in their pants so that, when they squatted to eliminate, the slit would automatically open. The scarcity of motor vehicles was obvious. The cars and trucks that were puffing through the street throngs were old and decrepit and were mostly of Japanese manufacture. Bicycles were common and out-numbered the motor vehicles and horse-drawn trolleys.

Sewage ran in open ditches at the sides of the streets and many Koreans carried honey buckets on their backs. Excrement of any kind did not remain in place for very long, as there was an active competition among the sweepers to get to the pile first and sweep it into their honey-buckets. The bucket collections would finally be sold to a collector with a honey-wagon.

The odors were almost intolerable. The crowd finally dispersed at the butcher site. The sweepers were busy with the remains as the bus of astonished Americans continued its trek north.

Both sides of the road were tightly lined with small shops that were nothing more than shacks. The Korean families usually lived in or imme-

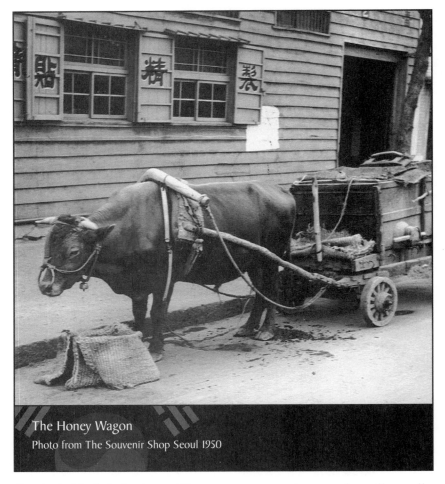

The Honey Wagon
Photo from The Souvenir Shop Seoul 1950

diately behind their shops. There were many shops and smaller stalls. Our bus driver stopped frequently so we could do a little shopping.

When the view no longer included the shops, the bus started its open-road climb into the foothills north of the city. We then had an opportunity to view a higher level of housing. The typical Korean family with means lived in a one story building on a hill, and facing south to capture the sun.

Top:
A close family of six.
Photo from The Souvenir
Shop Seoul 1950

Bottom:
A country home
Photo from The Souvenir
Shop Seoul 1950

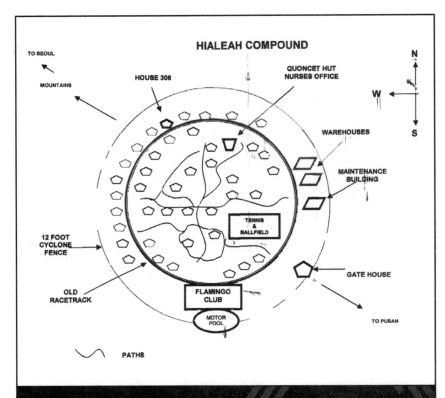

HIALEAH COMPOUND

TO SEOUL

MOUNTAINS

HOUSE 306

QUONCET HUT
NURSES OFFICE

WAREHOUSES

MAINTENANCE
BUILDING

TENNIS
&
BALLFIELD

12 FOOT
CYCLONE
FENCE

GATE HOUSE

OLD
RACETRACK

FLAMINGO
CLUB

MOTOR
POOL

TO PUSAN

PATHS

N
W   S

Compound diagram Sketch by author

Hialeah Compound

Sometime during their occupation of Korea, the Japanese built a one-mile horseracing track on a plateau just north of Pusan. It came to be known as "Hialeah", most likely a name given to it by the U.S. Military Occupation personnel. It was originally a dirt track but was eventually grated and graveled over by the Americans providing smoother vehicle access to the new homes they constructed.

Hialeah was a new American-style housing development in 1946. The first residents were U.S. military officers and their families; part of the U.S. Occupation forces. A few additional streets were cut across the circle and a 12-foot high cyclone (chain link) fence surrounded the entire compound. The fence would open only at the guardhouse gate on the southeast of the circle. The houses were constructed on both sides of the track perimeter and on both sides of the added streets within the circle. Storm drains 13 inches deep and 20 inches wide paralleled all of the streets. Birch, mountain ash and maple trees were tastefully placed and very nicely accented our landscape.

Homes on the old racetrack. Photo by A. Roth

We were assigned to the houses by number. My assignment was House #306 and Kelly was assigned to #308, right next door! It would be an understatement to say that we were surprised and pleased with the houses. The design was definitely American; a large living room with an adjacent dining area.

Inside author's house #306
Photo by author

The small kitchen behind the dining room housed a large sink, refrigerator, ample cupboards and a very small wood-burning cooking stove including an oven. On the opposite side of the living room, a hallway led to three bedrooms and a complete bath with tub and shower. All of the rooms had large and attractive paneled windows with Venetian blinds providing good views and plenty of light. The floors were highly polished oak partially covered with thick throw-carpets. There was a white picket fence around a small front yard. A large wood box in the back yard held a cord of firewood for the cooking stove.

The roof was covered with bright orange clay tiles. We were advised that when our families arrived we would each be assigned a "House-Girl" to assist with housekeeping and laundry. A "House-Boy" would also be assigned to carry in firewood and tend to the yard and garden. The compound had a sanitary sewer system and clean water supply. Our heat source was an oil-fired stove in the front of the living room. At any setting of the stove the house would become unbearably hot and the stove would have to be shut own.

I hurried to write a letter to Marion explaining these details to relieve her of any concerns she might have relative to the living conditions. Uppermost in her mind would, of course, be the birth of our first child, which she was now carrying into her third month of pregnancy. I was able to assure her that there were good doctors and reliable facilities in Seoul.

Three very large Quonset huts served as warehouses for appliances, furniture and a variety of machines, tools and materials. One large Quonset hut near house #306 included the nurse's office and was used for large meetings. It was screened in and used for picnic activities when it rained.

The Flamingo Club was the center of activity. A large one-story concrete structure; it housed a large galley, dining room, PX (Post Exchange) store and washrooms. There was a large cloakroom in the front lobby. The dining room chairs and tables were used for Friday night Bingo and were folded against the wall for Saturday night dances. The club was located close to the compound's guarded front entry gate. We felt comfortable with a visible level of security.

The Flamingo Club. Photo by A. Roth

Three meals were served each day and even though fresh meat was not available, the food was excellent. The beef and pork left in deep-freeze by the U.S. Military had turned green and was not edible. Very large prawns and fresh fish were in adequate supply. Chicken and eggs were not always readily available.

The Flamingo Club was the kingdom of Gerry Lucas. Gerry was in charge of almost everything associated with the club. In his mid-thirties, New York accent, single, handsome and very busy; he seemed to be everywhere at the same time. In charge of the galley, the bar, the food, the warehousing etc. He had a few people handling specific areas; administration, galley, maintenance, etc. There was also a registered nurse assigned to the compound; her name was Barbara Mella. A very tall and attractive young lady; she kept busy tending to the booster shots, colds, cuts and bruises, nuisance complaints etc.

The compound was located on a large plateau surrounded by a range of hills to the North and West. The plateau was the bottom of a gravy pitcher with the spout dropping off to the South and East toward Pusan City. Large fields of various crops like wheat, barley, oats, soybean and rice covered the plateau. Rice paddies occupied the largest portion of the land. Rice was the principal crop of South Korea and along with coal made up the bulk of the cargoes shipped to Japan in trade for fertilizer.

Sixty-two American families and several singles would share Hialeah Compound at Pusan. At the same time, there were over 1500 non-Korean civilians in the Seoul/Inchon area. Most of these were American employees (and their dependents) of one of the elements of the American Mission in Korea (AMIK), i.e., the Korean Military Advisory Group (KMAG), the U.S. Embassy, the Economic Cooperation Administration (ECA) and the Joint Administrative Services, (JAS).

Rice Planting Photo from The Souvenir Shop Seoul 1950

Harold Bennett 1946. Photo by Dorothy Bennett

The Railroad Man's Family

By Josselyn Bennett Winslow

Harold Bennett obtained a degree in Civil Engineering from Ohio State University in 1924 and went to work for the Baltimore & Ohio Railroad (B&O). He had a variety of jobs in Maintenance of Way (being sure the tracks, ties and railroad bed were in good shape), to Trainmaster (keeping the trains running on time, working when wrecks occurred to get the line open again). As a child, I remember that he was regularly gone two or three nights a week. Harold would go out, spend the day checking into railroad business and then frequently would spend the night on the private rail car of the man who had oversight of that part of the railroad. My father told stories of the delicious meals and the evening poker games on the private car. As the years passed, he worked his way up the railroad hierarchy. Then, when World War II started he decided that he had to join the Army.

Because of his railroad experience, he went into the Army Transportation Corps as a Lieutenant Colonel and spent his time working with the railroad system in France. After the war was over he returned to the B&O in March of 1946. When he found that those people who had stayed behind on the railroad resented him, it was an easy decision to say "Yes" in 1949 when the call came from old Army buddies to join them in working on the Korean Railroad as part of the Economic Cooperative Administration's program (ECA).

Harold arrived in Seoul and met General (retired) Burpee, the head of his office and Paul Oakes, a railroader from an Illinois line. Paul and Harold had a close working relationship and Paul and his wife, Gertrude, became very good friends of my parents.

His work in Korea was interesting and challenging. The transition from being a captive nation to an independent one left Korea with a good Japanese-built rail system, but with few trained to run that system. The men who came as part of the ECA program knew how to run a railroad but they probably had not anticipated the problems that would arise from the people they would be working with. In France, my father had found there were times when he needed to pat the forty-five on his hip to "encourage" someone to get something done, but in Korea that kind of tactic was unthinkable. The major problem in Korea was the division between the "educated" gentlemen and the workers. More than one evening my father grumbled over the fact that the well-educated Koreans who were in charge of the railroad did not understand that you could not run a railroad from an office; you had to get out, see the equipment, talk to the workers and be ready to solve problems. Several of the Korean men had graduated from Ohio State, but they had to learn that even the boss sometimes had to get his fingernails dirty.

Harold Bennett inspecting locomotive "You can't run a railroad from an office." Photo by Harold Bennett

Most of the evenings he was at home, but there were weeks when he was gone several days at a time as they worked to expand the line and make the rail system work better. During all of these operations, communication was always a challenge. One small example that I remember. My father returned from a grand ceremony of the opening of a new track. The story was that when all of the dignitaries arrived to celebrate the event there was a huge block of ice on the track. Finally someone asked, "Why the ice?" A Korean official explained that earlier when they were planning the ceremony an American had said, "It will be good to

Harold and Dorothy Bennett on bridge over railroad
Photo by Harold Bennett

break the ice," so the Koreans had promptly procured a big block of ice to be broken at the event.

Another interesting offshoot of my father's civil engineering career and association at Ohio State University was the gathering at our home, very early, the day after New Years in 1950. Ohio State was playing in the Rose Bowl and Harold had invited a number of Ohio State Alumni to come to our house and listen to the broadcast of the Buckeyes defending their honor on the football field. I wondered to myself just how much the Korean men enjoyed getting up early to listen to a football game from California. Somehow, I found it hard to believe that the Korean gentlemen would enjoy the game as much as my dad who was born and raised in Ohio.

He flew to Korea in July of 1949 and my mother Dorothy and I followed by military ship in August. It was no problem for my mother to follow my father wherever he went; she was accustomed to moving with him on his various railroad assignments. It was more of a challenge for me. I was half way through my college education as a student at Western College in Oxford, Ohio. However, the challenge of the adventure made it an easy decision so, Mother and I began getting ready to head for a new life in Korea. We were told that we should bring all the clothing we would need for at least a year and household items—but not furniture. As a result, Mother and I went on a shopping spree. We also sorted through household items to see what we would need to add to make a "furnished" house a home—like the extras for entertaining. In August Mother and I left Columbus, Ohio (and my grandparents there) and headed west by train. We went through Chicago, through Cheyenne and to San Francisco. We had reservations at the St. Francis Hotel, right in the middle of the city. We explored the city and went to Fort Mason to watch a departing troop ship. The military band played "Now Is the Hour that We Must Say Good-by." In spite of ourselves, both Mother and I had tears running down our cheeks—it was just the excitement of knowing that we had a great adventure awaiting us.

Early on the appointed morning Mother and I left the St. Francis Hotel in downtown San Francisco and reported to Fort Mason where we boarded the *General Aultman*—a military troop ship. We had a large number of soldiers bound for duty in Japan and a few soldiers and others who were to go on to Korea, including a number of dependents, families of military men and families of civilians working in Korea. We had a few special passengers aboard, the most memorable, Dr Helen Kim (PhD), the Korean delegate to the United Nations—and, as I was to learn, the president of Ewah Woman's University in Seoul. She and her traveling companion, both attired in modified Korean dress, provided an interesting contrast to the rest of the ship's passengers. The *Aultman* weighed anchor and we passed under the Golden Gate Bridge, bound for our adventure. Non-sailors quickly discovered the rolling wave motion just outside of San Francisco was a new sensation—but most of us grew used to the ocean's rocking rhythms in a short time. Mother and I had two cabin mates. One was the wife of a civilian worker in Korea. Her name was Hon (short for Honey) Harbison. She had the distinction of being the first person I had ever known with hair swept up and held in place with spray—enough that no sea gales could dislodge even a hair. Our other companion was a young (probably just twenty-one) Special Services girl, Betty Jane Smith. She would be working in the Seoul service club—directing a variety of social and recreational activities to keep the soldiers busy while they were far away from home. The August weather was good and our trip was easy. We celebrated when we crossed the International Date Line, but the event I remember the most was when the ship's captain invited my mother and some of the other passengers to the bridge. Mother got to steer the ship! We judged her steering prowess by a slight zigzag in the ship's wake. When we arrived in Japan the passengers who were going to Japan debarked and then the rest of us were permitted to go ashore. We traveled by bus to Tokyo. My memory of the city was that it was a flat, desolate plain—from the effects of the fires that were part of the final days of World War II. My other memory was of driving by General MacArthur's headquarters and getting to see him as he drove from his headquarters in his big car. In those days, General MacArthur was one of the most revered men in the world and everyone stopped to watch as he left his office. Back to the *Aultman* and more days sailing—around the southern tip of Korea and up the western coast. We arrived in Inchon mid-August. I remember being amazed at the strange sights and smells. My father met us and we rode by car into Seoul to the Sudo Hotel. The Sudo, and the adjacent Kookje Hotel were just one of the several small hotel complexes around Seoul where American families were billeted. We had a couple of rooms. Our meals were served in a common dining room. Being there was a little like living in a boarding home. There was some flexibility—but not much. However, it gave us a chance to learn a little Korean from the waiters who taught us to say, "Ko mop sum ne da"-"Thank you" in Korean. My father introduced us to the others in his office, including General Burpee, who headed the transportation organization and Andy, another staff member of the office. Shortly after our introduction, my father announced that General Burpee and Andy decided to move out of the house they were occupying in the Transportation Compound, the Hermitage, and let our family have it for a home. This house was in a compound situated directly across the main road from the Seoul Railroad Station—just behind the row of buildings that faced the street. The Japanese-built brick Hermitage would be our home for the ten months we were to have in Korea.

The Hermitage, a former Japanese home where the Bennetts lived before the war   Photo by Dorothy Bennett

Our Japanese-built house was in a compound just off an alley way. The compound was surrounded by a six-foot high brick wall topped with a row of jagged broken bottle pieces that were there to discourage any possible intruders. We had Korean guards at the gate. They seemed to know who to admit and who to keep out. Our compound contained about six houses. In addition to our place there was a large house next door occupied by the son of the president of a major Korean bank. He lived there with his wife and young family. Beyond their house was the home of a top advisor to the Korean government. Two other American families lived in the compound: John Baldridge, who worked for a US newspaper, and Dick Jones, who was also a journalist. Our cook, Henry, lived with his family in a Korean-style house in the compound. When we moved from the hotel to our new home we found it was "furnished" with a cook, Henry, and Yuan, a tall young man from North Korea who was the houseboy. He oversaw the cleaning, served the meals, and kept track of things. We also inherited a German shepherd, Poli, and a tough old tomcat, Elmer. We took a little lady from the hotel with us. Mrs. Yoo was to be the laundry person and help with the cleaning. The outside staff consisted of two men who were expected to fire the boiler for heat and hot water and to mow the grass. The house's original entrance was opposite the compound entrance. We reoriented to use an entrance near the compound gate as our main entrance. The low front door was built for Japanese people. We had to warn our visitors to duck if they were over about 5'8." They came into a corridor that had windows on one side and sliding walls on the other. Our low-ceilinged living room was sunny and cheerful. The furniture, provided by the Army, was built by Koreans who thought all Americans were big. As a consequence, neither mother nor I could sit on the couch and have our feet touch the floor. Off the living room was a small prayer room which had a vertical unmilled wooden beam beside the altar. The dining room had a Russian furnace on one wall. It was sunk into the floor. Half of the furnace was visible in the dining room. Part of it was open to the kitchen and the other section opened into Yuan's room. The high-ceilinged western-style former living room became my parent's bedroom. I had a bedroom with sliding walls. There was a family bathroom and a large bathroom at the back of the house that became Mrs. Yoo's laundry room. She did the washing in the bathtub until the Army was able to supply us with a washing machine. She normally hung the clothes outside—except for days when it was "pouring small" as she would report to my mother. We had been told that the Army would supply our furniture but we were to bring the extras. Mother had packed linen table clothes, linen napkins and the silver. We had also arrived in Korea with enough clothing to meet our needs. The weather there was very similar to what we had known in Ohio—hot and humid in the summer and cold and snowy in winter. The Korean people were not used to our modern conveniences. When the Army delivered a lawn mower, we were fascinated to look out and see our two-yard boys had enlisted a friend. They had looped a long rope around the top bar above the cutting blades. One of the men was pushing the mower and the other two were walking ahead in V-formation pulling the rope to make the job easier. We also saw the Koreans use a similar technique with a shovel. They tied a rope around the handle. One would use the shovel and the other two would help lift and toss the load. We were fascinated at Koreans ability to make do or to fix things. Our furnace was a good example. One day, during the cold weather someone let the boiler go dry. As the boiler grew hotter and hotter, someone discovered the mistake and rushed to add water. The water hit the red-hot boiler—and it cracked. Everyone was sure that the boiler could not be repaired—since it was made of cast iron, but the Koreans fixed it.

Outside the compound was a different and challenging world. The smells were a combination of honeycarts and charcoal—the universal fuel. During the days streets bustled with people hurrying. Transportation was by foot, bicycle, and streetcar. A result of Japanese planning. Very few Koreans had private transportation. The Americans had military sedans and Jeeps. A car picked up my dad for work. When mother or I needed to go somewhere we called for a military sedan. The fellows in the Army had their own Jeeps to get around in. Mother got involved with other American women and with some of the wives from the diplomatic corps. Because the circle of people was so small she was invited to most special events—including tea with Mrs. Sigmund Rhee, the Austrian-born wife of Korea's president.

Mother was never one to spend all of her time engaged in social activities so she soon was working to learn Korean and she taught English to students at one of the local high schools. I decided I needed to continue my education. My choices were limited since I could not speak Korean. I finally enrolled in two classes at Ewah University, a women's school and two at Chosen Christian University, the men's university next door to Ewah. I made friends with two Korean girls. Both of the girls visited my house. One girl, Pak Pong See, was an Olympic discus-throwing champion. She was shocked when she came to visit me and discovered I had on a pair of straw slippers I had bought in the market place. She informed me they were "beggars" shoes. Normally the military sedan would pick me up for class early in the morning. Our drive from the center of Seoul—near Nam de Moon-South Gate—to the west of town took us over dusty roads. The hillsides were stripped of trees and other vegetation by Koreans who needed wood and other fuel. The road passed a steep hillside where a Korean family had dug out a cave for their home. One Korean phrase the driver taught me was "Nam da ga nom ne da"—"dust is flying." It was an appropriate phrase on many occasions. Classes at both schools were held in big stone buildings. My clearest memory of the classrooms was during the wintry days when students attended fully clothed for winter—because there was little or no heat in the rooms. Windows were tightly closed to keep any warmth in—and the overwhelming smell was that of kimchee– the spicy vegetable mixture Koreans ate to enhance their daily diet of rice. Kimchee is made of cabbage, turnips and Oriental radishes. It is prepared during the summer when the vegetables are fresh. They are cut up and put into big jars to ferment, similar to sauerkraut. By mid-winter Kimchee eaters could win any contest against garlic eaters. The school cafeteria served noodle soup in large brass bowls. They gave us chop sticks and a brass spoon for utensils. I was only semi-competent with chopsticks. I learned to hold the soup bowl right under my chin and scoop up the noodles with the chopsticks—but the spoon saved me. At the end of one of the long, cold wintry days I was glad to get back into a waiting sedan and head back to the cozy Hermitage. Some of our instructors were sent by church organizations, which had helped to found the universities. One, Helen Daniels, was from Canada. She taught at Ewah and was friendly and helpful. Another instructor, at Chosen Christian University, was Jim Phillips. I particularly remember one of his classes. All of the other students were Korean men. This was the spring of 1950. There was a big discussion about the situation between North and South Korea. Typical of students, many of them felt very strongly about issues between North and South Korea. That day I was not at all sorry to leave the heated discussion and return to my seemly safer world.

Korea's markets and small shops held treasures beyond imagination. There were few big stores, but if you were willing to look, you could find all sorts of things by wandering through the little side-street shops. The fabric shops had lovely silks: the traditional stripes to make the sleeves of the festive dresses worn by children and gauzy silk organza and heavy woven silk fabrics in amazing colors and designs. My friend, Betty Jane, who introduced me to Frank, was looking for white fabric for a wedding dress. The shop keeper pulled out bolt after bolt of white silk with damask-like patterns woven into the material. We chuckled when we spotted a gorgeous piece of white silk with a pattern of tennis racquets, balls, bats and other sports items woven into it. Betty Jane, the Special Services girl, was marrying a young officer who was also in Special Services. Both of them planned activities and other recreational events for the troops. Betty Jane said, "I love my work, but not enough to have a wedding dress with tennis racquets on it." I'm sure the Koreans might not have understood that sporting equipment didn't really fit with exquisite formal fabric.

In 1950, Korean soldiers wore uniforms much like the American Army, but most Koreans wore their traditionally styled clothing. The men had white bloomer-like pants and a jacket which lapped over and was fixed with a half-bow tie. Older gentlemen wore high see-through black horse-hair like hats. Women wore black or white skirts and a cropped-top which lapped and tied much as the men's. Americans noted that young Korean mothers who were still nursing their babies had only to push the top up a little to provide a quick lunch for the baby. For parties and other special occasions, men usually wore western-style dress and women wore fancy Korean dresses. During the summer the dresses were made of layers of light silk. In winter, the fabrics were heavier. Students wore simple dark uniforms of jackets and pants or skirts and the ubiquitous schoolbook pack on their backs.

Girls seemed to have their hair braided. Students had short hair. Women wore their hair pulled back into a bun and held with fancy pins.

The Koreans were fascinated with the differences in American clothing and styles. Once when I was out for a ride in a jeep we stopped in a small town. Children crowded around. They wanted to feel the kind of fabric my clothing was made of. They were interested in my short, curly hair. And they were fascinated by my red-polished fingernails. They wanted to know if my toe nails were red, too. My limited Korean kept me from explaining that it was only fingernail paint.

Leaving the compound to explore Seoul on foot was an entirely new experience. To the right we could climb a dusty road-path through Korean houses and shops. In one of the little shops, I found, and bought, an unusual tea set made of pottery. It was only one of the many things we abandoned when we were evacuated from Korea at the start of the war.

Turning left a short distance took us to the main street across from the railroad station. That street was lined with shops. One Sunday Harold, mother and I wandered along, in and out of the shops. We looked at the paper-made Korean umbrellas. When I attempted to open one it jammed and ripped. Looking further at more durable items, I noticed a long row of similar Korean pots. They were all decorated in the same manner. I picked the one I liked and asked the price. The Korean shopkeeper nearly doubled up laughing. "Korean piss pot," he said.

Other shopping trips were more worthwhile. There was one large department store in Seoul. Mother and I meandered through the floors and looked at many items. We finally decided to buy a personalized Korean chop-like the wooden stamps (with ink pads) used by government officials to substitute for their signatures. Our chop would have been a great remembrance-if we had gotten it home.

The real shopper paradise was the Bon Chong-a narrow winding street which had every conceivable kind of shop. Fabric shops with hundreds of stacked bolts of silk in every unimaginable color were designed to tempt the ladies. Stores did not have ready-made clothing but it was easy to find a dressmaker who would come to your house and make any kind of clothing you described. Dressmakers never used a pattern; they just took your measurements and listened carefully to what you wanted. In about a week she would return with the finished article. A small special item that was readily available was inexpensive sterling silver buttons made with a simple carved out surface.

We bought most of our food from the military commissary. Because Korea was at the end of the U S government's food chain we did not have milk nor were there many fresh fruits or vegetables. Before we left for Korea we had been informed that we should not eat local produce-unless it was cooked because Koreans used "night soil"-human waste that men collected in their "honey buckets" to use as fertilizer. The problem was that Americans would not have built an immunity to many of the local germs. We were told that some things, like an apple with a firm skin, could be okay. But the officials still recommended that you "peel the apple before you eat it"-a phrase that was ubiquitous.

However, Mother found that Korean eggs were fresh and far superior to the ones shipped across the Pacific. She would send Yuan out for a "stick"; ten eggs wrapped in a sheaf of rice straw, which was tied at the ends and in between each egg (the perfect packaging). We also decided the local apples were a safe bet, even when not peeled since they were grown by farmers who carefully wrapped each blossom to protect them from bugs and the weather and, they grew that way on the tree. We have wondered since Korean days what kind of apples we ate because they were one of the best variety our family had ever tasted.

Early fall brought fresh persimmons. They were ripe and delicious. Mother even got out her Indiana recipe and made persimmon pudding.

Some things in the local market looked very tempting-like shucked-out local oysters-but we decided that they were too much of a risk to try.

The other "shopping" came when people like "Trader Annie" brought things to the house. In addition to shopping in the market and little stores, there was a brisk commercial trade brought to the Americans' own homes. Somewhere I heard that it was not legal for the Koreans to trade merchandise, but no one seemed to care about that legality.

The Korean guards at the gate let special Korean guests in and they also let people like Trader Annie in. Every week or so a grandmotherly Korean woman arrived at our house. She carried a large bundle tied in fabric. When she came into the living room she would set the bundle on the floor and untie the fabric corners to expose a world of treasures. Sometimes we would not be interested in her wares, but at other times we would find an item we really wanted—like the green cloisonné powder box mother bought. When we asked the price it would be quoted in three currencies: in US dollars or "green dollars," in Army Military Payment Certificates or Army script, and in cartons of cigarettes. For the Korean "Green Money" was the most favorable exchange since the

Korean economy was somewhat uncertain and American money could always be exchanged.

The military script was good, except that the military deliberately kept the MPC exchange rate the best kept secret. Old script became worthless if it was not cashed within a few hours notice. If Korean traders who accepted military script could not give a legal source of the money the military would refuse to exchange it. There were many stories of Koreans standing outside of military compounds with handfuls of old script begging an American soldier to exchange it before it became worthless.

Most Americans had few "green dollars" to spend. Koreans would pay dearly for American cigarettes so the best way to purchase an item was with cartons of American cigarettes. Every American adult received a ration of cigarettes each month. Because I didn't smoke I had my monthly ration to use to barter for the items Trader Annie brought. My proudest purchase was an oriental coffee table that cost me two cartons of cigarettes. At that time, cigarettes cost about $2 a

Military Payment Certificate.
Author's collection.

carton. Of course, the coffee table stayed when we left Korea, so it did not turn out to be such a good buy.

Some of the items Trader Annie brought were really special. Word was that the Chinese families who were being pressured by the

Communist soldiers were smuggling their treasures out of the country. Many of these treasures found their way to Korea and to the Americans who had money to spare. A friend of ours took us to see a wonderful lacquered oriental screen. It had several panels with Chinese figures. The faces were carved ivory and there were beautiful jewels inset in the scenes. He purchased the screen and being uncertain of the stability of the situation in Korea, had it shipped back to the states. We heard later that customs intercepted it and he was forced to turn it over to a museum.

The same undercurrent of uncertainty made my mother start worrying about her sterling flatware which she had taken to Korea. After pondering a while she decided that the tableware provided by the Army was good enough and that she would ship her sterling home to my grandmother. When the package arrived in the states, the silver was held by customs. Mother was most aggrieved with the hassle it caused— until she realized later that she would have lost it if she had not sent it home when she did.

My mother wrote the following letters to a friend in the States.

Seoul. Korea

September 15 1949

Dear Helen:

Now that we have been here nearly a month, we feel like old timers so I will try to give you a brief account of our experiences so far. Josselyn and I took the train to San Francisco after Harold had been advised to sell the car. He flew on the 23rd of July and made the trip in about 48 hours from Washington, going by way of Minneapolis, Anchorage, Alaska, one stop at an Aleutian island and one other at Tokyo. He says the trip is very tiresome and that is far from the case with the ship. Josselyn and I had four days in San Francisco during our processing time and think it is the most beautiful city we have ever seen. We shared our cabin with a girl of 21 coming out to do U.S.O. work and another wife in her thirties coming to join her husband, so we just hit it off grand. The girls were reporters for the ship's paper, getting all the news and gossip. It was a small Army transport, the load was light, so we were permitted to roam the ship as we wished. Josselyn and I were up for most of the sunrises. They can be compared only with the sunsets on the Pacific; movies out on deck, dances and bingo games kept us well entertained. The weather was perfect, having only two rainy days, and I have seen Lake James much rougher. Altogether, it was heavenly and then Harold met us at the port of Inchon, Korea. We had to drop anchor a mile out and come ashore in small craft, as the channel is quite shallow. (ed. Inchon and Bay of Fundy have the world's largest tidal changes) I forgot we had two days in Yokohama where buses took us sightseeing, one being a trip to Tokyo.

After Harold met us, we drove to Seoul which is about 25 miles and on the only paved road in the country. We stayed for ten days in a hotel and have been in our house for two weeks.

You hear much of thieving here, but our house is in a small compound of six houses; around the compound is a wall, two guards at the gate and two patrolling the premises. In spite of all that, while Harold is gone this week, Josselyn and I sleep with most of the lights on, in the same room, and with our 22 pistol by the bed. Since Harold is No. 1 (as they call it) Railroad Man, we have one of the nicest houses in town. Our neighbors are the Korean Minister of Transportation and Mr. Lady, American Advisor to President Rhee. The house has ten rooms, two of which are for the servants, and is a rambling Japanese style. We had to retain the house staff, people who had been here for several years—so we have Henry, a cook of 40 years standing; Jun, a house boy who sleeps in; Yoo, a laundress, and Sur, the yard boy. The last is about 60 and looks just like a little gnome. He helps with the cleaning and at the moment is doing the windows at my elbow. All speak but few words of English so I am getting good at sign language. The other day I found a package of carrot seeds and thought it would be grand to have fresh ones as we have a little greenhouse in our compound. I showed Sur the package, he grinned, bowed and disappeared for half an hour; then in he came with a huge geranium plant and apologized because it had no flower. Every leaf had been washed, and he was so sweet that I didn't try to explain that I had been too stupid to take the seeds from the package. He thought I wanted a flower the color of carrots and believe it or not, one popped open this morning. He was so pleased when I showed it to him.

One confuses them so easily, and I know that I am to blame most of the time. I asked for a fly swatter and got a glass of ice water, so you see how it goes. Harold and I went walking and stopped in a native shop as I saw a pretty bowl with blue flowers painted on it. I asked "How much" The man told me the price and asked, "what for?" I said, "for flowers". "OK" he shrugged, "but Korean piss pot." Well, I thought Harold would explode, and I backed out without buying anything. Of course, Harold thought the story was too good to keep so now it is all over town. I was presented with "the pot" the other night.

On our ship was Dr. Helen Kim, president of Seoul's EWHA College, a school for women established by Methodist missionaries. Doctor Kim (Ed: *who later represented Korea at the UN*) is a wonderful woman, and we became very well acquainted. She taught us a Korean game, and we helped her with various card games. Josselyn has been in school for two weeks now and is loving every minute of it. She is taking literature, history, drama and religion. Yesterday she came in all excited, as she had been asked to teach the seniors basketball and modern dance. After one of the assemblies, a teacher told her that Dr. Kim had told the girls all about her and that in the future they hope to have exchange students from other countries. Josselyn says it has its handicaps. She is expected to be an authority on the U.S. and an English dictionary. Before the Japanese 1941 attack on the US, English was taught in the public school and many classes in college were in English. All the girls are required now to take English, but as Dr. Kim explained, they are necessarily slow. I am to work with conversation classes at the YWCA and to help with a cooking class. Life is far from monotonous.

Harold is conducting a Washington, D.C. man on a tour of mines and railroad installations this week. They left Wednesday, went by train for 7 hours, will go by jeep to the mines and arrive at the east coast where they will take President Rhee's yacht for an 18 hour trip down the coast to Pusan; then back by rail. All this is not as easy or wonderful as it sounds, as we are not permitted to eat native food so that must be provided. I helped Harold shop for breakfast for 7 men, also luncheon; another man and his wife were providing for three days and then Harold has to provide the food for the return trip. When you get everything from salt to coffee, it's quite a job. You also take along your own bedclothes (a blanket) as a Korean hotel, outside of Seoul, gives you a room 6x6 with a block of wood on the floor for a pillow. Even at this point, I could write a book, but I won't and the memories I shall keep for years.

The poverty here is unbelievable; rather it is like pictures you have seen and things you have read. The 'exotic scent' of the Orient is plain stink and most of it seems to arise from the honey carts. As there are no fertilizer plants here, all human refuse is put in big jars and collected much as our garbage back home. This in turn is ladled out by the bucket-full to gardeners, and I am told that the worst possible thing that can happen to you is to run into one of these honey carts. You go to the hospital for fumigation if you live that long. This means of fertilization is the reason we cannot eat food grown here unless it is well cooked. Every thing we get is either grown by the Seventh Day Adventists or frozen. I might add that the Lord seems to favor the Koreans, as their vegetables are many times bigger and better. All of our water must be treated with purification tablets or boiled so you can see there are a few discomforts.

I can only say that I hope we stay the two years for it is a wonderful experience. The people try so hard to please and to learn that, for the first time, I can understand the thinking of a missionary. I probably won't learn too much of the language although I get a few words each day from the laundress. She by the way, does the washing in the bath tub or on the tile floor, depending on the size of the piece. This morning when she came there was a slight drizzle; she calls it "pouring small."

I didn't think I would ramble on this much and now must do errands. There is a motor pool which provides a jeep or beaten up sedan; we are not to use local streetcars or taxis. Disease, of course, is always with us and at the moment, there is an epidemic of sleeping sickness so we are all in the process of taking shots. Many people wouldn't venture out on the streets for the world, but we wouldn't miss it, although we always go in pairs. You put away your pens, pencils and watches, keep a firm grip on your purse, and get along all right. Harold's interpreter, a native, has lost three watches, one a wrist watch, so that gives you an idea of the situation. Again, I must get going, write me the news of the family and tell me about your school this year. I sent a card to Harriet and Vance but told them I would ask you to forward this when you had read it. Please do for I don't often settle down to writing. We think of all of you and Harold has spoken of Vance's coming out several times. We decided that it was no place for small babies or even young children. Most of the homes we have seen are very poor living quarters, and we are just fortunate to be situated so well.

With love to you and all the family,

Dorothy

December 17, 1949

Dear Helen,

It was so nice to get your letter of December 6th that I decided to get an answer off at once. Hearing of all the things you did this summer and the news of the family makes it seem like a good visit. I know Paul and Grayce will enjoy having their own home and we would have called them if we had had any time going through Denver.

Josselyn and I have been quite busy with our English classes and teach at the high school four mornings a week; the other mornings I go to the YWCA, or perhaps I told you about that. I have signed up to take on seven of the high school teachers for two days a week; the way that came about was rather interesting. With Dr. Kim, President of Ewha College, on the ship was her secretary and professor, Miss Lee. She suggested me to this high school group so she took me out for introduction. This is a new school, privately owned and very lovely. It is literally built on the side of a mountain and is made of stone; it is very high up, just away from everything. I was taken on a tour of the building and it was a pleasure to see that everything was spotless-one of my biggest objections is that everything is dirty and run-down here-the domestic science room had cabinets for dishes and in it were rice bowls, Korean teacups with lids and other native china. It all looked so different yet the room was planned after the American way of doing things. Instead of gas or electric stoves, each desk had an hibachi or charcoal stove. On it, one pot of food can be cooked at a time. They use no ovens here so do not have bread, as we know it. Later the girls brought us samples of the food they were making, just as a school at home would do, and the dish was a combination of vegetables and mushrooms, very good. In it were pieces of bread as they use, made of rice flour and water, nothing else so it is almost like trying to chew a piece of glue. That I didn't like. Another room had laundry tubs like ours and they teach washing and dyeing of materials. All good housewives must dye material for it fades when washed. Most things are pasted together and when washed must be reglued. The better things are sewed but are all taken apart for laundering and put together again. I have seen some beautiful clothes but they are very expensive. The satin brocades run about ten to fifteen dollars a yard and velvet is from thirty, up. Josselyn is having a wild formal made-the background is kelly green with red and purple brocade flowers. The dressmaker looks at a picture and there you are.

Last Sunday Harold had the interesting assignment of riding the train to the 38th parallel to pick up the two Americans who have been held there for 80 days. (Sept 24-Dec 12) There were four American newsmen and two from the State Department, plus six Koreans. We had the fun of planning a steak dinner and buying the food for their first meal and they surely needed it. They have been confined to a small room for seven weeks and given two bowls of this eternal rice with a few vegetables over it, each day. One had lost nearly sixty pounds and both are nervous. They were questioned for hours and hours when they first landed but two weeks ago were taken to a hotel for their first bath and haircut. Harold took some pictures of the location and the two armies are facing each other just a few kilometers apart. He said the North Koreans kept calling to them and telling them to break away from the Imperialistic Americans and join the free people. Everyone thinks there will have to be war to reunite Korea for the power and natural resources are all in the north part while down here it is mostly agricultural.

Today at the Post Exchange we were able to buy some electric lights for our Christmas tree, other than that, we will be making most of our decorations so will have a real old-fashioned tree. We have been saving tinfoil and cellophane and are going to cover stars and string popcorn. We think it is lots of fun and want our Korean friends to see what we do for Christmas. Of course, most of them are not Christian and when you actually realize that, you feel that Christianity is what is back of our country and its principles.

Josselyn has a Korean boy who has a crush on her. He is 20 and in college, studying law, and will complete his education at Harvard. The family is very nice and we have been to their home for dinner but we feel that Josselyn should confine her social activities to family affairs. Jai Kin wants her to go to the theater, etc., but I think the fact that the army was here has made a difference in the attitude of people. Yesterday he brought her silver chopsticks and a rice spoon with "Merry Christmas" engraved on the spoon. We are making candies and cookies to fix up boxes for several of our Korean families. They love any American food, as it is much richer and sweeter. Their sugar is yellow and unrefined, as is their salt. They buy coffee, Chase & Sanborn, etc., on the black market for $3.00 a pound.

You hear so many cute things such as, the men say "ha, ha, ha" and the women say "ho, ho, ho". We were discussing American poetry with one of the girls and she asked us if we knew "the Barefooted Gentleman". Josselyn and I nearly doubled up laughing but she got the joke too when we explained. If I were a young teacher, I surely would try to see some of the world and get my teaching in as well. ECA sends teachers to many parts of the world for American children but most of teachers in the native schools are connected with some mission.

Josselyn has gotten a great deal from her own schoolwork. I know it has taught her patience for she is asked hundreds of questions a day and answering is no simple matter. She has had to do much outside reading for her courses as some of the regular textbooks are in Korean.

I know you will have a wonderful holiday and I want this to be waiting for you when you get back.

The best of everything and lots of love from,

Dorothy Bennett

June 8, 1950

Seoul Korea

Dear Helen:

Last week Harold received a letter (not available) and I just had to make a copy to send to you; it gives you a slight idea of the way these people think. Mr. Kim is an interpreter in the railway division. He is a graduate of the University of Tokyo and is now going to the Seoul University at night to study Shakespeare. Their idea of higher education is entirely literary for that gives a man the privilege of sitting back and meditating which is called an Oriental virtue. Anything that requires physical exertion is frowned upon and, as Josselyn says, we have "lost many faces" by cutting the grass, pulling a few weeds, or even moving the furniture. To them (the Koreans) there is no pleasure in pushing a lawn-mower—but that is a story in itself—I was able to get a mower through our supply office and no one around our compound had ever seen one before. Well, I showed the boys how it worked and one ran for a rope—then four pulled and one pushed—I explained that it was only a one-man job but you would have to see five men use a shovel the same way to believe how hard it was to convince them. They are like children, always wanting to do things together and everyone has time to stop and watch.

Harold is on a trip and this one is about two weeks long -I'll be more than glad to see him when he gets back six days from now. We, including Josselyn and a young officer whom she dates, took a trip recently. We took the sleeper (only one car in Korea) to Pusan. The berths are six feet long so most Americans have to double up a little. Both the Japanese and Koreans are short and small so sheets and blankets are just 30 inches wide-even I couldn't keep both sides covered at the same time. Instead of the usual bag of rice, we had a bag of straw for a pillow but since there were no bugs or fleas, we felt fairly comfortable.

We drove to Chinhae in a jeep. It took us three hours and a half to drive the 37 miles so you have some idea as to the conditions of the road. Chinhae is a beautiful seaport completely surrounded by mountains on one side and huge rock islands on the other. During the war, it was used by the Japanese as the harbor for their warships and the Allies were never able to locate it from the air. The Commander (Achurch ret.

USCG) took us for a tour of the harbor in his little boat and it is really a lovely place.

The next day we drove inland and came to a town on market day. For miles, as we approached, people were walking in with things to trade or sell; many were women with perhaps twenty or thirty eggs in a basket. When we reached the town, it was crowded with people and booths set up for trading. Josselyn and Hal got out of the jeep to shop while Harold and I stayed to watch our luggage and cameras. People instantly closed around us for most of them had never seen a white woman before. At first, it was a little frightening but they were just curious so I said my few words of Korean, most of which are "I don't understand Korean". That pleased them, but I surely felt like a freak at a sideshow, having them reach in to touch me or my clothes. I had on a bandanna and they wanted to know if I had ears so I displayed them; when Josselyn came back, I explained that she was my daughter.

Further along our trip we stayed at a Korean hotel, a very fine one as hotels go. Each room had one piece of furniture, a large low table for use for eating. There is one bath for the hotel -the tub is about 4x5 feet and four feet deep. It is filled and a fire is made under the tub to heat the water; you are supposed to wash in one tub with running cold water and then get in the other to soak. Each takes a turn, or I suppose you could all go together, anyway, you will use the same water.

Comment by editor who lived for many months in Japanese— Korean homes: *"Dorothy describes what is probably her sole bathing experience away from her assigned quarters plumbed to American expectation with hot and cold running water. She describes two tubs in the bath room: one with running cold water and one with hot water which is not running but heated by a fire. Typically the place in the bath room with the source of running (or more likely, carried in) cold water was not a tub that one sat in but rather it was a place tiled with a floor drain where one stood or sat on wooden stools to soap up using a mix of cold and hot water dipped from the hot tub—the equivalent of a modern shower. Practically, the objective of bathing to become clean was completed without getting in the hot tub. In fact, US military advisors who stayed in places with such hot tubs never got into them and made certain that no one fouled the hot water supply by immersing themselves in it."*

For dinner that night we had fried chicken, chicken rice soup, omelet with spinach and green onions, kimchi (mixed vegetables that have been put down in a jar and kept all winter), toragee (root of blue-bell plant), rice with curry sauce and coffee which we had brought. For breakfast, we had exactly the same thing except that the omelet was cold; in fact they eat the same for all meals and breakfast is the largest.

When you are ready for bed, they bring in three pads, one to sleep on and two as a cover. They were the usual 30 inches wide but very nice and clean. We got up early and hiked to the mountaintop to see the sunrise at a Buddhist temple, it was beautiful and worth the effort. We have been reading up on the oriental religions, and I hope I am located near a school when I get back. I want to take a course in geography for I never felt so stupid about the earth and its people.

Josselyn is planning to leave sometime in August so as to be back in time for school. Her plans are not complete, but she will be going somewhere. She has a total of 22 hours over here but does not know how many will be recognized at Western. If she is not able to have senior standing, she will be going to Ohio State as she feels she would not be happy with her classmates leaving before she does. In a university, it doesn't make much difference but class spirit is a large part of the life at Western. I am leaving it entirely up to her for, as you once told me, I couldn't rear her to be independent and then expect to make an important decision for her.

In TIME (magazine) of June 5th, (1950) you will find an interesting article on Korea. We know Mr. Gibney as he spent some time here on his assignment; we have also met the LIFE correspondent so feel that we have a little personal interest in the news. We went to a nice little tea on Sunday recently -just twelve were there and it was to meet the new Minister of Education-Josselyn has known him for some time, as he is President of the University where she has been going for her class in History.

Dorothy

Harold was evacuated on 27 June by air to Japan and a week later he flew back to Korea to continue assisting Koreans in railroad management.

And finally, Dorothy Bennett wrote the following very interesting article for the Baltimore and Ohio Magazine in early 1951:

"Before World War Two, Korea's 2,000 miles of railroad were operated entirely by Japanese personnel; so that when the war freed Korea it had few experienced railroad hands. As a result, Harold found rolling stock and especially motive power in bad shape. His first task was to quickly teach the Koreans sound railroad operating methods and, above all, proper maintenance of equipment. And the job was made doubly hard by rugged terrain and the even worse language barrier. But as a railroader, Harold enjoyed the challenge and practically ran his own railroad system.

Our year's stay in Seoul was filled with minor clashes and guerrilla warfare along that nearby 38th parallel and, while everyone realized war might come, we had grown used to these disturbances. Then early one June Sunday the North Koreans attacked a village near Seoul. It caused little concern until the approaching crash of big guns and bombs told us this was it.

Harold was called to his office. I'll never forget his dashing away to the railroad calling back—'Don't worry—if the planes get too close, run for the air raid shelter!' And Josselyn and I were alone—-with the battle approaching and the streets becoming a mass of fleeing humanity. Then midnight brought the word: 'Pack what you can carry and report at 3 a.m.' Evacuation was at hand.

Joining the other evacuees, we reached Seoul's waterfront, where more than 700 American women and children were quickly crammed onto a small Swedish freighter. (Ed. Note; a Norwegian freighter) It had a crew of 40 and only twelve staterooms. So to shelter us from the torrential rain, a rope ladder was improvised, the whole 700 of us clumsily climbed down into the ship's dingy and smelly hold—and we sailed for Japan.

We slept as we could, on the floor, each having an army blanket. With the ship's galley built to serve only the small crew, we lived on canned-meat sandwiches—-once having stew which, with no spoons, we ate from cans. The trip to Japan took three days—our only consolation the accompanying planes.

The men had evacuated from Seoul by plane the day after we left. But Harold immediately returned to operate the South Korean railroads, and was attached to the 8th Army until released in December.

Now safely back home and Harold again with the B&O, we realize as never before how precious is freedom in a hate-filled world ready to explode. What we saw in Korea taught us how vital it is for every American to get busy and help rush our war preparations, while opposing Communism in every way we can; for I know its brutality when in control.

In Seoul, Josselyn attended the Ewha University, being the only 'white student'. And it was weird for us to find so few Christians among so many people. But doing what we could among the natives, one soon became accustomed to many strange things. Most important—one gained on the spot factual knowledge of the South Koreans that I wish we all had, to end the misconceptions of some about these wretchedly suffering yet courageous people—as we who have been there know them.

Korea is among the most ancient of lands, its present calendar year being 4284. Small in stature, the people are not a mixture of Japanese and Chinese as commonly supposed, but a pure strain of the original Yellow race, with an ancient language of their own. Their customs and dress have changed little through the centuries. Men and women, alike, wear white. The men's full bloomer-pants are drawn tightly at the ankle. The women wear long loose skirts. Both men and women wear the same style blouse—white cotton for ordinary dress, white silk for special occasions. On their festive days they dress in brilliant colors, though women over 30 do not wear red.

South Koreans have a rich culture, are peace-loving and want only to be left alone. The ox is the beast of burden, and its easy pace seems to mark the South Koreans' tempo of living. Despite their sufferings, their's is a certain peacefulness and patient tranquility you learn to love. They are great visitors, and when you visit them, you are expected to come early and enjoy their hospitality for the rest of the day.

We were guests in many homes. Arriving, you leave your shoes at the door, as is the custom. House floors are immaculately clean and covered with straw matting or heavy oiled paper. You sit on the floor to eat dinner, and believe me, it isn't easy to 'stay put' for the three hours the meal usually covers. Each dish is served as a separate course and is nothing you have ever heard of. Ever try eating slippery, brown sea slugs with chopsticks? In time, you acquire the knack and learn to like sea slugs. Rice is part of every meal. Fish and chicken are used to make soups. There is little meat, due to the lack of grazing land. All food is boiled, steamed, or fried, for cooking is done over small pots of charcoal. Fortunately, we had an old-fashioned wood stove in our home—undoubtedly installed by the American army officers who had previously occupied it. Our cook, 'Henry' (short for Kim Sung Fu), thought it wonderful. We never did understand how he prepared such good meals on it.

As part of our efforts to aid the people, I taught English in a Korean high school and to a class of adults in the YMCA. And I quickly learned that the South Korean people have a high regard for education, literature and art. Young and old—my scholars gulped my teachings and wanted more. But the schools have suffered great damage, like everything in a war-torn country. They are without heat—and how cold a schoolhouse can become! I wore fuzzy wool slippers; but the students wore only socks—leaving their shoes at the door.

That eagerness to learn had much to do with causing the Korean conflict. Under the friendly influence of American occupation and the help it provided, South Korea grasped Democracy and patterned its government after ours. In North Korea, Russia, with an entirely different motive, restored industrial plants, befriended the people, and supplied many needs the Japanese had denied. Here seemed proof of Communism's benefits—so North Korea accepted its teachings as readily as south Korea accepted Democracy.

Yet, while Democracy encouraged the peaceful nature of the South Koreans, Russian Communist teachings made North Korea a land of war-minded fanatics. Mr. Bennett realized this growing difference when on an inspection tour of the northern country before war broke out. The people, under Russian influence, had become hard, cold and unfriendly. On his return, the South Koreans welcomed him warmly.

Let us not forget that Communism's infiltration, propaganda and false 'friendliness' first deceive a people—like China or North Korea. Then, at the opportune time, Communistic propaganda creates a war-mania, with the 'friendly' Kremlin providing the implements and, if necessary, an army of soldier 'advisors.' From that time, speak out of turn—and disappear. I asked a Korean doctor about Communism. He answered: 'Do you know what it is like to live in fear all your life?'

By these tactics Russia has absorbed nation after nation, while its Communistic teachings of hate have grown new armies of Stalin worshippers who, without conscience or religion and recognizing only the Kremlin's flag, have learned to fight like demons.

This is what America faces in a world gone berzerk. Against it, we must quickly prepare our defense—whatever the cost. Otherwise we will pay a far greater price in destruction and countless lives; for as we saw Communism in Korea, it knows neither nationality nor boundaries and has but one terrible purpose—world conquest."

Jossylen continues:

Being a college-age student and in a strange country did not keep me from enjoying the social scene. After all there were a good many young American officers and enlisted men, as well as businessmen representing oil companies and other commercial enterprises. Some gatherings were at peoples' homes, but more were in military and civilian clubs. The main officers' club was at Sobingo, a military compound. The club itself was situated in a Japanese mansion, probably the former general's quarters. After the Japanese were forced out, the US Army had turned the facility into a club. The main ballroom had seen different uses. Although it was a ballroom when we were there, you could look closely at the wooden floor and see the fact that the room had also been used as a basketball court. The Korean band knew all of the latest American dance tunes and added a few oriental tunes that we all got to know, like "China Nights". Tables surrounded the dance floor and so people eating could watch the dancers. One memorable couple were from South Africa; they could match any professionals in their rendering of all of the Latin American dances.

Shortly after I arrived in Korea, I heard that there were going to be square dancing classes at the club on Friday evenings. I called my friend, Betty Jane, and asked her to look around for someone to be my square dancing partner. She called back to say that she bad found a young

Lieutenant, Frank Winslow, who was also looking for a partner. He agreed to pick me up on Friday. I really don't remember our first date, but I do know that we enjoyed the square dancing crowd. They were enthusiastic and energetic. Our caller was Captain Beimfor, a JAG (legal branch) officer from Texas. He had the ability to call the dances and to instruct us thorough the intricate patterns. In our beginning classes, as he commanded us to do an allemande left and chain to the right, he would often have to stop the group and remind someone to use their "other right hand". Although new couples would join the group, the old hands would be able to pull them through the squares, so that it didn't take too many Friday evenings before we became committed square dancers. And that was how Frank became my "Friday-night date".

Most nights if you wanted to go out for dinner or a social evening that meant going to the club. It was always fun to see who was escorting whom. Some people went steady or were committed to each other, and there were a number of wives who had joined their husbands by the fall of 1949-but with a somewhat limited number of eligible women, and a rather stable number of men, it was not unusual for people to date one person on Friday and another on Saturday. Both Frank and I had other people who were our "Saturday-night dates", but that didn't mean that we, and any of the others, would spend the entire evening with the person who took us to the dance. We all moved from table to table being sociable with each other. Sometimes the only way you could be sure who was someone's date was to wait for the last dance to see who paired off for "Good Night, Sweetheart". Other memorable tunes from the club were Army Blue, and the Light Cavalry Overture. Numerous officers turned their chairs into charging horses and galloped back and forth across the dance floor to that music. Someone introduced the Varsouvianna, a European style dance, and we all learned to "Put Your Little Foot".

On special occasions, the women would have new dresses, designed and made locally. Despite the grand occasions, transportation was still by jeep. Frank tells of the time he picked up his date for a formal dance. It had rained earlier and the jeep had acted like an upturned tub in the storm. As they were turning on the way to the club the water swished forward and soaked the bottom of her long dress. Fortunately, for our future happiness, that person with the soaked formal was not me.

Traveling through Seoul during the dark, evening hours was eerie. There was a very limited amount of electricity for the Korean people. The streets were poorly lighted. Shops had carbide lamps but many people used candles. Most military housing had electricity. We were not afraid to go out but everyone knew that there was unrest in the country.

One evening my father, mother and I went to the USIS-the United States Information Service–building for a meeting. The USIS had displays about the United States and generally supplied information about our country. That night there was to be some sort of presentation for the Korean people. As the talk of the evening progressed the mood of the crowd became ugly. My father quickly hustled us out. We were glad to escape back to our compound. I never was quite sure what had occurred but it was clear that not everyone was delighted with having Americans in Korea.

We did take a number of day trips. We visited the kings' burial mounds. We had an outing with several families on a boat on the Han River. We drove into the countryside to take pictures. Brightly dressed Korean children played a teeter-totter sort of game, standing on a board that they would jump on. Most Americans had a picture of a girl rocketed high in the air above the end of the board.

One memorable sight was that of a Korean funeral procession. When a person of note died the villagers all joined in a long procession that would wind along the road. The honored dead was carried in a colorful bier topped with a canopy of brightly striped fabric. Musicians and ceremonial dancers were included in the procession. Professional mourners in coarse straw-colored attire were a part of many funerals.

Outside of Seoul, the country was from a different age. Rice fields dotted the landscape. Villages were made up of Korean houses of mud with rice straw roofs. One house that we visited had very simple furniture, low Korean tables and chests. The Koreans slept on mats on the floor. The most unique thing about the houses was their heating system. They build a fire in the kitchen but the flue went under the floor and heated other rooms in the house. Even in cold weather, their thousand-year old technology of in the floor heating kept their homes comfortable.

Children at Play Photo from the Souvenir Shop Seoul 1950

The military people had maps. There were only a few main roads. Once, when my dad was out of town, a friend invited mother and me to drive to Uibigonbo, towards the 38th parallel. We wandered along the roads until we came to a woodsy, military looking establishment. We tried to find someone to ask about the place-to see if we were near Uibigonbo, but no one seemed to be around. We finally found a sign with both Korean and English writing by the roadside. We got out of the jeep and read the words. We discovered that we were in a leper camp! We dove back into the jeep, did a fast U-turn and headed back for Seoul.

My father, mother, another officer and I took a road trip to the south, to Taegu and Taejon. We traveled to see some of the historical sites in Korea. We visited the first observatory, built, as I recall, in 67 AD. It was a simple conical tower with an open top that would allow observers to see a specific part of the sky and be able to record the changes with the hours and the seasons. We also went to Bulguksa-a lovely old Korean museum and inn. We stayed in the Korean-style rooms, with matting on the floor, sliding doors and a "slit-trench" toilet. I was fascinated at the simplicity of a toilet that was just a porcelain trench in the floor, but easy to use—and I am sure, easy to keep clean. The hotel staff provided us with bedding, including mats, covers and a "pillow." The "pillow" was made of porcelain and about the size of a cracker box. We decided that it was one Korean amenity we could do without-particularly if we wanted to sleep that night. Our trip was over the usual dusty roads, with lots of ruts, but non-the-less most memorable. And it gave us a much better appreciation of Korea and its historical and cultural past.

Summer time is always the time when the Army makes the majority of its reassignments. A number of our friends, including Frank, had received orders for new posts in the states. I planned to return to the states to college at the end of the summer. There were a series of farewell parties.

The comfortable social scene was interrupted by the North Korean invasion of South Korea in the early morning hours of Sunday, June 25th. My father, mother and I spent the day wondering what would happen next—and listening to the Armed Forces radio station to keep up with the news. By evening, we were notified that the North Koreans were advancing on Seoul. All military and civilian dependents were told to pack and be prepared to evacuate. I vaguely remember trying to decide what to pack. At my father's urging both mother and I packed two bags—for as he said, "You can always throw one away if you can't carry it." We agonized over what items to take and what to leave. In the end, we chose a mix of what we would need to wear and what we would like to keep. Mother had a particularly lovely round, green cloisonné container that she treasured. She had put dusting powder in it. I remember her standing in the middle of her bedroom and saying, "I can't take this; the powder will spill." Much later we realized that she could have just dumped the powder on the rug and packed the dragon-decorated container. My other strong memory of the night was hearing Guy Lombardo's rendition of "Enjoy Yourself, It's Later than You Think" played, quite appropriately, on the radio.

In complete darkness, we traveled to a designated area. The women and children said good-by to the men, boarded busses and traveled in a dark convoy from Seoul to Inchon. It was distressing to see one of the girls who had been square dancing with us be turned away from the bus because she was Russian and could not to be included for evacuation with the group of US citizens. It was light by the time we were at the harbor. We got into the small boats, which took us out to board the Reinholt, a fertilizer ship that was standing by to evacuate the women and children to Japan. It was a chaotic scene as families climbed aboard the ship. Mother and I carried our bags to the main deck. We hung over the ship's rail watching as others came aboard. Many families had small children. At least one man, a civilian worker, was included. He apparently had been so stressed by the events that he was brought aboard in a straight jacket.

The crew of the Reinholt found sleeping space for us in the ship's holds. Our bags stayed on the decks—which was no problem until it rained and everything that we packed got wet. Somehow, the crew managed to feed everyone and everyone managed to share the limited number of latrines, except women of the Chinese Embassy who had to wash their hair. The late June weather was warm enough that we could be on deck and the water was smooth so seasickness was not a problem. After two days of travel down the Yellow Sea, around the south west corner of Korea, and through the Korea Strait to debark at Fukuoka.

I later learned we sailed at 4 p.m. with 682 passengers; and that we not only had combat aircraft, F-82 and B26, over us for the trip but at dawn two US Navy destroyers escorted us to Japan.

The Army took the families to a military camp with big, old Army barracks. We were assigned beds, ate in the Army mess hall and used the common latrine, which had a long row of toilets. One of the kids rushed back to tell his mother that a couple of the toilets had pink seats and he had used that. It was reported later that the Army made it a practice of having special colored toilet seats for use by soldiers with VD.

Within a short time, my mother and I moved on to Tokyo to a downtown hotel to await my father's arrival from Korea. When he came in by plane from Kimpo, he reported that he had a phone call back in Seoul from Frank Winslow to tell me good-by. Little did we know what the future would bring for our family and for him.

Typical coastwise shipment   Photo from The Souvenir Shop Seoul 1950

Out to Sea

Our five ships, dressed in gleaming new paint, were an impressive sight for ship lovers. Although smaller than the average ocean-going merchant vessel, they were very large by 1940/50 Korean standards. They had a gross weight of 2500 tons and 250-foot length. They were highly maneuverable and drew a light draft for navigating and docking in the sometimes-shallow harbors of South Korea. Junks, barges and inland trucking had carried out much of the inter-coastal trade.

Three of our vessels, the *Whitney*, the *Whidden* and the *Winsor*, were assigned to carry rice and coal from Korea to Japan and fertilizer from Japan back to Korea. The other two ships, the *Lester* and the *Brown*, had the job of transshipping between Pusan and the southern and western Korean ports of Yosu, Mokpo and Kunsan. Typically, when loading rice, the product was bagged and the bags were placed on wooden pallets. The Korean longshoremen had the responsibility of bringing the product to shipside and the winch operators would load the pallets with the ship's own booms and winches. On one occasion, the Koreans had a work stoppage. There were hundreds of loaded pallets on the dock when the winch operators suddenly walked off. Our departure was delayed and unless we did something about it, we would be in Mokpo for many days or perhaps even weeks. I believe the dispute was over food quality and rest periods. I had never operated a ship's winch but after a little practice, I got the hang of it. I would handle the vertical winch and Chief Engineer Murphy handled the horizontal movement of the load with another winch. Captain Kitts took a position at the hatch being loaded and directed our movement of the pallets into the hold.

Normally, Koreans would be in the hold properly stacking the bags. Without them, we simply dumped the pallet loads into the hold. After many hours, we winched the hatch covers into place and departed Mokpo. We got menacing looks from the Korean shore-gang throughout the operation. After all, we were "scabbing."

Unloading chemical fertilizer was a different operation altogether. Discharging in Kunsan at the mouth of the Kum River a hundred or more Koreans wearing coolie hats, facemasks and two buckets hanging from a yoke-frame on the shoulders, formed an endless human chain from shore to the ship's hatches. The air was so thick with fertilizer dust that at times it was difficult to see the shore from the ship. A narrow plank was placed across the hatch and each coolie would pause over the hatch long enough for his buckets to be lowered into the hatch, filled with the dusty chemical and raised back to his yoke. It was fascinating to watch them scale the narrow planks from shore to ship and ashore again; then start another round. There was a definite talent and rhythm to their well-synchronized work and we were surprised at how rapidly they could unload an entire cargo of many tons. We could not have challenged a walkout during this operation. It is difficult even to imagine three Americans in coolie hats scooting across the planks barefoot. Perhaps I shouldn't refer to those workers as "coolies." That implies a kind of slave labor. I am really not sure but their expert plank prancing and bucket shuffling demonstrated a lot of experience in this kind of work. It could be that they were the last of the coolies. By definition, a coolie is an "unskilled laborer" and these men were certainly not unskilled.

The Korean crew was organized in the traditional American con-figuration, that is: Captain, First, Second, Third and Jr. Third Deck Officers, Boatswain, Carpenter, six Able-bodied Seamen (AB's), and six Ordinary Seamen comprised the Deck Department.

Armed guard on the S.S. "William Lester" Photo by author

Two Koreans made up our Armed Guard.

The gun-tubs on the bridge were empty however, and our armed guards carried only loaded forty-five caliber automatics. They were on board to counter any violence on the part of the crew; especially mutiny.

The Engine Department was comprised of Chief Engineer, First, Second, Third and Jr. Third Engine Officers, Electrician, three Pumpmen, six Fireman/Water-Tenders, six Oilers and three Wipers. The Engine Department is commonly referred to as the "black gang."

Officers of the "William Lester." L to R: Assistant Radio, Interpreter, Chief Radio Pak Kee Long, Third Officer, Captain.
Photo by author

The Steward Department was made up of Chief Steward, Chief Cook, Second Cook/Baker, Third Cook, three Messmen and three Bedroom Stewards (BR's). There was one prominent exception, "Cook for American", who was added to ensure that the Americans would enjoy a semblance of digestive order. "Cook for American" was a Korean and, no matter what American menu he was struggling with, the meal looked and tasted much the same as the Korean meal being served at the same time. The total crew numbered 70 and approximately half of them were experienced with the other half being trained.

Each of our ships carried three Korean Radio Operators. One of them was more experienced than the other two and his shipboard title was Chief Radio. The other two were cadets being schooled in marine radio operation. I was surprised to learn how well they knew the code and relieved that I would not have to teach it to them. During the first few weeks, I spent most of my time on board assisting them in becoming familiar with the American radio equipment. Chief Radio Pak had been operating Japanese radio equipment for several years, and, of course, the common denominator was the code. Once the receiver and transmitter were tuned to the desired frequencies, they could easily communicate with shore stations and other ships. Each day we would take out the equipment instruction manuals and schematic diagrams and spread them out on the counter. Chief Pak knew enough English to follow me and he would interpret for the cadets. We would open the piece of equipment being discussed and viewed on schematics and, tracing the circuitry, discuss the method of operation. For every sentence I spoke there followed about five minutes of English/Korean interpretation by Pak Kee Long.

The three of them would babble back and forth in their language, pointing first to certain parts of the equipment and then to the schematic diagram and instructions. They were good students and learned quickly. These five-minute breaks in Pak's instructions gave pause to lean back and prepare for the next lesson. We would cover only one piece of equipment each day and in the afternoon, I would give Pak a written Q & A that he translated into Korean and gave to the cadets. I insisted on an eighty percent passing mark and then covered again any incorrect answers. They were very enthusiastic. After all the equipment had been thoroughly covered, we took the same approach to proper maintenance, including the ship's batteries. Finally, after a few weeks and a few coastwise voyages, the cadets were cleaning the equipment and shining brass and it was time to bring on fresh radio cadets.

On the second day of a stay in the port of Mokpo, a young Korean boy came on board and delivered a message to Captain Kitts inviting the three of us to dinner at the mission-home of the Columban priest. We dressed clean and casual and were getting ready for the walk of a mile or so to the mission when we heard the noise of a gathering crowd on shore just aft of our ship. A young man of about 25 years was in the river just below the crowded sea wall. He was swimming slowly out into the fast ebb-tide current of the river. (There is approximately a 32-foot difference between high tide and low tide.) He disappeared and reappeared three or four times and then was gone, an apparent suicide. The crowd dispersed.

We left the ship for the mission escorted by the same young boy who had delivered the invitation. The four of us walked the cobble-stoned main street while our escort explained why the man swam to his death. He had stolen a bicycle and was caught. He said, "That's it. There's nothing else to tell."

The priest, an Australian, welcomed us and made us feel as though we were royalty. We were treated to many courses of carefully and well prepared food dishes, wine and desserts. His Korean wait-staff was very efficient. In spotless and well-starched white blouses, dress and apron they moved quietly and gracefully to and from the kitchen. The priest spoke of the history of his Mission, the Columban Fathers. He was very curious, inquisitive about our purpose, and objective in Korea. We lit up cigars offered by the priest and we chose from a variety of liqueurs. While Capt. Kitts filled in the priest on our mission in Korea, Milo and I retired to the billiard table for a couple games of snooker.

It was very late when we made our way back to the ship without escort. It had been a wonderful evening with a great host. Back "home", in Hialeah Compound we told of our Port of Mokpo shore leave to an interested audience at a chicken barbecue. Chief Engineer Des Mann, after hearing our tale, said their ship had called at Kunsan and their Radio Officer, Frank Crosby, had visited the Columban Fathers there. The priest asked Frank if the ship could take some baggage to Mokpo. Capt. Scanlin didn't hesitate. He sent a message back to the priest agreeing to do as he requested. A few hours later three large trucks showed up at shipside loaded with a variety of goods.

The load visibly increased the draft of the ship. When they arrived at Mokpo, they anchored off the port waiting for a berth. The priest, bearing a striking resemblance to Barry Fitzgerald, came out to the ship in a very large launch with many Koreans who off-loaded the cargo from Kunsan. Captain Scanlin and Chief Mann were invited to dinner at the mission.

Frank had already gone into the town with his camera. At the mission the priest offered drinks after dinner and advised Chief Mann that his deep-freeze machine had failed. Chief Mann fixed the machine and they had more drinks. An in-depth discussion on the subject of religion followed during which, according to Mann, the priest showed great restraint.

Posing on the steps of the Mission School in Mokpo, left to right: Ch.Engr. Des Mann, Columban Father in charge of school, Ship Captain Jim Scanlin.
Photo by D. Mann

The Disappearing Uniform

On another coastwise voyage, I discovered during a routine inspection that the ship's batteries needed water. The distilled water was kept in 5-gallon glass jugs and strapped to the bulkhead on the stern housing. It was necessary to climb a ladder to reach the bottles, cut the strapping and somehow lower the bottle to the deck. I should have called on Chief Pak and his cadets to fetch the water but Milo Atkinson, in full dress uniform, gold-braid and all, volunteered to assist. He stood at the bottom of the ladder while I held the neck of the heavy bottle and slowly lowered it toward him. When he announced that he had a grip on it, the bottle suddenly slipped from his hands and crashed to the deck at his feet. He was soaked from head to toe in what we thought was simply distilled water. Either the Japanese vendor who supplied the ship in the Yokohama shipyard had chosen to add acid to the water, or it had been ordered that way. The result on Milo's clothing was disastrous. After hanging his clothing to dry, Milo's uniform dissolved into thin air. His gold braid and shoes were also damaged beyond repair. The debate over who was at fault ensued for several weeks. Every time the event was discussed, it drew smiles and snickers from the crew and officers. We were not surprised when Milo appeared once again in full braid dress. He had stored a spare set.

Strawberry Dessert

The most desired commodities in South Korea that were missed by Americans were ice cream, fresh milk and, while at sea, fresh fruit. We were not blessed with ice cream in our ship's freezer but we did have a rationed supply of frozen strawberries and pint bottles of "Avocet"; an American-made milk substitute with the consistency of whipping cream but sweeter. Every other day the three American officers would hide away in the Captain's quarters and delight in ice-cold strawberries and cream. A real treat. Each of the officers had a key to the freeze-locker and the refrigeration locker. The Captain kept a careful count of the treasure and discovered the supply was diminishing faster than the three of us were consuming it. He asked Milo and me to turn in our keys. We did, and nothing else was said about it. We continued our dessert sessions in the Captain's quarters with the Captain in control and he reported the inventory had stabilized.

The Collision

The S.S. *William Lester* steamed along the coast on a calm sea and overcast sky. It was near midnight and the 12 to 4 watch was preparing to relieve the 8 to 12. The rest of the crew was sound asleep when suddenly there was a loud "blam-blam" and the ship lurched hard. Our engine was stopped, then reversed, then stopped again. The crew, some half-dressed, scurried about the decks turning on the cargo floodlights. Aiming the lights on the sea, it was soon apparent that we had struck a large junk. The junk was split in two, sinking fast, and there were men in the water to both the port and starboard of our ship. We quickly launched two of our lifeboats, one on each side of the ship, and picked up the swimmers. We had no idea how many were in the crew of the junk. After getting them on deck and handing each a blanket, the Captain of the junk announced to our Korean captain that his crew of 19 was all present and accounted for. We led the victims to the warmth of the midship passageways. Captain Kitts opened the ship's stores and gave each of the shivering crew a carton of cigarettes and a quart of whiskey for them to share. We disembarked the unfortunate crew at the Port of Yosu and the local authorities were invited on board to record the event. In the ensuing weeks, a lawsuit was initiated and the case went to court. After the first day of the trial, the case was quickly settled by giving the captain a new junk and a certain amount of cash. Everyone was satisfied. The officers and the lookout on watch on the *William Lester* at the time of the collision swore that the junk displayed no navigation lights. The Captain of the junk swore in court that he did have an anchor light displayed.

8

Family Arrivals

March 1950

Mr. Alonzo King, attached to the State Department in Seoul, advised that I bring a handkerchief and a small bottle of perfume with me to Kimpo Airport. This was to ease the shock that Marion would feel as she stepped from the airplane into the objectionable odors of Korea farming for the first time. He was right. The wind carried the odors from the nearby fields and gardens to the aircraft exit as the door was opened. When Marion stepped out onto the accommodation ladder her hand shot straight to her nose. She was repeatedly asking, "What is that? What is that?" as I gave her a big hug. I slipped the perfumed handkerchief to her and said "Welcome to Korea, you'll get used to it."

(L to R) Author, Dottie Kelly, Alonzo King, Marion.
Photo by Joe Kelly

Her pregnancy was starting to show. She was more beautiful than ever. After gathering her luggage in the terminal, we were whisked away to the Banto Hotel in Seoul in a car with a chauffeur provided by our helpful Mr. King.

As we entered the lobby of the Banto Hotel, the Armed Forces radio broadcast station (WVTP) behind a large glass window caught my attention. I quickly introduced Marion and myself to the two broadcast engineers (Army personnel) operating at the console; explaining to them that I was also "in radio". We chatted briefly about my assignment to Pusan, exchanged amateur radio call signs and parted with a promise that we would chat more later.

We were given a large comfortable room; a bottle of wine and a bouquet of flowers graced the table. The decor was impressive with ceiling-to-floor drapes, over-stuffed furniture and large ceiling fans. We even had room service. The bathtub must have been three feet deep and we had a good laugh because the water was up to our necks.

We were treated to a welcoming reception that evening which many of the higher-ranking American personnel attended. Most of them held positions in the State Department, the American Embassy, the Korean Military Advisory Group or the Joint Administrative Services (JAS), all elements of the American Mission in Korea (AMIK). We enjoyed a fabulous smorgasbord including the largest shrimp we had ever seen.

The next morning we were put on the train to Pusan with a package of cheese sandwiches and a can of pineapple juice. We were given a small compartment that had a small bench seat but no berth that would have allowed Marion to rest better. A small basin with a very slow-running water-tap graced the corner of the compartment. After departure, we asked one of the train attendants where the lavatories were and in his very poor English, we finally understood the facilities were two cars back. I escorted Marion to the designated car and thought it best that I stay outside the entrance and wait for her. Seconds after going in she came back out. She looked like she had just seen a ghost. She said, "I'll tell you about it back in the compartment." After hearing her report on the facilities, I had to return to see for myself. I opened the door to the "lavatory" and could hardly believe the scene. A trench, about a foot wide, ran the entire length of the car and male and female alike were squatting over the trench. The odor was unbearable. The waste in the bottom of the tank car sloshed back and forth as the train pitched from side-to-side. On my way back to our compartment, I asked an attendant if there was any other kind of lavatory on the train. He soberly informed me, "Most Americans use bowl in compartment."

Marion's arrival was followed by the arrival of Joe Kelly's wife, Dorothy "Dottie" Kelly. Joe met her at Kimpo accompanied by Alonzo King.

Next arrival by air was Frank Crosby's wife, Doris Crosby from Lima, Peru. Doris was strikingly beautiful, but conceit and lack of charm offset her beauty. She also lacked personality and was somewhat anti-social; a spoiled child of well-to-do Peruvians. When Doris arrived, she was eight months pregnant, would have her baby in Korea and then return immediately to Peru with the baby.

The Mrs. Atkinson, Peterson, Scanlin, Kressen, and Mann arrived in Pusan on board the *U.S. Army Transport President Cleveland*. They had many stories to tell about their crossing the Pacific from San Francisco but, since the men were not privy to all the chitchat, their factual report-

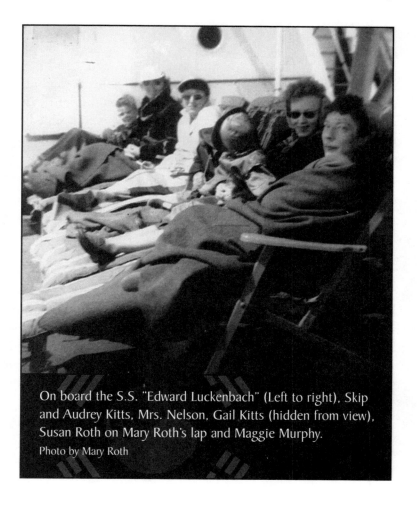

On board the S.S. "Edward Luckenbach" (Left to right), Skip and Audrey Kitts, Mrs. Nelson, Gail Kitts (hidden from view), Susan Roth on Mary Roth's lap and Maggie Murphy.
Photo by Mary Roth

Audrey Kitts & Mary Roth.
Photo by Mary Roth

ing is not recorded here. Some gossip made it through the screen but let's just say that one of them on board was flirtatious. After all, it was only gossip.

The Mrs. Kitts, Nelson, Roth and Murphy arrived in Pusan on April 23 on board the S.S. *Edward Luckenbach*. Son Skip and daughter Gail were with Mrs. Kitts and daughter Susan was with Mrs. Roth.

The compound occupants went through a dramatic change. The men no longer lingered long evening hours at the club bar. They no longer played poker all night long. The foulness of their language cleared up; their personalities changed. They accompanied their wives to dinner at the club and retired to their respective homes at a decent hour except when Bingo or some other entertainment was scheduled.

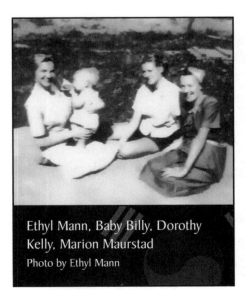
Ethyl Mann, Baby Billy, Dorothy Kelly, Marion Maurstad
Photo by Ethyl Mann

Saturday night was dance night. The club had a good speaker system and the acoustics were excellent. The room would fill with our favorite tunes. After a week or so, everyone was pretty well settled in and daily life was more routine. The men, their wives and children, were reunited and prepared to spend a year in South Korea with an option to renew contracts for an additional year. No one seemed to have any idea about what was boiling just north of the 38th parallel.

The Good Life

Marion inspected the house and she was delighted. She was not expecting an American-style home. There were some questions about the size of the kitchen and the stove. When I told her we would be taking our meals in the clubhouse her face beamed in a big smile. I had done my smiling the first time I had looked at the meal-pricing three months before; Breakfast 25 cents, Lunch 50 cents and Dinner $1.35. She remarked that not having to cook would be like vacationing. She sighed with relief when she saw that we had a flushing toilet. That was the final clause in a contract of acceptance.

Now that the wives and children had arrived at Hialeah, life in the compound settled down to an enjoyable routine. The need for the ship officers to be at sea frequently was not something new to the families.

Marion at her new home
"She was delighted"
Photo by author

They were experienced in keeping the home fires burning for their seafaring men. The coastwise voyages in Korea were short compared to the lengthy voyages of one to three months on the Atlantic or Pacific. In our Korean shipping operation, we could depend on spending almost twenty-five percent of our time ashore. There was ample entertainment and recreation. There were card games, movies, bingo and billiards in the clubhouse. Baseball, tennis, volleyball and horseshoes on the compound grounds, tending to gardens, housekeeping and shopping.

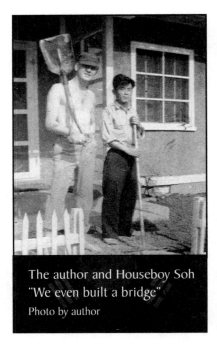

The author and Houseboy Soh
"We even built a bridge"
Photo by author

All our letters to and from the states were handled by the Army Post Office at domestic postage rates. The usual delivery time was approximately 10 days. The Pusan mail was taken to the Seoul post office every day by train and went from there to Japan and the U.S.A by air.

The Fish Pond

During one of my stays ashore I decided to build a goldfish pond in the small front yard of our house with the assistance of our houseboy Soh. We found cement and tools in the warehouse and after gathering stones of various sizes we set to work designing, outlining, digging and constructing.

We felt a great deal of satisfaction when our project was complete. We had even built a bridge across the center of the 8' x 2' pool and planted two small pine trees nearby. Soh managed to find a half-dozen goldfish and ceremoniously lowered each one into the pool the next morning. The word got out fast and we had more than the usual number of visitors to look over our decorative achievement.

Shopping trips to Pusan City were a biweekly highlight. There was always transportation of some kind. There were jeeps or small buses waiting at the front door of the clubhouse. The same vehicle would stand by at an agreed-upon time and place for the return trip.

The streets were narrow and, although the shops were small, they were bursting with merchandise that was primarily from China, Japan and India. These, when added to the variety of local handicraft items, offered many choices. There was an endless variety of woven products provided locally.

Man in a dog fur hat. "We did not see many dogs"
Photo from The Souvenir Shop Seoul 1950

Shopping with Korean money was somewhat of a problem. The exchange was a few thousand Won to the U.S. Dollar. It was comical to watch the wives trying to stuff enough Korean bills into their pocket books for a half day of serendipity. Following adequate warning about the frequent purse snatching in the city, their purses were secured both over the shoulder and around the waist. The purse then held no other valuables than the large bulky bundle of bills. In spite of the precautions, there were several occasions when fast thieves with sharp knives would cut the straps and make off with the money. After the first excursions into the markets, headdress of any kind was left at the compound. It was quickly discovered that hats, bonnets, caps and scarves were favorite targets of the market thieves. The thieves were youngsters with great speed and they would quickly disappear into the crowd.

There were many shoes, boots and hats on sale with brims and linings of attractive fur in various shades of black, gray and brown. Some with patches or streaks of white. When we asked what kind of fur it was, we were shocked when told that it was dog fur.

No wonder we did not see many dogs around the streets of Pusan. Later, we did see a pack of 10 or 12 dogs tethered together and herded through the town by a man who was very likely heading for the slaughter-pens. A heartbreaking sight for dog-lovers.

One evening, while the Kellys, Marion and I were enjoying dinner in the clubhouse, a very large young man who was vaguely familiar to me approached us. He said, "Hi Ray! Hi Bernie!" Then I recognized him. It was Bob Clinton, who had been one of my 1944 classmates in radio school in Boston. While there, a girl by the name of Bernie had come to Boston to visit me. I had introduced her to Bob and, apparently not remembering her very well, he was addressing Marion as Bernie. After I explained, Bob was embarrassed, apologized and bought a round of drinks for our table. After dinner, Marion retired to our house. Bob and I kept the bar busy until closing, reminiscing about radio school. What a small world!

There was an American Embassy Annex near Pier One and it housed the only other restaurant in Pusan that served genuine American food; the other one being at Hialeah Compound's Flamingo Club. This restaurant had a reputation for excellent chicken and seafood dishes. After a busy shopping trip in the city, we decided to have dinner there and we were seated next to the windows on the back of the building. The staff was made up of several Koreans and the manager was a foreign national. I thought I detected an Australian accent when he greeted us. We didn't notice the scene outside the window for the first few minutes.

Then, with a small gasp, Marion nodded toward the spectacle outside. There was a garbage heap immediately outside of the building rear entrance. It was at least 30 feet in diameter and about six feet high. The pile of garbage alone was enough to spoil an appetite but it was topped off with more than two-dozen small Korean children and several adults each carrying a sack or pail. Scratching through the mess, they would quickly put each "discovery" into their containers and hurry back to scratching. Dozens of birds were competing with them and both the diggers and the birds seemed accustomed to each other's company. Marion jerked her head toward the door and I knew she felt as I did. It would be impossible to enjoy a meal here. On the way out, I caught the manager's attention and complained about the activity outside. He apologized and remarked that if they were able to have the waste removed more often they would do so. He said that it was removed about every six weeks. We had learned another lesson in economic aid to South Korea.

Sergeant Barber drove over to our house one day with a small brown dog. We immediately fell in love with the puppy and Barber told us we could keep him. Because the dog arrived in a jeep we thought it appropriate to name him "Jeepo." Our first concern was whether we could housebreak him. We opted instead to keep him outside if he would not run off. Testing that option, we were pleased to find that he was satisfied to sleep on either the front porch or the back stoop. He would follow us to and from the clubhouse and would wait patiently outside until we came out with a treat for him. He had found a home and we were happy to have him. We would allow him inside a few times a day and if it rained or was very windy, we would allow him to sleep just inside the door. He quickly learned to do his duty only outside.

It never occurred to us that someone would steal him and deliver him to the slaughterhouse. After he had been missing for three days we concluded that the monetary temptations, or the hungry home table demands, were just too much for a Korean compound worker to resist. We shed our tears and missed Jeepo for some time to come.

The Monkey

Joe and Dotty Kelly were visiting with us for a few hours at home. When we showed them out, we hesitated on the front porch. Young Skip Kitts and his sister Gail were across the street, walking toward us and holding a monkey. The monkey stiffened suddenly when he saw us.

Gail & Skip Kitts holding pet monkey
"The little fellow is in love with you"
Photo by Mary Roth

Then, in two long leaps he landed on Marion's chest and threw his skinny arms around her neck. He was instantly in love with her. He hugged her tight and didn't want to let go. Marion appeared mesmerized and she was visibly shaken. Joe tried to remove the monkey's arms from Marion's neck but each time Joe touched the monkey he snapped at him. Skip and Gail laughed and easily removed the animal. "The little fellow is in love with you. Would you like to keep him?" Marion quickly replied that in no way would she entertain the thought of having a monkey jumping around in her house. As they left with the monkey on Skip's shoulder the monkey continued to stare wide-eyed at Marion. We never thought to ask them where they got the animal and we never saw it again. I suspect that their father, Captain Kitts, brought it home from one of his recent voyages.

The Thief

He was Korean, but he did not look Korean. He was taller than average, thinner, and his hair was long and stringy. He was perhaps thirty years old and wore eyeglasses that were in need of repair. He could have used repair himself in the way of more frequent bathing. He toured the compound almost daily and would show up at our house once a week. He carried a folded bed-sheet over his shoulder as a sack to hold his wares. The merchant was always welcomed, especially by the wives, since he carried such an interesting variety of items. These included silks, brass, ceramics, carvings of wood and ivory and an impressive variety of jewelry and coins. He would spread his bed-sheet on the living room floor and carefully lay out his offerings. We would sit on the floor with him while we shopped. There was never a price on anything and it was difficult to judge a good bargain. The ladies usually used cigarettes for payment. They cost us only a dollar a carton but were worth much more on the Korean market. He preferred cigarettes rather than Korean money. Joe and Dotty would join us and that helped the negotiations. He would spend as much time as we allowed and he would not pressure his sales. Instead, he listened carefully, and his response in English was fairly good. After serving him American coffee, he tried to increase the frequency of his visits to our house but we discouraged that.

The Kept Man

Perhaps the most colorful characters in Korea were the gentlemen we dubbed as "Kept Man." Aged to retirement, he was credited with having great wisdom. These grandfathers were dressed, at all times from head to toe, in carefully laundered all white garb. He was treated with great respect by all, in particular his family members. More often than not, his appearance included a long-stemmed pipe. He was very dignified, wore a black stovepipe hat and always stood out in a crowd. Tourists would follow him with camera in hand and he was accustomed to posing for them. His tunic had long sleeves where various personal items could be stored, e.g., his pipe, when it was not in use. We were told that the kept man was well cared for by his family for the rest of his life.

A "kept man", well-kept & respected

Photo from The Souvenir Shop Seoul 1950 .

Another colorful character passed right by our house daily. House 306 sat on the north border of the compound marked by the 12-foot wire fence. Immediately outside the fence was a well-worn path that paralleled the fence for the entire one-mile circumference of the compound. The path was used frequently by the local population moving from one side of the compound to the other. This population included many women carrying big loads on their heads.

What made this passing parade colorful was that the women were almost topless. Sometimes totally bare from the waist up. We had not noticed this in the city. There seemed to exist a greater demand for modesty when visiting the city versus the country, a double standard of sorts. On the other hand, was it perhaps the same in the city and we hadn't noticed it? After all, we had been in Pusan for only the colder months so far and everyone had been dressed warmer. Now in the warm spring scene, Joe's mouth was hanging open and Dottie punched him awake.

Marion and I had been sitting together on the back stoop of our house with Joe and Dottie. Marion remarked that she had been cautioned by Soh not to wear shorts or short skirts, as it was taboo. Dottie ran next door and put on her shorts. Marion put on a shorter dress, as she couldn't get her shorts on over her pregnancy. Now, when the passing women arrived at our property and observed the two American women with bare legs, they would break into a faster gait or run with their faces turned away from our porch. It was obvious that the Korean topless women were embarrassed in much the same way as the American women were. Miss Chun and Soh did not approve of our actions. They had retreated to the front of the house during the dress parade. Soh shook his head and remarked, "Evahbuddy be bad."

Large Honey-Pit for Sale

When the U.S. Army occupied South Korea and Hialeah Compound in late 1945 they did not have a plumbing system before the homes were built. They dug their very large latrine near the western perimeter of the compound and it served them well until the home construction was completed in late 1946. The latrine cabins were then torn down and the pit was covered. Now in the winter of 1949-50, a small group of Americans gathered to discuss a moneymaking idea. I was invited into the group, which was headed up by Sergeant Barber. I could hardly believe that their moneymaking idea was to

Korean mother carries lunch to the field workers. "Dottie ran next door and put on her shorts"
Photo from The Souvenir Shop Seoul 1950

sell the contents of the latrine pit to a local honey buyer. I knew there couldn't possibly be enough money in such a business venture, especially after splitting any profit six ways. Barber assured me that the goal was to get rid of the pit contents whether there was any money involved or not. There were four of us from the marine group; Capt. Kressen, Engineer John Murphy, Radio Officer Frank Crosby and myself. Alonzo King came down from Seoul and joined our group at the Flamingo Club on a Saturday morning with a honey buyer and his interpreter in tow. Gerry Lucas also joined us and we all moved from the club to the covered latrine pit. The honey buyer lifted one end of a wooden cover, poked around with a stick for a few minutes, put the cover down again, huddled with his interpreter for a few minutes. Then his interpreter announced, 'I sorry, American honey has also too much paper. No sell, no buy." That was the end of the honey sale and I couldn't stop laughing for a while. We were all laughing. We had fun. Variations of the failed plan were told in the Flamingo Club for a couple of weeks. The participants, including myself, took quite a razzing. Within two weeks, the honey-pit was being emptied. I asked Gerry Lucas if the project had been renegotiated. He winked and said the club paid the Koreans to remove the contents and fill in the hole.

High Wire Electrician

Captain Woods, Engineer Murphy and I were returning to the compound from Pusan when, with only a few hundred yards to the entrance gate, I had to stop the jeep for a crowd in the road. There were a few vehicles, several bicycles and a few dozen pedestrians in the road. They were all looking up at a man lying across the power lines about 100 feet off the ground. Smoke and sparks were flowing from one of the man's ankles where his flesh met with a live wire. Two men were climbing the tower with slings and lines but they were hesitating every few feet and shouting to someone on the ground. I guessed they were waiting for someone to shut off the power. Then suddenly the man's shoe, with his foot in it, fell to the ground. Up on the wire the sparks continued for a few minutes between the man's leg and the wire, and then stopped altogether. The two men continued their climb, were able to put the man in a sling and lower him to the ground. We assumed the man had been electrocuted and had seen his last day. I edged the jeep through the crowd and continued on to the compound. In the next Stars & Stripes newspaper, there was a short piece about the accident and it was reported that the man survived after amputation of the injured leg.

The Handkerchief Dance

There were times when we would be pleasantly surprised with entertainment at the Flamingo Club. One evening in particular comes to mind. Everyone in the compound had gathered in the clubhouse for the dinner special. Tiger Kim*, in police uniform draped with his many medals, entered the dining room with his assistants and bodyguards. A hush fell over the room as they were seated.

Not to be confused with the Tiger Kim of North Korea.

We all 'ooooh'd" and "aaaah'd" when the food was served. The prawns were the size of dinner plates. None of us had seen Tiger Kim in person and he had arrived unexpectedly. He had come to see the Flamingo's Saturday night entertainment and with his arrival, we sus-

Entertainer using musical instrument Kayagum "They moved in unison with the music" Photo from The Souvenir Shop Seoul 1950

pected the show must be something special, and it was. Gerry Lucas came to the small stage above the dance floor. The room became silent again as Gerry tapped the microphone, asked for attention, then announced, "I am pleased to present the Korean Dance Group of South Korea performing the Handkerchief Dance." Without hesitation, the stage filled with a dozen beautiful young Korean girls. The silence was slowly interrupted by the sound of string music.

It was eerie and wistful at first and a strange new sound for the audience. The music picked up the beat and the rhythmic dance started. Slowly and with grace, the dancers started to move about the stage, swinging, swaying and twirling their vibrant kerchiefs. Their silk gowns of many pastels were flowing with every graceful movement. At times, they seemed as one body as they moved in unison with the music. The finish of the dance was greeted with foot stomping, whistling and applause.

There was some commotion from the back of the room. We all turned to see what it was. A group of Hawaiian men got up from their tables and headed for the dance floor. These men were the crew of the S.S. *Jacona*, a World War I battleship that was converted to a power plant for the purpose of supplying power to the city of Pusan. One of the men walked to the jukebox, put in a coin, and ran back to join the group that had formed a line in front of the stage. Within seconds the music of the Hawaiian War Chant filled the room and the Hawaiians started grunting and gyrating with great agility and showmanship. As the recording came to an end so did the silence of the audience. Gerry Lucas had put another coin in the machine and the war chant was playing again. The Hawaiians started dancing again. The entire audience got up and joined in as Gerry announced that the drinks were "on the house."

Haeundae Beach

Haeundae Beach was just a few miles from Pusan. In 1950, it was mostly desolate and barren. A couple of small buildings housed some maintenance equipment and there were a few vending stalls. You can see from the shadows almost directly underneath them that they were there at high noon. At a later and warmer date Joe and Dottie Kelly joined Marion and me for a return visit to the beach.

The Hunt

Sgt. Barber knocked at the door. Over his shoulder, I could see his jeep parked in the road with two Korean teenagers in the back seat. "Wanna go hunting Ray? We can bring home some fresh meat. Got a deer 3 weeks ago. Got a gun for you." He was smiling from ear to ear. It was five o'clock in the morning.

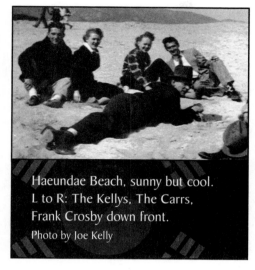

Haeundae Beach, sunny but cool.
L to R: The Kellys, The Carrs,
Frank Crosby down front.
Photo by Joe Kelly

I quickly put myself into what I considered the proper hunting attire. While dressing, I wondered why he had not asked me sooner so that I could have planned on it. He introduced the boys as Kim and Kim Two. He said Kim Two would be my gun bearer. I felt a certain level of excitement as I had on many hunting trips for pheasant and deer as a teenager in Minnesota. The hunting season in Korea began in September and ended in April. In addition to deer, you could hunt wild boar, bear and wolves. Eagles, hawks, pigeons, quail, dove and pheasant were also fair game.

At the curb, Barber showed me the gun he brought for me to use; a 12-gauge Remington shotgun. Four extra shotguns were laid across the floor in the rear seat. Barber assured me they were not loaded. He filled my jacket pockets with #6 buckshot shells. He had an M-1 rifle in case we spotted any deer. Birdshot in my gun meant I would be looking for birds, not deer, and that was fine by me. Barber remarked that the boys would not be allowed to shoot and cautioned me to not let them carry a gun if it was loaded. We zoomed out of the compound and headed North with Barber at the wheel.

The countryside was strikingly beautiful at dawn. We wound and wormed our way up the dusty roads between greening hills, rising hillsides and along fast-running streams. We finally pulled off on a plateau north and west of Tongnae and some 50 miles North of Pusan. The view was magnificent. The hills dropped away to the sea like a huge rolling carpet and I stood spellbound for a few moments marveling at the sun's brilliant reflection on the sea.

The Korean boys flushed out cock-pheasants and fetched them after we brought them down. Carrying large burlap sacks slung over their shoulders, they appeared to be enjoying the sport even more than we were. I felt sure their enjoyment was closely related to Barber's promise of payment as well as a share of the meat.

What happened next is difficult to remember in my fading memory. We had become separated from Barber and the older teenager. I brought down two pheasants quickly and Kim Two ran to fetch the first one. The second bird was only wounded, ran across a clearing and over an embankment and I went after it. On the other side of the bank, the ground dropped away steeply and I lost my footing. I was sliding down the hill feet first. I let go of the loaded shotgun and fought to regain my balance but only tumbled head over heels down the small hill. I came to a sudden stop and feeling dazed I decided to stay there for a few minutes to recover. I saw the bird laying a few feet from me, still breathing and looking at me. What's this? Guilt? Me? I had a deep sense of foreboding and couldn't reason with it. I felt very sad and thought of blood and death. Then I heard a voice "You okay? . . . You okay?" It was a deep baritone and not the voice of Kim Two. I was looking up at the voice up side down and above me. I rolled over and looked up at an elderly Korean man and Kim Two was standing behind him. I climbed slowly up to them retrieving my gun on the way and told them "I am okay . . . okay." The man started slapping Kim Two's burlap sack with the back of his hand repeating "Bird for me . . . bird for me." I pointed to Kim Two and then to the bird at the bottom of the hill. I gave both birds to the old man and he walked off toward a hut in the distance. I assumed the man owned the land we were on and wanted to be paid for its use.

Now Kim Two was patting the back of his head and pointing at my head saying "P'iananun . . . P'iananun" (blood . . . blood) I ran my hand down the back of my head and came up with a streak of blood. I must have hit or scraped my head on the way down the hill. Barber's repeated shots reminded me that he must be bringing down many birds. We were soon reunited and Kim and Kim Two chatted excitedly as they transferred birds from Kim's bag to Kim Two's bag.

The floor of the jeep was soon filled with as many pheasant as we dared to take. The boys began pointing to a large stand of trees and kept repeating, "pidulgi . . . pidulgi! Barber said, "They are trying to tell you there are many pigeons over there in the trees." Sure enough, although at first difficult to see, there was one branch of a distant tree lined with dozens of small pigeons or doves. "Ko-yo hada, ko-yo hada" the boys quietly repeated as we moved toward them. Barber interpreted for them in a whisper "Quiet, Quiet" When we were in range we fired together and brought down 10 to 15 birds. This may sound a little greedy but in each bird, one of the breasts made only a mouthful. We had more than 50 pigeons and our cache of a couple dozen pheasant when we decided to head home.

On our trip south, we encountered some very exciting hunting. As we came over the crest of a high hill; there before us lay a beautiful fast-running stream and, struggling to stay with the current were a dozen or more ducks and geese. Perhaps I should not describe this as the most exciting hunting as these fowl were more or less "sitting ducks". In any case we could not afford to spook them so we crawled along the road-side on our bellies with an agreement that by a signal from Barber we would rise in unison over the stream's embankment and fire at will. It was important to position ourselves downstream from the birds in order to retrieve them. We did this and the birds rose from the stream in a noisy flurry. Firing off several shots resulted in seven birds floundering on the surface of the fast moving water. The birds were now floating with the speed of the stream. We dropped our guns and ran into the shallow water to fetch them. After an ample soaking in the knee-deep water, we returned to the road with the best bag of the day; three geese of about 15 pounds each and four ducks of about 4 pounds each. It was now time to go home, for sure.

On the way back to Pusan, Barber dropped the two boys off in the suburbs and gave each a few birds and some money.

When we arrived back at the compound the keepers of the galley volunteered to dress out the many birds while we drank beer, boasted and watched. The next day we had the community at the barbecue. It was a good day for a meat-starved group of people.

Frank Winslow in Seoul, Winter 1950/51
Photo by Frank Winslow

The Army Lieutenant

1948-1950

Frank J. Winslow was a 22-year old Army lieutenant assigned to the 123rd Signal Photo Detachment serving XXIV Corps in Seoul, South Korea. That was in September 1948. Here is Frank's story in his own words:

"I trained at Ft. Monmouth, New Jersey in the Signal School Officer's Associate Basic Course from 19 April '48 to July 21 '48. The classes were held in Hangar #4 that was used for WWI Signal Corps aeroplanes. Behind the hangar was the Pigeon Breeding and Training Center established during WWI. Homing pigeons were still used to carry messages during WWII.

I came out of Camp Stoneman/Fort Mason California (near San Francisco) and spent ten days on the U.S. Army Transport ship *General Aultman* from San Francisco to Yokohama and visited burnt-out Tokyo for several days. I then boarded a small Japanese built ship up the Yellow Sea to Inchon South Korea. This curious vessel's accommodations included a vast expanse of Tatami mats for sleeping. In Korea, cultural shock set in the first night when I found slit-trench toilets in the Bachelor Officer's Quarters.

I was assigned to the 123rd Signal Photo Detachment serving XXIV Corps where General Hodge commanded his Corps troops along with a depleted 7th Infantry Division. The U.S. 6th Infantry Division had been inactivated in 1947. Major Bill Burkel was Corps Photo Officer and Capt. Norman Flint Commanding Officer of the Signal Photo Detachment. As the detachment's power generators became inoperative, we had to print photos between midnight and 5 a.m. using 60 to 80 volts. At this time of day Seoul's trolley cars were not running thereby making available some of the diesel generated power from the *Electra*, a power barge permanently docked at Inchon. The steam generated coal burning power plant at Yongwol was intended to be the major source of electrical power after the Russians cut the south off from the north's hydro-electric power in May 1948, but I was aware only of the Inchon power barge which continued supplying power until June 26, 1950.

The Power Plant at Yongwol. Until the Soviets cut it off in May 1948, two-thirds of the South's electricity came from big Jap-built hydro installations in North Korea. ECA Photo

Carbide lamps were the main source of illumination for people of Seoul. U.S. Forces made do with candles in their quarters and unheated clubs. We dipped hot water from a metal bucket on top of a space heater for shaving and bath. The water source was the five-gallon water can. Food was dreary, all from cans, Vienna Sausage 3 times a day. Nothing fresh—a weight loss diet for everyone. Serving of rice (even U.S. grown rice) was prohibited to avoid complaints that the U.S. Forces were eating Korean rice.

December 48 to May of 49, I was with Company A, 76th signal Service Battalion. I continued photo service, training film and projectors mainly used for Hollywood movies distributed by another organization to U.S. Army Forces in Korea (USAFIK). Col. "Baldy" Collier was Chief of Staff. Col. Francis Miller was signal Officer. USAFIK's troop unit was an infantry regiment. We built a photo lab and film/projector exchange in an old Japanese Army compound occupied by the 76th Signal Service Battalion on the north side of Nam Sam Mountain and east of the Cathedral. Officers were quartered in a Japanese built home in the residential section of Seoul not far from the 76th Signal compound. In May we were billeted in a new 6-story hotel called the Traymore and operated by the State Department, whose policies did not segregate men and women.

In May of 1949, I was assigned to KMAG headquarters USAFIK. The remaining U.S. Army of Occupation troops including the 76th Signal Service Battalion departed Korea. The U.S. State Department's Ambassador John Muccio represented U.S. interests in Korea with two major programs; one, Korean Military Advisory Group (KMAG) to advise the Republic of Korea (ROK) Department of Defense, including ROK Army (ROKA), Coast Guard (Commander Achurch at Chinhae & Commander Speight at Seoul) and National Police; and the other: the Economic Cooperation Administration (ECA) to help get the one year old government and its economy on its feet.

The families of KMAG officers, State Department and ECA employees arrived in May and June 1949. Most appreciated were the single young women employed by the State Department and Army Special Services. I hasten to add that one of the ECA dependents was the 19-year old daughter of a B&O (Baltimore and Ohio) Railroader who was hired to advise the Ministry of Transportation and its inexperienced managers of the Korean railroads who succeeded the Japanese in 1945.

During the 40 years that Korea was part of the Empire of Japan the Japanese designed and operated the railroads in Korea and had no reason to train the Koreans to manage them. The same condition applied to all parts of the government structure. Following Japanese Empire rule in Korea was U.S. Military government from late 1945 to 15 August 1948 when the Republic of Korea was established following United Nations oversight of the first-ever election of a government in Korea.

June of 1949, we built a new KMAG photo lab on the first floor of the Mitsui Building. Other tenants included the Army Post Office, RCA Telegraph Office (they used circuits on the Mukden, Manchuria buried cable that went through Seoul and then undersea to Japan). Message traffic from Japan to USA went by high frequency radio (sky waves and rhombic antenna fields). Perhaps traffic went by undersea cable across the Pacific, but I lack such information. KMAG PX (Post Exchange) occupied the second floor. Directly across the street was the Banto Hotel, which housed the offices of the ambassador, his military attaches, the ECA, and Lt. Hughes' crypto room. Directly behind the Banto through a historic park was the Chosen Hotel where the senior state department officials lived and earlier where the colonels who comprised the Army Headquarters in Korea lived. During the 18 months before the war, I had the only U.S. government photo facility in Korea. A customer of our lab was The U.S. Air Force Office of Strategic Intelligence. I was also the Public Information Officer for KMAG (hometown releases).

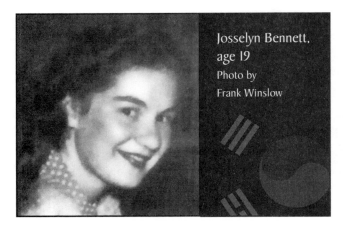

Josselyn Bennett,
age 19
Photo by
Frank Winslow

In May 1950 LTC Edwards, the embassy's military attaché, asked me to photograph the execution of 39 North Korean guerrillas who infiltrated the south to wreak havoc in the country-side. Their presence in the mountains caused one third of the Korean Army to be devoted to their capture. As the jail filled to capacity, there would be a trial and execution. My execution photos had arrived in the post office from the Kodak Color Labs during the week I was on leave.

Frank Winslow's story continues in Chapter 17.

Guerrillas about to be executed. Photo by Frank Winslow

11

The House Help

April 1950

Housegirl Chun and Houseboy Soh "I make garden grow faster... bigger" Photo by author

The day after Marion arrived we were introduced to our house help, Chun, the house girl and Soh, the houseboy. It was difficult to determine their exact ages but we guessed they were both in their mid to late teens.

Both were shy and quiet but obedient. Soh was a hard worker and Miss Chun was a bit withdrawn and lazy. Her job was most of the indoor work while Soh chopped wood, kept the wood-box full, tended to the garden, cleaned windows, disposed of trash and kept the hardwood floors clean and polished. Miss Chun was responsible for keeping the kitchen and bathroom clean, making beds, doing the laundry work, dusting and the sort. We were advised that we should pay them with an eighty-pound sack of rice and two U.S. dollars each month. We object-ed to that as being too meager but were told that we had better not pay them more as that arrangement was a "hard and fast" rule and was all that was expected. Breaking the rule would incur problems; especially the bickering that would follow between the more than 100 house-helpers in the compound. Both Soh and Chun would arrive on a bus in the morning and depart the same way in the evening. If one or both of the house-help stayed overnight it was an exception to the rule and usu-ally requested of them when the house would be otherwise empty or unguarded. There were occasions when Marion would overnight with one of the wives who had a husband at sea.

Marion and Soh got along especially well. Now in her sixth month of pregnancy, Marion liked to take short walks around the compound and Soh would walk with her. "I make sure that Sir not fall down." When he wasn't busy and Marion wasn't resting, Soh was constantly at her side. He always called her "Sir". He started with "Miss Sir" but later refined it to "Sir". I was always "Mistah" but she was "Sir". Several ses-sions of tutoring on genders and proper addressing failed completely so we just gave up. She would be "Sir" and I would be "Mistah." Marion would sit with him and teach him English words and he would teach her Korean. "Thank you" came first; "Ko-map-sim-ni-da" as they pro-gressed through the simple and most commonly used words in both lan-guages. Marion asked Soh to teach her how to say, "I love you" in Korean so that she could say that to "Mistah" Maurstad. Soh blushed and hesitated but finally responded with "Nanun tangsin sarang imni-da". At that moment, Miss Chun had walked into the living room from the kitchen to hear Soh say only, "I love you" to Marion in Korean. Miss Chun very quickly covered her face with her hands; swung around and ran out the back door. Surely, the bus carrying out the house-help that evening was buzzing with gossip. Later in their language lessons Soh asked Marion to teach him how to say words to "shunshine song."

For the next two months our house and yard were filled with song; "You ah mah shunshine, mah oni shunshine, you may me hoppy aw day rong." Soh loved the song and he would sing it even as he walked from the house to the bus each evening. He no doubt was a star in his home village with his newly acquired talent.

Our knowledge about the homes and families of Soh and Miss Chun was very limited and there was a certain reluctance to discuss their lives outside of the compound. Soh did, however, boast about his father's big apple orchard and would bring us a few apples every day. The apples were sweet, crisp and juicy, but after we enjoyed the first ones there followed two weeks of recovery from dysentery. Thereafter, we soaked the apples overnight in Halazon treated water.

We enjoyed fresh baked bread from the kitchen in the clubhouse. A few varieties of canned meat were available so that we could make up sandwiches. Fresh meat, milk and vegetables were not available. We dared not consume the locally grown vegetables as experience had shown that nary a single American digestive system could process them in a civilized manner. The most sought after of the missing items was lettuce. Lettuce for sandwiches and salads. It wasn't long before I had a lettuce bed in full bloom on the west side of the house. The crispy cool taste of those large green leaves between two pieces of bread smeared with potted-meat, canned ham or Spam and mayonnaise was a gourmet's delight for a week or so. The neighbors would visit for sandwiches and coffee. It really hurt when it had to end. I went out one morning to pick a few leaves and the odor was just too much. I looked for and found Soh, and told him of my disappointment with the garden odor. "Oh Mistah, I make garden grow fastah, biggah." I told him the garden was now all his to do with what he pleased as long as he did not apply any more of his liquid honey-mixture. I never did figure out where he got the stuff. He either planned to take over the garden or did the deed innocently and in accordance with his garden programming at home. With perhaps as much as 18 more months ahead of us in Korea, I preferred to believe the latter and to settle the situation diplomatically. We soon learned to soak all fruits and vegetables in Halazon treated water no matter what the source.

It became apparent that these teenagers were having difficulty adjusting to American ways and, as a result, they accidentally provided us with some bizarre entertainment. Marion and I had been in the city for the day and on returning we could hear a loud moaning coming from the house. When I opened the door Soh was in the middle of the living room looking very frightened. He was nervously wringing his hands and shuffling his feet. That was something he would do anytime he felt something was wrong or something needed fixing. The moans were coming from the spare bedroom where we found Miss Chun rolling back and forth on the bed and writhing. She was obviously in pain and was gripping her midsection. Marion tried to make conversation with her in an attempt to find out why she was suffering so, but the girl would only continue moaning and rolling. I guessed it must be an attack of appendicitis so I told Soh to run quickly and get Nurse Mella. Nurse Mella managed to quiet Miss Chun enough so that she could press and explore her abdomen and quickly ruled out appendicitis. Then Soh appeared in the doorway with an empty Exlax tin and sheepishly remarked, "I think Miss Chun eat candy." We closed the door to the bedroom and left the door to the bathroom open. We dismissed Soh and he headed for the bus stop. We thanked Nurse Mella and she returned to her office shaking her head. Marion and I went to the club-house for a couple of hours. When we returned Miss Chun was resting quietly and there were distinct footprints on the toilet seat. She slept quietly most of the night with only one or two more trips to the porcelain relief station. We let her off the next day and saw her onto the incoming morning bus where she encountered many questions from the Koreans arriving to start their day. Miss Chun quietly seated herself and covered her face without replying to them.

After returning from a long trip to Seoul and back, we arrived at our house mid-afternoon. We had asked Soh and Chun to wash all the bed linens and other soiled clothing and hang them out to dry before our return. The bathroom door was open and we found both Soh and Chun in the bathtub, fully clothed and up to their necks in water. Our linens and clothing were also in the tub. We then realized that we had failed to introduce them to the laundry facilities in one of the outbuildings. They were aware of the facility but they had never been shown how to operate the machines. They had decided to take the most expeditious route available to them and to wash the clothes they were wearing at the same time. We assisted in rinsing and hanging the laundry outside then led the two of them to the laundry building and put them through the paces on the washer and dryer.

After Soh and Chun left for the day, Marion wanted my attention in the bathroom. She showed me long strands of black hair in her toothbrush. Fortunately, we had spares.

On yet another occasion, we returned from a day of festivities in the compound including baseball and a delicious chicken barbecue arranged by Gerry Lucas. This time the offender was a strange and terrible odor throughout the house. We traced the odor to the cabinet underneath the kitchen sink. There we found a large dish pan covered by dish towels and on closer inspection discovered that either Soh or Chun, or both, had decided to concoct their favorite dish; Kimchi. The mixture of cabbage, radishes, fish, salt and sugar must have been there for a few days but it was not until fermentation had progressed to the point of bleeding that it escaped the cabinet. Now it had permeated the wallpaper and it would stay there for a few weeks. We aired out the house day and night and may have slowly become accustomed to, or unaware of, the odor. We asked Soh to remove the dish from the house and it was gone that same evening.

Could this have been any worse than one of our Scandinavian dishes popular in Minnesota; Lutefisk?

We had a good laugh telling Joe and Dotty Kelly, our next-door neighbors, about these incidents. They related some similar experiences that they had with their house-help; "Joe" and "Cho". We wondered what we would have thought if Koreans had come to our country, built a Korean home on the river and, hired us as house-help. Would they then expect us to perform in accordance with Korean customs and culture?

The Capital at Seoul
U. S. Army official photograph. National Geographic Magazine.
June 1950, page 778

To Seoul Again

April 1950

Marion was handling her pregnancy very well but she did occasionally hunger for pickles and ice cream. In any case, it was time to see a doctor for a checkup. Most non-Koreans visited the doctor at the 7th Day Adventist Hospital in Seoul for the more serious attentions of medicine. Certainly, there may have been some good Korean doctors in the Pusan area but once the doctor in Seoul had been labeled, that was the place to go. Considering the number of non-Koreans there were in South Korea, I have always wondered why the U.S. did not have a doctor assigned.

On our trip north and somewhere near Taejon our train blew its whistle and came to a screeching, jerking stop on a bridge over the Kum River. Our car was directly over the water and the lifeless body of a young man lay half in and half out of the water. He had been on the bridge and apparently could not outrun the train to avoid being hit. The water was turning red at his feet and a small crowd gathered. The crowd turned in unison to look at an approaching woman; most likely his mother. Her hands went to her mouth and she dropped to her knees. Our English-speaking conductor told us that she would have some difficulty moving the boy's body as it was customary that whoever last touches it is responsible for the costs of funeral and burial. I found that hard to believe. Our train moved on.

We were expected at the desk of the Kookje-Sudo Hotel. Someone had pre-registered us. After signing the guest book, we were assisted to our room. Opening the sliding rice-paper door revealed a large platform about one foot higher than the entrance and that is all there was; no furniture, no cabinets, no toilet facilities; nothing except a light blanket and two wooden "pillows" wrapped in silk. Marion was delighted but skeptical. She had seen so many different and fascinating pictures back home in school and now she was living the pictures. She wondered aloud, "I hope we can sleep on those pillows." We didn't. We used our clothes wrapped in a roll that night. The bellhop explained in broken English that the toilet was down the hall, just around the corner. We piled the luggage in a corner before going on the bathroom search. We couldn't find the ladies room so I asked Marion to wait for a minute outside the men's room while I used the facilities. Returning to the hallway, I assured Marion that there was no one in there so she should go in while I stand guard outside the door. I hadn't checked it very well. She came out again after just a minute or two. Red-faced, she told me that she had sat down and then saw a man's shoes in the stall next to hers. The man also came out; smiled and continued on his way. We finally located the ladies room on the floor below ours. Marion would remember my poor surveillance job for the next 50 years.

We taxied to the Banto/American Embassy restaurant for dinner that evening. During dinner Marion's face turned red again. The same gentleman was at a nearby table and had just nodded to her in recognition. He was apparently amused with her embarrassment.

Seoul heavy traffic—1950
Photo from The Souvenir Shop Seoul 1950

After her check-up with the doctor in the morning, we decided to walk in one of the parks nearby. It was a beautiful morning and we walked while holding hands and admiring the beauty of the flower gardens. The cherry trees were in full blossom and completely covered the walking paths. A group of small children followed us, pointing at us and snickering. The group was growing larger as others left their swings and sandboxes to join the parade. Marion was the first to realize why we were such an attraction; we were holding hands and perhaps her pregnancy stimulated their mischief and curiosity as well. A few of the children dared to walk backward in front of us while holding their eyes wide open with their fingers. I laughed and responded by stretching my eyes into narrow slits. We all laughed together. My thoughts flashed back to my days in grammar school when we teased Asians by stretching our eyes. Now we had become a major attraction in the park. I decided to

Korean soldiers enjoying the view—summer 1950
Photo by Frank Winslow

give them a real treat and took Marion in my arms while I gave her a long passionate kiss. Well, that did it; the children dispersed like a flock of birds on the highway with a bus approaching. We enjoyed the children and they enjoyed us. Our teasing and laughing together was a healthy form of communications.

When we arrived back in Pusan, Joe Kelly informed me that a man from the State Department had been visiting Hialeah Compound. He confidentially told Joe that the North Koreans "will attack South Korea after the rainy season starts." (June through Sept.) First, I didn't believe it. Second; that was two months away. Anyhow, Joe said the man was drinking heavily. I didn't repeat it and I put it out of my mind.

Seoul, Korea, May 10 (AP)—DEFENSE MINISTER SIHN SUNG MO WARNED SOUTH KOREA TODAY THAT INVASION BY COMMUNIST NORTH KOREA WAS IMMINENT. MR. SIHN SAID INTELLIGENCE REPORTS INDICATED THE NORTH KOREANS WERE MOVING IN FORCE TOWARD THE SOUTH.

Amateur Radio

I was very proud of being a professional radio operator, without much respect for amateur radio operations. After graduating from the U.S. Maritime Service Radio Training School in Boston Harbor in April 1945, I operated radio on several ships, on Wake Island for Pan American Airways and at Grand Forks, North Dakota for Northwest Airlines. I had mastered 45 words per minute in code while operating high-speed circuits between the islands of the Pacific; operated radio teletype circuits and guided aircraft into Wake Island by radio oscilloscope direction finder and maintained traffic control circuits for commercial airlines. Pompous and conceited about my professional status as a Radio Officer, I applauded myself for having graduated from the lower ranks of amateur radio. My view of amateur radio was an organization of people who could not pass the examination for a commercial license and had to settle for amateur status. How wrong I was! I was very wrong!

February 1950 I found myself in South Korea with no reasonable or dependable telephone service. There was no way for me to satisfy my thirst to talk with Marion and the folks at home. Frank Crosby had an amateur radio station but he operated strictly in Morse code. I could get a message out to the states but then would have to wait patiently and too long for a reply. Frank did not have a microphone. His pounding the Morse key was his first love, after photography, and he would chat that way with the stateside amateurs for hours.

A real stroke of luck came my way when a cargo freighter, the S.S. *Pioneer Wave*, called at the port of Pusan. I should mention that, more often than not, when ships called at Pusan, the officers would find their way to Hialeah Compound to take advantage of the Post Exchange, the meals, and the bar. Not necessarily in that order. George Terhune was the Radio Officer on the *Pioneer Wave* and he asked about radio operators while he was enjoying a drink. I was called over to the bar to meet him. George was from Chicago, 15 years my senior and a professional in electronics. We hit it off right away, talking ships, foreign ports and radio. In the course of our conversation, and a few more beers, I brought up the subject of poor communications with home. George sympathized with my plight and invited me to the ship to see his personal amateur radio station. I confessed my feelings about amateur radio and he quickly responded that I should not be negative without knowing more about it.

George returned to his ship. I followed first thing the next morning. The *Pioneer Wave* was docked at Pier 1 and several Americans were visiting. Just as the visiting sea-going personnel enjoyed raiding the Hialeah Compound, so did the shore personnel enjoy the shipboard change of diet that included steaks, fresh milk, vegetables and ice cream. The *Pioneer Wave* was 459 feet long, 63 feet abeam and 40 feet deep with a 25-foot draft. Her speed was 15.5 knots. Well maintained and in fresh paint she was a beautiful sight to see.

After a brief introduction to the ship's Captain, George escorted me to the radio room. He was obviously a very good housekeeper as even the copper tubing lead-ins from the antennae were shining bright. The tiled deck was squeaky clean and the non-skid carpet well vacuumed. The Bedroom Steward performed these latter two tasks. George's pride and joy was his amateur radio station. Dwarfed by the huge console of commercial equipment behind it, the amateur equipment was made up of four units. The radio receiver was a National Radio Short-wave NC-200. The transmitter was a black box Meck T-60. (60 watts) The VFO (Variable Frequency Oscillator) was a Millen with a variable arm for very fine-tuning. The microphone on a stand was a Turner D150.

I had now entered into the world of amateur radio for the second time. The first time had been in St.Paul, Minnesota in 1937 when a neighbor boy and classmate friend by the name of Charlie Zahn had invited me into his home to see his father's ham radio. I remember being mesmerized by the bright blue light of the mercury-vapor tubes. I soon built a crystal radio with a cat-whisker for tuning and listened to local broadcast stations. Then, when I went to Cub Scout camp in Turtle Lake, Wisconsin, I rigged two-hundred feet of wire through the trees from my tent to another and slowly sent and received Morse code with a fellow camper on battery-powered Morse keys.

Now George would do something illegal to convince me that I needed my own amateur radio station. He fired up the transmitter and took the microphone in hand. Carefully moving the dial of the receiver, we soon heard California stations signals booming through the speaker. George chose one of the stations and clicked his microphone to the "on" position at the same time tuning the little transmitter to its best output and then spoke; "Hello, this is W4AYE Maritime Mobile near the coast of Korea." This was the illegal part. International telecommunications agreements did not allow a station to transmit from a country without that country's express permission. George was breaking the rules and knew it, but he was determined to make his point then and there. Immediately after his call, there must have been thirty or forty stations answering George's call, rendering the accurate copy of any one of them impossible. After a wait of two or three minutes the din of signals died down to a point where it was possible to understand a few of them. George transmitted again, "Ladies and gentlemen, this is W4AYE Maritime Mobile again off the coast of Korea. We appreciate the many calling stations but the collective interference is too heavy to maintain communications with you. Please transmit on a frequency within twenty kilocycles either side of this frequency and we will pick out one of you to talk with. Go ahead, this is W4AYE Maritime Mobile."

Again, there was a deafening collection of stations calling on top of George's transmitting frequency but several of them had moved off to the sidelines. Then George was able to pick up one of them and invite him in. The station was in California and he announced that he was very pleased to reach a ship near Korea and at the same time announced that he had "phone-patch" facilities and wondered if he could connect anyone to a telephone number in the States. I quickly wrote down my mother-in-law's telephone number in Minneapolis and George gave it to the California station. Within a minute or so, I was chatting back and forth with Marion. The signal in both directions was clear as a bell and we chatted for one half hour or so. After hanging up, we asked the California station where we could send a check to cover the landline charges from California to Minnesota. He advised us that he would not accept any reimbursement. "It is my pleasure, gentlemen, just send me a card acknowledging that we have had this contact." As

George signed off, we could still hear the hundreds of stations calling. There would be another day.

George sat back and smiled, "Well, have you had that experience on amateur radio before and what do you think of it now?" I told him how pleased I was and told him that I would be trying to get some G.I.'s in Japan to price out some radio equipment for me. I could not pass up opportunities like the one he had just presented. George rose from his chair, still smiling, and put his hand on top of the transmitter. "You know Ray, this little gem has been with me for a number of years and, as much as I love it, it is time I look around for a replacement. If you want, I will let you have this entire station for two hundred dollars, and that's half what it is worth." After our jeep ride back to Hialeah with all the equipment in the back seat, dinner and drinks were on me along with the check. I was very pleased. This was amateur radio and George was not only a professional but he was also an amateur radio operator. My respect for amateur radio was on the first block of a new avenue.

I set up the equipment on the writing desk on the dining-room side of the living room. I was so anxious to get on the air, I just ran a copper wire from that corner across the living room into the bedroom hallway and tacked it to the walls about six feet off the floor. At eight o'clock in the morning, the signals from the states would roll in like local broadcast. At that time in Korea it was 6 PM on the West coast of the states and the hams, having just finished dinner, would be listening for stations in the Far East. I soon found out that it was not necessary for me to put out a lengthy call like "CQ CQ CQ from Korea." In 1950, the propagation of signals on 10, 15 and 20 meters was at its best. I had only to whisper into the microphone "This is South Korea" and I would have a response. It really was that good and it really was that easy. I knew that I could get into trouble if I did not secure a license to operate from Korea. I sent a copy of my commercial license to the Chief of Communications in Seoul and within a few days, I had my South Korean license and call letters "HL1CE". The South Korean government granted my amateur license in recognition of my commercial license and in a reciprocity agreement with the U.S. Government. I was, of course, delighted. Marion arrived before I changed my antenna to the outside of the house.

April 1950

When Marion would no longer tolerate a "hot" copper wire running across her living room, I decided to build an antenna that would beam my signal to the states. At the warehouse, I found enough copper tubing and a 25-foot section of steel pipe. With the assistance of Joe Kelly and Frank Crosby, I assembled a 3-element Yagi for the ten-meter band. We stapled the tubing to three wooden slats. We mounted the assembly on one end of the pipe and secured the pipe to the side of the house. The results were phenomenal! Many of the responding hams in California had 1000-watt stations and beams aimed on Korea. It was not unusual for one of those stations to pin the signal meter on my receiver providing what we referred to in amateur radio jargon as "armchair copy." It simply meant that the signal was perfect and comfortable to the ears. I also relocated my equipment to the second bedroom immediately under the location of the new antenna and strung copper wires up in the air for the other radio bands.

When the word got around that we had direct communications with the states, there was a high demand from the residents of Hialeah for communications with their homes in the United Sates using my radio. I had to organize a priority list and put their names on a schedule limiting a morning's work to three callers. I would put the coffee on at seven o'clock and they would come in at 0730, 0800 and 0830. It worked like a charm. I can't say enough for the kind cooperation of the operators in the U.S. who would connect their telephones to their amateur equipment and connect our caller with his or her party for two-way communications. Then talking to home was as easy as one, two, three. We always asked the ham radio operator in the states to make the telephone call a collect call however, more often than not, he, or she, would pay for the call.

I would be back on board ship by ten a.m. and put in a full day. When we had to leave port for another voyage the radio operation from the house would have to cease, of course, but on a few occasions I transferred my equipment to the ship and would operate as "HL1CE/Maritime Mobile." Now the callers were limited to the American Captain, Chief Engineer and myself and the connections were just as good as they were from the house. We kept our families well informed of our activities.

6/9/50—AMBASSADOR MUCCIO ADVISED CONGRESS THAT THE THREAT TO THE REPUBLIC OF KOREA WILL CONTINUE AS LONG AS THERE EXISTS IN THE NORTH AN AGGRESSIVE COMMUNIST REGIME DESIRING THE CONQUEST AND DOMINATION OF THE SOUTH.

The new communications link with the states improved morale noticeably both in the compound and on board ship. Frank Crosby continued to provide written message exchanges and Captain Nelson did his part to provide both voice and message service with microphone and key. Before long, these amateur stations would prove to be of much greater use than anyone could have anticipated.

"Highball"

6/19/50—Ambassador Dulles visited the 38TH parallel on June 18 and the next day told the Korean National Assembly: "You are not alone. You will never be alone so long as you continue to play worthily your part in the great design of human freedom."

John Foster Dulles "The Korean Decision" by Glenn D. Paige 1968 The Free Press, A division of The Macmillan Company, page 74

When we met the radio broadcast engineers, Francesco and Al, on our arrival at Seoul Radio WVTP in the Banto, we discussed amateur radio. They wanted me to know that they had a personal amateur radio station at the Embassy with call letters HLIUS. I paid little attention since, at that time, I had no amateur radio equipment and did not plan on getting any.

After buying George Terhune's radio station off the S.S. *Pioneer Wave*, I made several radio contacts with HLIUS. We became better acquainted with Al and Francesco. They were enjoying the good radio propagation and were providing much the same service for American personnel in Seoul as we were in Pusan; patching them through to their families in the States.

June 25, Sunday Morning

It was just another morning. I put the coffee on and settled into my chair at the radio with my first cup. The sky was overcast and there was a stiff north breeze coming through the screen window behind my equipment. I thought of closing the glass to prevent moisture from entering the radio equipment. On second thought, I was enjoying the fresh morning air and left the glass open. I tuned across the radio bands and could hear many U.S. stations busy at their radio hobby. I had no residents scheduled to talk to the states that morning. Then something out of the ordinary happened. A bird slammed into the screen and fell dead to the ground outside. Marion was just getting up and I called to her, "I don't like that, dammit!" She replied, "You don't like what?" "Oh, a bird just crashed into the screen here and dropped dead." In a low tone she said, "Oh-Oh." She knew what I was thinking. Now she was next to me with her coffee. "You better get a call through to home and find out if everyone is okay!" "Yah, I agree, I'll do that."

We were not superstitious types. I could walk under ladders, challenge black cats, and step on sidewalk cracks. However, throughout our family, when a bird died at a window, it was an omen of imminent illness or death.

I started to spin the dials again and was soon in contact with Minneapolis, Minnesota. Marion's mother was on the line and we both chatted with her casually, not revealing the bird incident. Everyone seemed to be doing just fine. The next call was to my father in St.Paul and the same results; everyone was okay.

At 0700 hours, Frank Crosby came bursting through our front door, out of breath, and announced that he had just received a call from a friend in Seoul reporting that North Korea had invaded South Korea in force. We spent the better part of the morning checking with officials in the compound and in the port. Nobody had any more information than we did. We got on the telephone at the clubhouse and called the radio station WVTP in Seoul. Al answered and confirmed that we were being invaded and that everything was in a state of confusion . . . "don't know how long this telephone connection is going to last" . . . "we are trying to wrap things up here and prepare to evacuate" . . . "Ambassador Muccio hasn't given us any instructions yet" . . . "we may have to get out of here fast" . . . "guess you folks down there should be pretty safe for now."

Before we hung up Al reminded me that the code word "Highball" would alert us by telephone or radio when they reached a point where they would have to abandon everything and try to get out. It would mean that the North Koreans were taking over the city. Al mentioned that, in addition to keeping WVTP broadcast station on the air as long as possible, they would try to keep their amateur radio station operating. In any case, "Highball" would mean they would destroy the stations to preclude any use by the North Koreans. They would throw a handgrenade into the equipment at the last moment.

Frank Crosby and I agreed that we should attempt to set up dedicated radio channels with the U.S. Military in Tokyo in order to ensure on-going communications should Seoul fall to the enemy. We both knew that the major links of communications out of South Korea were sourced out of Seoul; cable, telephone and wireless. If Seoul was captured, South Korea would have no link with the outside world. (At the time, we were not aware of the Mukden-Japan cable terminal in Taejon). We felt like the David under Goliath but would try anyway. Frank would send SOS (QRRR in amateur radio language) on his Morse key using the 20-meter band. I would send out a "MAYDAY" using voice on the 10-meter band.

It was 7:40 a.m. I updated Marion on the Seoul activity. She filled a thermos with coffee for me and I sat down to the radio. I re-tuned the antenna to 28,500 kilocycles (the ten meter band), flicked on the transmit switch and addressed the microphone: "MAYDAY MAYDAY MAYDAY THIS IS AMATEUR RADIO STATION HL1CE IN SOUTH KOREA WISHING TO ESTABLISH A DEDICATED 10-METER CHANNEL WITH TOKYO TO REPORT THE INVASION OF SOUTH KOREA BY THE REPUBLIC OF NORTH KOREA PEOPLE'S ARMY . . . THIS IS DISTRESS . . . PLEASE STATIONS IN JAPAN ONLY ANSWER TO HL1CE . . . OVER . . .

Captain Joseph H. Ziglinski, assigned to the 71st Signal Service Battalion in Tokyo, had just filled his coffee cup in his home in Grant Heights, Tokyo. Joe sat at his radio and tuned across the ten-meter

Capt. Joe Ziglinski at his ham radio station, Tokyo "He heard Mayday Mayday Mayday"
Photo by Joe Ziglinski

band. He heard, "Mayday Mayday Mayday" and the message that followed. Joe: "This is ja2kk in Tokyo, the name is Joe, go ahead"

"This is Ray hl1ce in Pusan and are we ever glad to hear from somebody in Tokyo . . . We are worried stiff about things here . . . The North Koreans are attacking South Korea and are reported to be moving into Seoul . . . What are you hearing over there?"

"We have nothing yet Ray, . . . I'll try to contact hllus in Seoul . . . They are closer to the fighting . . . Can you please get on your landline phone Ray, and call Francesco or Al for me? Tell them I will be looking for them on the 20-meter band . . . It's more reliable . . . Do you have landline to Seoul?"

"Yes, I think so and will do Joe, but keep in touch with us too . . . We want to know what to do down here . . . Will stand by . . . We will find you on 20 meters later and establish a dedicated channel there . . . This is hllce. . .Back later."

"OK Ray, we will all meet on 20 meters until this thing clears up . . . This is ja2kk shifting to 20."

When we signed off there followed a cacophony of signals from calling stations. The mixture of hundreds of stations calling made it impossible to copy any one of them. I would not have answered the stateside stations in any case as there was more important business requiring immediate attention. I ran to the clubhouse, called WVTP radio station in Seoul on the phone and got a message through to Francesco and Al to get on 20 meters with Joe JA2KK in Tokyo. Gerry Lucas was in the kitchen with his cooks and I called to him to come out to talk. He had just heard from a KMAG officer that the North had invaded. I told Gerry of our radio operations and the need to centralize our equipment in the clubhouse. Gerry said we could use the room behind the kitchen where there was a large table. I went back there to look it over and it was perfect. There was a large window that would accommodate our antenna connections. We would spend the better part of the morning checking with officials in the compound and in the port. Nobody had any more information than we did. The North Koreans were on their way south, that's all.

Meanwhile, Frank was tapping out his distress signal on 20 meters. At his home in Tokyo, 1st Lieutenant Donald P. Dickinson, also a ham (JA2DD) with the 71st Signal Service Battalion, picked up Frank's distress call, "QRRR" and Don responded. They moved off the frequency to avoid the build-up of interference from the states and established a morse code channel on 20 meters. Captain Robert K. Slaven (JA2CO), another member of the 71st had also responded to Frank from his home. Frank advised Slaven and Dickinson about the invasion. Landline contact was established; MacArthur's intelligence office was alerted. Then Slaven and his wife went over to Don's house to split the watch with Don so they could maintain round-the-clock operations.

(Captain Slaven had been in Korea in 1947 through 1949 and was involved in the major train-wreck at Napnin.) (See Chapter 1)

On the way back from the clubhouse I stopped at Frank's house and told him, "Frank, this isn't going to work."

"What do you mean?"

"Well, who are you talking to?"

"JA2DD and JA2CO in Tokyo . . . did you get anybody?"

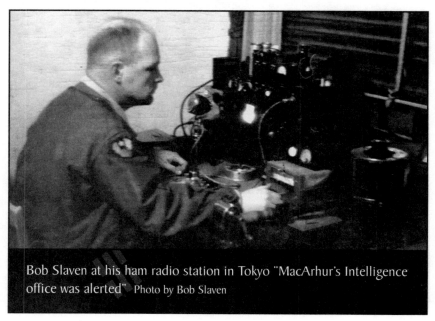

Bob Slaven at his ham radio station in Tokyo "MacArhur's Intelligence office was alerted" Photo by Bob Slaven

"Yah, I got Joe JA2KK in Tokyo and Joe is trying to get HL1US at Seoul on twenty meters now . . . We better put our stations together at the clubhouse . . . Gerry said we could have that back room by the kitchen . . . we don't have any information for Tokyo anyway and we should take advantage of the lull.

Lt. Don Dickinson's ham radio station, Tokyo Photo by Author

Frank told Slaven and Dickinson . . . "Signing off, back later" and pulled the plug. "OK Ray . . . let's do it."

I told Marion we were going to move to the clubhouse and that she should come with me. With hands on hips she said, "Oh no I won't, I'm staying right here. I don't think we're in any danger yet. Just load the shotgun for me."

"What are you going to do with that?"

"Well if anyone comes after me there is going to be one hell of a mess! I took the Remington shotgun out of its cover in the second bedroom and put four shells in it. We went over the safety lock feature several times until she felt comfortable with the gun. She had some experience with shotguns while pheasant hunting on the farm back home.

I moved my equipment to the clubhouse in an old wheelbarrow. Frank did the same. Both of us pulled down our dipole antennas, including the coax lead-ins, and brought them along. My radios were positioned on one side of the table, Frank's on the other. Rigging the antennae on the roof was the most difficult part of the move. Fortunately, there was a railing around the perimeter of the roof. We used old broom and mop handles for masts, secured to the rails with tape. We used wooden clothespoles to prop the antennae as high as we could. Raiding the warehouse again, we found more copper wire and coax and cut dipole antennas for the forty and eighty meter bands so that we would have all bands covered for changing propagation. We used the flagpole halyard in front of the building to raise the 80-meter antenna but we kept the flag raised.

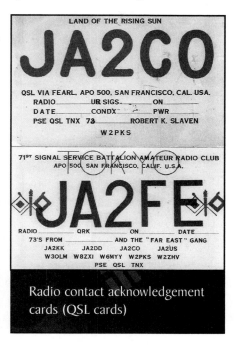

Radio contact acknowledgement cards (QSL cards)

At 9:30 A.M. Ambassador Muccio in Seoul cabled Washington D.C. to report the invasion.

At 9:35 A.M. the Military Attache in Seoul reported the invasion to G-2 Intelligence in Washington D.C. All communications were copied to General MacArthur in Tokyo.

Back on twenty meters at seven p.m., we found HL1US in Seoul talking with JA2KK in Tokyo. We were lucky to have ideal conditions for the propagation of radio signals to and from both Seoul and Tokyo. The distance between Korea and Tokyo is approximately 600 miles as the crow flies. At about eight p.m. Francesco reported from Seoul that the North Korean troops were in the city. He went off the air for about thirty minutes. Then he was back on the microphone:

"WE DON'T KNOW WHAT TO DO NEXT . . . THINGS ARE GETTING HOT HERE!"

Joe at JA2KK: "STAND BY THERE, I AM PATCHING YOU THROUGH TO MACARTHUR'S HEADQUARTERS . . ."

American officers of the Korean Military Advisory Group in Seoul used the channel to MacArthur's Intelligence office to relay reports of the North Korean advance south.

Then Francesco's station went off the air again. It was about eight thirty p.m. After twenty minutes Francesco came on the air and said, "JEEZ . . . STANDBY. WE'RE UNDER AIR ATTACK".

There was another long pause. . "IT'S OKAY NOW . . . THEY SHOT DOWN ONE OF THOSE YAKS AND THE OTHERS SCATTERED . . ."

For the next three hours the KMAG officers in Seoul kept Al and Francesco busy passing messages back and forth from and to MacArthur's intelligence office and the 71st Signal Service Battalion. The invaders continued their advance into the city. Ambassador Muccio finally came on the air from Radio WVTP at 11 p.m. and requested that all women and children dependents board the buses to Inchon.

At midnight Francesco came on the air and said "THINGS ARE LOOKING UP . . . WE'RE GOING TO HAVE A HIGHBALL!" These were the last words spoken from HL1US. Translated, these prearranged code words meant that the situation in Seoul was hopeless. Staying longer would mean capture or worse. They threw hand-grenades into the radio transmitters and "highballed" it for Kimpo airport.

We thought our ham radio station in Pusan was now the only link to the outside world. We found out later that a group of signal officers and radio operators had evacuated Seoul and moved south to Suwon then on to Taejon where a cable connection to Japan was being utilized. It was not until Taejon fell to the North Koreans that our little amateur radio station was the sole contact between South Korea and the rest of the world.

Communications in Korea

By Francis J. Winslow
(US Army Signal Corps Officer in Korea 1948 to 1951)

This chapter tells of the happenings in Korea centered on General MacArthur's afternoon message on 27 June 1950 that announced a complete reversal of US foreign policy on Korea. The text of messages that passed through KMAG's * high frequency radio from 25 to 28 June 1950 are the basis for this chapter. But first, a review of communication systems used in Korea to serve both military and civil interests.

KMAG is the short title for United States Military Advisory Group to the Republic of Korea. There was a KMAG, but there never was a "Korean Military Advisory Group."

Introduction

In my research effort for this chapter, authoritative information about the communications systems in use by the Japanese during their 40-year rule of Korea was sketchy. None of the histories of Korea, to include that from the three year US Military Government period, acknowledge the existence of or give a description of the overall communication system of Japan's colonial period in Korea and Manchuria.

The otherwise comprehensive historical survey in XXIV Corps' *KOREA* (see bibliography) describes a wide range of topics affecting life in Korea, such as the railway system, but the only mention of communications is a communications bureau in the National Police. The bureau leased circuits to create a dedicated national police telephone network to assure security of police information.

Lacking any other informational source of communications, I went in search of my fellow KMAG signal officers and had the luck to find, through "Google.com," Joseph H. Foerch, Jr. Joe was a 33-year-old captain who advised the ROK Army Signal operation office. KMAG's small group of eight Signal officers were all much older than this 23 year old lieutenant who was well suited during the three days of this report to be a KMAG duty officer. It is therefore a great pleasure to discover Joe Foerch and have him review and validate what I have written, and to add his first hand information in this account from 1950. I remember the energetic officer (Capt. Paul Wells called him "Jumping Joe) in the Korean Army Signal Operations office where he worked with his Korean Army counterpart, and sidekick, Major Bae beside him, whistling into the telephone transmitter to hit the 1000 cycle ringer frequency to connect Major Bae with Koreans manning a cable repeater station.

Basic Communications: Open Wire

In Korea, as in the development our own country's primary communications, telephones connected to switch boards in towns and cities were interconnected across the country by long distance trunks carried by bare wires on insulators strung from cross arms mounted on poles that seemed to accompany most highways and railroads. The ROK Army used this open wire system and KMAG was dependent on the Korean Army for telephone communication. The bane of communicators in wartime Korea, as in peace time United States, were people with rifles (soldiers and gun owners) who use telephone wire insulators for target practice. They had no concern that a telephone repairman would have to find and repair the damage. Korean open wire poles became supports for US military insulated field wire laid for one-time use in uncountable and unidentifiable strands by US Army units along the Main Supply Routes of wartime Korea.

Communication System: The Mukden Cable

KMAG Signal officers referred to the Mukden cable during 1949 and 1950. To be politically correct today one would when discussing the cable substitute Shenyang for Mukden. Japanese names have long been out of favor in Korea.

The least known but the most valuable fixed communication system in Korea was the buried telecommunications cable the Empire of Japan installed prior to August 1945 from Mukden (Shenyang) Manchuria down the length of Korea and undersea to Kyushu, the most southern

Japanese Island. This cable must have been tied into other cables to provide the long haul backbone for the telephone and telegraph system serving the Japanese colonial government and the Japanese business interests who dominated Korea for 40 years.

Obviously, sometime between 1905 and 1945 the Empire of Japan built the cable in phases to support each of its territorial expansion aims beginning with occupation of Korea in 1905, the occupation of southern provinces of Manchuria (subsequently named Manchukuo in 1932), and its attack on China in 1937 through its Korean/Manchukuo pathway. During this time, Japan must have incorporated technological advances in undersea cable segment and in-lead covered cable circuit capability beginning with Morse code telegraphy. Capacity was later increased progressing to voice and adding a carrier system to obtain additional multiplexed circuits. Signal regeneration on the 8 to 16 pair occurred at repeater stations every 40 or so miles. DC batteries recharged by a German generator supplied the power. The cable was laid in the railroad right of way that extended the length of Korea.

Japan's surrender on 14 August 1945 provided the US Army of Occupation in South Korea the means to communicate via several cable connections with the Pentagon. And, presumably, it gave the Soviet Army of Occupation in North Korea the means to communicate from North Korea through Mukden and thence via Russian cables to the Kremlin.

Between 10 September 1945 and 25 June 1950, the Mukden cable south end, i.e. from 38th parallel to Pusan, provided permanent circuits to Seoul's RCA (Radio Corp. of America) telegraph office in the Mitsui building and across the street to the "Washington" switchboard and communications center (teletype and encryption) in the Banto Hotel. The Banto was Lt. Gen. Hodge's XXIV Corps headquarters and was occupied by successor commands, the last being Ambassador Muccio's American Mission in Korea (AMIK) established in July 1949. No doubt, the Japanese extended Mukden cable circuits to the Banto when it was occupied by a Japanese Governor General. From September 1945 onward, the cable continued to serve the basic long-haul telecommunication needs of the US interests in Korea. KMAG's use of the cable was in a way never foreseen, that is, to make a series of temporary connections at cable repeater stations as the North Korean Army drove the ROK Army and US Army down the peninsula towards Pusan.

Except for interruptions caused by the forced relocations southward from Seoul to Sihung, to Suwon, to Taejon, and finally to Taegu. General MacArthur's staff in Tokyo again used the Mukden cable circuits to communicate with US forces in Korea. Writers have told of Brig. Gen. Church driving 17 miles south of Suwon to a cable repeater station to talk with General MacArthur in Tokyo several times from 27 to 30 June 1950. Marguerite Higgins, a correspondent for the New York Herald Tribune, told about fellow correspondents having unrestricted access to their Tokyo offices from a cable circuit in Taejon's (vacated) US Information Service office before "Jumping Joe" had it moved across town to US Army headquarters. There the correspondents had to queue up to use the circuit at night, (see Higgins in bibliography) allowing it to be used in the daytime by Signal and other staff people. The only other cable circuit in the Taejon headquarters terminated in G-3 operations.

Some time after 1945 the US Far East Air Force acquired a couple of dedicated circuits on the Mukden Cable extending from Kimpo airfield to its headquarter in Japan. This largely unknown termination at Kimpo continued to provide communications to Tokyo some three hours after the Banto hotel cable connection was terminated.

Communication System: High Frequency Radio (Wireless telegraphy)

Wireless telegraphy was a term used for HF radio when first used in the 1905 Russo-Japanese War (Pleshakov, Bibliography). Given the utility of the Mukden Cable, there would be little need for the Japanese in Korea to use high frequency (HF) sky wave or ground wave radio propagation to link Korea with Japan or other distant parts of the world. Before the US installed transatlantic cables, the United States used high-powered HF sky wave communications with distant countries. Such sites were recognized in 1948 from a highway in New Jersey, by huge fields of end-to-end rhombic antennas pointed at Europe.

ROK Army made use of lower powered high frequency radio using CW (Morse code) and voice frequency modulation and the long wire antenna. Teletypewriters in the Korean alphabet did not exist but eventually would. A math professor at Purdue University, a Mr. Choe, moved back to Korea before June 1950 to teach math at Seoul University. He had his students study the frequency of use of Korean characters in newspaper stories to design a Korean characters typewriter keyboard. After acceptance, he would convert the typewriter keyboard to a teletypewriter keyboard. He persuaded Remington Rand to manufacture two Korean language typewriters, one of which survived the trip to the Pusan Perimeter. Mr. Choe put his Korean keyboard project aside to become Colonel Choe and the deputy Signal Officer of the Korean Army. During the Pusan Perimeter days, Colonel Choe established a ROKA Signal School for 300 soldiers. The reader is on his own to pursue the history from 1950 onward of the development of the Korean language typewriter and teletypewriter. Some one please tell me whether Mr. Choe, or others, attained his goal of expanding the speed and capabilities ROK Army HF communications beyond CW and voice modulation.

The US Army regularly used high frequency radio, both fixed and mobile, to send telegraphy (or CW) and later voice, teletype, and multiplexed circuits. The ever-changing ionosphere challenged HF communicators to remain in contact with the distant station.

KMAG used the largest tactical field radio of the post WWII Army, the SCR 399, mounted in a hut on a 2.5-ton truck which towed a trailer mounted gasoline generator. It had the telegrapher's key, voice and teletype. The lower powered SCR 193 mounted in a half ton had voice and telegrapher key to serve advisors to ROKA divisions. Later, in the war, a smaller HF AM radio mounted in 3/4 ton trucks were assigned to advisors at regimental level.

The following description from:
http://www.gordon.ary.mil/museum/scr-rc2.htm

SCR-399 Mobile HF Station, 2-20 Mhz, 400 W CW, 300 W AM; (two BC-342 receivers, Hallicrafters BC-610 transmitter, BC-614 speech amplifier, BC-939 ant. tuner, BC-1052 multimeter, RA-63 rectifier, in HO-17 shelter on 6 X 6 truck; PE-95, -197 power units in K-52 trailer). Developed into AN/GRC-26 & AN/MRC-2. Also, see SCR-299, SCR-499 TM 11-281, 1945. MC-543 provides added equipment for two-kW RITTY operation. Gnd, mobile; set is similar

SCR 399 Radio mounted on truck. Photo by Frank Winslow

to Radio Set SCR-299-C except set is installed in Shelter HO-17 combined w/power plant normally carried in Trailer K-52. Shelter HO-17 may be mtd on a Truck 2 1/2 Ton 6 X 6 (not supplied w/set), or on level grid for fixed operation; xmtr freq range is 2.0-18.0 mc and may be extended down to 1.0 mc by use of Frequency Conversion. Kit MC-509, not supplied.

When the Japanese installed cable communications between Far East Command in Tokyo and the American Mission in Korea in Seoul was terminated at 1030 hours on 27 June 1950 to allow evacuation of the last of the AMIK staff, it became apparent that General MacArthur's Far East Command had no alternative means of communication in FEC's supporting Signal Battalion. It had no HF radio capability. The story of how amateur radio operators living in Tokyo's US forces housing area saved the day for FEC is told in the analysis.

Communication System: VHF Line-of-Sight Radio Relay

During Army of Occupation period (September 1945 to June 1949) the 76th Signal Service Battalion in Seoul installed and operated a multiplexed carrier system providing four voice channels or combination voice and teletype circuits between Seoul and Pusan to augment both the open wire network and the long haul circuits on the Mukden cable. Some five radio relay mountain top sites were required to elevate highly directional VHF antenna to obtain line-of-sight shots of 40 miles or more between sites. A story about this system by Capt. Slaven is in Chapter One.

KMAG's Captain Foerch said during July 1950, as a contingency in the event of the collapse of the Pusan Perimeter, he pulled this VHF equipment out of storage to establish a 190 mile communications link from the 6400-foot mountain on Cheju do (island) to Pusan.

The US war against North Korea began on 27 June 1950

Of the 58 messages that serve as the basis for this chapter, one has great historic consequence. The message effectively halted the nearly completed evacuation of Americans, ended the US Secretary of State's control of US interests in Korea and put General MacArthur's Far East Command in charge of making war against North Korea. General MacArthur's message to Col. Wright, chief of KMAG was signed at 1355 hours Korea /Japan time, 27 June 1950.

At the time MacArthur's message arrived, the number of Americans in Korea had been reduced by the evacuation to less than 100 Americans in Korea (15 Embassy and 60 KMAG in the north and perhaps others in Pusan who had not sailed on the two evacuation ships).

Author's Note: Approximately 100 male Americans remained in Pusan until other ships were available.

HF Radio Messages for June 25 through 28 June 1950

I compiled the following chronology from a stack of 58 typed messages on 1950 vintage carbon copy tissues. The stack, labeled "Be of Good Cheer" file, was given me in July 1950 in Taegu by my boss, Major Lynnford S. Wilson, the deputy Signal advisor in KMAG's eight officer signal section. Earlier he had caused the "written down in any form" messages sent or received by KMAG's SCR 399 to be retrieved and transcribed. KMAG's radio kept the US Ambassador's organization in Korea in contact with the Far East Command and the Department of State during the turmoil of the first four days after the North Korean attack. HF radio became the sole means of communication with FEC when the

Mukden cable connection in the Banto was shut down by AMIK at 1030 hours on 27 June to allow evacuation of communications personnel.

Major Wilson was very proud of Private First Class Shipp from Arkansas who was a SCR 399's CW (continuous wave) operator who copied Morse code for many hours at a time without sleep. Wilson told me that during the drive south on the 28 June from the Han River to Suwon Shipp while sound asleep in the truck's cab his hand was endlessly keying Morse code.

I made two mistakes during this 4-day period. One was to decline Major Wilson's invitation on the Han River's north bank to go with him to find a way to ferry the SCR 399 radio truck across after the bridge blew at 0220 28 June 1950. I missed the chance to have slept all the way to Suwon on the floor of the radio truck. The other mistake was the footwear I had on when I sleepwalked to Suwon with Lt. Col. Sturies' group of fifty or so KMAG members and Marguerite Higgins. Before setting off 20 hours earlier for evacuation from Suwon I jokingly asked Capt. Wells whether I should wear my well broken in OCS combat boots or my new Korean made high shine low quarters to Japan. He responded "Winslow, look like a gentleman when you arrive in Tokyo." I cursed my stupidity as I filled my shoes with sand and Han River water as I splashed ashore on the south bank. All too soon, I had developed big blisters on the hike to Suwon.

Until Ray Maurstad decided to do this book, I never had cause to read and critically analyze, as I do now, the data in the sheath of carbon tissues I had moved around for 52 years, including 28 years as a Signal Corps officer.

Analyses of these messages produced two conclusions:

1. Lack of HF radio capability in FEC seriously impeded its mission

MacArthur's Far East Command in 1950 was not only unprepared to send its depleted occupation army forces stationed in Japan into combat but also failed to have in place communication equipment capable of carrying out its basic mission to handle military contingencies. In 1950 such equipment was standard HF AM radio to net with KMAG's

SCR 399 as it moved about the Seoul area. FEC simply failed to provide standard military HF radio equipment of the type operated by KMAG. Had FEC done so, it could have obviated the need for rescue by amateur radio.

FEC's communications center relied for four years ('45 to '49) on the Japanese installed "Mukden"cable for voice and teletype circuits terminating in Seoul's Banto Hotel, the headquarters of its Army of Occupation. During the fifth year (mid '49 to mid '50) Department of State's American Mission in Korea (AMIK) took over the Banto Hotel's communications system to Tokyo using it to connect with US Government communications to the United States.

FEC's sole responsibility for Department of State's functions in Korea was to support implementation of plan Cruller to evacuate Americans in Korea to safety in event of hostilities. KMAG, who took direction from the Ambassador, reported directly to Department of the Army at the Pentagon on administrative matters. The only FEC entity stationed in Korea was a very small office of the Far East Air Force's Office of Special Investigation. It was supported by KMAG's (my) photographic laboratory.

FEC's lack of a communications alternative to the Mukden cable was immediately evident on Tuesday 27 June when at 1030 hours all communications in the Banto were shut down. Communications were terminated to allow AMIK staff to depart for Kimpo Airport to get aboard C-54s. About the same time about 390 KMAG personnel departed ROK Army headquarters for Suwon airfield to get aboard C-47s. At 1500 hours Chief, KMAG led his party of 33 to Sihung, the location of the Korean Army Command Post. The Ambassador and his staff accompanied KMAG to Sihung. HF radios (SCR 193) maintained contact between groups at Sihung and Suwon. The SCR 399 would maintain contact with FEC and, through FEC, to the Pentagon. In Pusan, Americans in all categories were boarding the Letitia Lykes and the Pioneer Dale for Japan.

Author's note: Women and children only. No males were allowed to board the two ships.

While these actions were taking place FEC's Chief of Staff was expecting KMAG to comply with his order (delayed receipt), to place an officer in the Banto, to be a relay between Seoul and Tokyo to make connections at the Banto switchboard (abandoned before message received), and to allow FEC chief of staff to talk directly with Col. Wright at his telephone served by the Korean Army switchboard (abandoned before message received) at DND. In a later instance when KMAG had returned to Seoul, Col. Wright dealt appropriately with Brig. Gen. Church's imperative that Wright, travel to Suwon on the night of 27 June to consult. Wright said, in effect, he had more important duty where he was.

These two examples reflect the dichotomy that arose between KMAG and some in FEC in the period covered by the messages. KMAG went mobile, motivated to act upon matters most essential to its duty to support the ROK's military. But some FEC members remained fixed in mind, place and time. They seemed duty-bound to the exercise of superior authority to issue orders and demand immediate compliance with standing procedure, insensitive to the events taking place at a rapid pace in Korea. The situation was exacerbated by the FEC Signal officer's failure to have back-up communication, such as HF radio, when the Mukden Cable was shut down in Seoul.

My superior, Lt. Col. Carl Sturies, told me in a near empty Korean Army Signal supply warehouse in Taegu in late July 1950 that the FEC Signal officer blamed him for poor communications with FEC in the first few days of the war. I was outraged by the charge, but Sturies, always the highly principled officer, chose to be resigned and disgusted. The attempted shift of blame gives me reason to believe that the FEC Signal Officer was unlikely to have informed his superiors that he was remiss in not having HF radio back-up for the Mukden cable. It was also unlikely he told them that amateur radio operators in the Tokyo housing area were the sole means of communication with KMAG's SCR 399 in the Seoul area from mid morning on Tuesday 27 June to mid morning on Wednesday 28 June 1950—the most critical period in which President Truman reversed US foreign policy in the Far East. It was possible for the FEC Signal officer to obscure his failure by shifting blame for communications slow-down to an incompetent KMAG signal that ignored

FEC instructions and failed to adhere to standard communications criteria, or whatever words were conveyed to that effect.

Military and civilian amateur radio operators have a long record of outstanding service in emergency situations going back to early days of wireless telegraphy. But I suspect that their story of filling a communications void during 27-28 June by being the sole means of communication between Tokyo and Seoul headquarters was not fully or adequately told. The full story was unlikely to be told in the aftermath of the Korean War because it would have revealed a serious flaw in the performance of General MacArthur's Signal officer. Several of the amateur radio operators involved were members of the Signal Battalion directed by the FEC Signal officer.

Delay of message traffic was the major element in the blame placed on the KMAG Signal Officer by the FEC Signal Officer. Some of the delay was due to frequent relocation of KMAG's 399 in the Seoul area. Delay is inevitable when a radio capable of operating conventionally at machine speeds had to operate with the manual system of amateur radio.

Further delay was introduced by the distance between the FEC communications center and the amateur radios in the housing area. Traffic between the two locations had to be read over the commercial telephone and copied down by hand in each direction. If traffic was encrypted, code groups had to be copied by hand and read back for error detection. This consumes time and invites errors.

None of the delay cited in the comments is attributed to failure of amateur radio or to be taken as a criticism of amateur radio. My only purpose is to defend the good name of my superior officer and to enable the amateur radio to tell of its exploits of which it must be proud—without pulling its punches to obscure the mistake of a senior Signal officer.

The discovery that FEC had no HF radio capability, either fixed or mobile, would be like hearing the Far East Air Force say it had no C-47s to take the 390 KMAG evacuees out of Suwon. Both the C-47 and the SCR 399 were basic military items, not in short supply, and not costly to keep available for contingencies. The Air Force was prepared, but FEC's Signal officer was not.

2.   Misuse of Message Date Time Groups

Rarely do military or foreign service people find themselves in a situation moving as fast as they did 25 to 28 June 1950. Confusion at critical times about such fundamental matters as date and time can produce chaos or inaction. Mistakes are easy to make in converting date and time from one of the world's 24 times zones to another. Mistakes in written communications are intolerable. Communications policy must minimize DTG conversions. When all operations take place within one time zone, only that time zone should be allowed in message DTG. Policies to require all DTG to be in Zero meridian, UTC, GMT Zebra or Zulu time invite conversion errors as FEC and KMAG demonstrated in the message list.

Fifty-two years later, it is probable that people still do not know how to convert time zones without error. Policy makers probably think that GMT should be the standard for all messages regardless of the mistakes and confusion such policy invites. But my concerns are projections of the confusion of messages such as KMAG 271620.

Explanation of Terms Used in Message

The following data is to aid in reading messages and in analyzing for messages selected for inclusion in the Full Text Messages File. I have made corrections to obvious transcription errors:

- DTG means Date Time Group (two digit day of month & four digit 24 hour clock) by sender. DTG acts as message identifier for a given month and year.

- All DTGs without a time zone letter are in Item time zone, which is local time for Korea and Japan

- Zulu time (Greenwich) DTG messages were put in brackets and also converted to time zone I.

- To convert Z to I time add 9 hours and a day to Z time.

- To convert Z to R time (EST) subtract 5 hours from Z time.

HF radio call signs:

- APA is Far East Command (FEC)

- APK is KMAG , which served AMIK (US Embassy)

- APK 1 is Army Support Command (Ascom) Later moved to Suwon

- APK 2 is Taegu

- V and DE mean "from"

- R or TOR at end of message text means time of receipt of message either incoming or outgoing.

Titles of persons whose last name only appears in messages:

- AMIK—Ambassador Muccio, Counselor Drumright

- KMAG liaison Maj. Holland. Communication officer for embassy and AMIK Mr. Morgan (Provides telecomm cable services: telephone switchboard, teletype and encryption. Obtains HF radio teletype service from KMAG)

- KMAG —Chief, Col. Wright

  KMAG rep at Suwon Lt. Col. Mahoney

  Senior Signal Advisor Lt. Col. Sturies

  Deputy Signal Advisor Major Wilson

  Signal advisors at HQ ROKA Capt. Fealty & Capt. Foerch

  KMAG provided HF radio for its advisors and to AMIK, KMAG provided crypto services and, in emergencies, HF service. Advisors used the ROK military telephone system.

FAR EAST COMMAND (FEC)—General MacArthur

  Chief of Staff—Maj. Gen. Almond

  G-3—Brig. Gen. Wright

  FEC advance command in Korea—established upon arrival in Suwon at 1920 hours on 27 June of Brig. Gen. Church

Signal Officer—Brig. Gen. George I. Back (provides cable telephone and teletype service except HF radio.)

Abbreviation DND stands for ROK's Dept of National Defense. DND was the common term for ROK Army HQ where KMAG advisors worked with their ROKA counterparts. DND was located about half way between Nam Sam mountain and the Han River in Seoul's Yongsan / Sobingo area. The US embassy, AMIK and the communication center were downtown in the Banto hotel. Across the street was the Mitsui Building's RCA telegraph office with its connection to the Mukden cable.

Message texts are quoted in full, or in part, or are gisted. Some of the longer or more informative or critical are identified by *FTMF* and may be read in a Full Text Message File located at the chapter's end. My comments on individual message are in italics. All DTG in this list are in local time. Their Item time zone identifier is omitted. All messages bearing a Z time DTG are converted and used in local time. The Z time DTG is enclosed in brackets for cross-reference.

The List of 58 Messages

Sunday 25 June 1950

250400 North Korea Attacks South Korea (telephone reports from advisors)

252200 assumed for No DTG AMIK Muccio to All Stations "Reference our emergency plan 'Cruller' the US Ambassador has ordered all dependents to prepare for evacuation." FTMF *Comment: Evacuation Plan Cruller applied to all Americans in Korea. Carrying out the evacuation was the only responsibility General MacArthur's Far East Command had for Korea.*

The order to execute the plan for dependents came over Armed Forces Radio station WVTP and over other means. When on Tuesday morning I sent my photographer, Cpl. Thomas Anderson, across to the Banto to take some photos, the Military Attaché, Lt. Col. Edwards, told him to destroy the equipment of WVTP.

Monday 26 June 1950

On morning of 26 June AMIK with assistance of KMAG established a net to aid evacuation of American civilians. AMIK established a voice circuit (radio-phone) on 4045 kcs, between Embassy, Yongwall, Inchon, ASCOM, Kimpo and Sobingo:

260225 ASCOM to Seoul. "Sgt. Fries arrived Inchon equipment trouble Gaffney on way down."

260553 Yongwall Mr. Hong (east coast) to Seoul " We are shutting down"

260605 ASCOM to Seoul Info: Capt Secor (KMAG Mil Police) " Two captains arrived from Seoul 0540 hours Report road condition good and traffic light."

261440 Inchon Holland to Seoul. "Washington and Security lines out. Request you contact Mr. Sinclair at Wash 301 and have him put someone on direct Frisco line to Inchon."

260230 KMAG to FEC "station using call words Dusty and Navigate on 5845 kcs jam one of our important nets". R.260234

260310 (251810Z) FEC to KMAG ref your 262330 {251430Z} Gist: A reply to net frequency interference by USAF station R260415

260350 KMAG to FEC for Haneda Gist: Crew of C-54 disabled at Kimpo with us. All ok. No injuries. R 260352

260700 assumed for No DTG msg Far East Air Force to Comdr., District 8 (CWO Nichols) Office of Special Investigation in Seoul. "Keep DI and OSI informed all changes from line positions" *Comment: Source Frutrell (See bibliography.) CWO Nichols telephoned the invasion news to the FEAF duty officer in the Meiji building at 0945 hours on Sunday, 25 June*

260800 assumed for no DTG msg. KMAG (Sedberry G-3) to FEC Gist: Request airstrikes in three areas: Uijongbu, Mansan, and Korangpo. Want air support party with VHF radio for G-3 HQ ROK Army. FTMF

Following five messages (with -) on KMAG's net Inchon-ASCOM-Seoul on 26 June:

- 261421 ASCOM Foerch to Seoul, Felty "Check with Morgan JAS Communications to give me estimated time trunk circuits Washington and Frisco will be back in service have no trunks now."

- 261425 Seoul Wilson to ASCOM, Foerch. "Approximately one hour."

- **261425** ASCOM Capt Constantine to Seoul "Sgt. Lop will proceed to Seoul with list."

- **261505** Seoul Wilson to Intone "Mr. Sinclair now at room 507 trying direct line. Suggest radio phone contact."

- **261532** Inchon Brandy to ASCOM. No further need for me here in this position moving to barge *Electra* will call in when in position." *Comment: Diesel powered electrical generator on barge powered the Seoul's streetcar system and other essential services. See Chapter 22 for before and after photos of the two power barges.*

2616 00 assumed for no DTG from Gaffney or Fries at Inchon to Seoul "an attempt was made to establish radio contact with the two freighters the 'Reinholt' and the 'Norelg' however they were guarding 500 kcs and we had no equipment that would cover their frequency." *Comment: the Reinholt having unloaded its cargo of fertilizer took on 682 passengers, mostly dependents and sailed at 261600 with F-82 fighter protection and at dawn next day with US Navy destroyer escort to Fukuoka.*

261600 Seoul Wilson to net "received instructions to shut down ASCOM-Inchon- Tokyo- Seoul net effective 261600."

261610 assumed for no DTG msg. KMAG to FEC info DA Report on combat force deployment by Col Wright KMAG. 2 pages DTG of 261500. FTMF

261940 KMAG Det Wonju to KMAG Gist: Report three officers and three enlisted in Wonju. (Msg. phoned to G-3)

Tuesday 27 June 1950

270720 OIC ADA (FEC) Stations APK 1 and APK 2 will report in this net. APK 2 will be Taegu and APK 1 will be ASCOM

271030 KMAG to FEC "Switchboard removed. No phone service to Tokyo. Conversation with C/S FEC interrupted. Request his instructions by radio." *Comment: refers to AMIK's Washington switchboard. See FEC's 271320 reply to request for instructions. Good 2 + 50 elapsed time*

271150 KMAG Wright to FEC pass to DA. R: 271300

1. Gist: One group of 98 KMAG airlifted from Kimpo at 271000. Second group of 312 KMAG airlifted from Suwon at 271115. Balance of KMAG consisting of 16 officers and 17 enlisted estimated departure Seoul at 1500 for Sihung. Korean Army CP shifts to Yong Dong Po at 1200. Next move of residual KMAG after Sihung not certain, but probably under cover darkness." Gist of para 2,3,4, Ambassador to remain DND Seoul until 271500. TOR 271300. Comment: Departure time for Second Group of 312 incorrect. 271316 reports group of 360 Americans are still on ground with first plane of 30 departing at 271345.

271150 FEC Wright to KMAG Wright "Can you confirm report that 1,000 NKA effected a landing 30 miles north of Pusan?" *Comment: See reply 271230 fast response 0+ 40*

271205 {260305Z} American Ambassador Muccio to SEC-STATE info FEC NIACT 27th Gist: Report on disposition of Embassy staff by name and others

At 271000 Drumright and six others left by motor to follow ROK government south. Muccio plus seven to remain at ROK Nation Defense HQ and leave at 1500 with last KMAG party for Sihung and perhaps to Taejon. Others include 33 KMAG, 20 UNCOK, 14 Chinese, 5 British, ECA and JAS (two elements of AMIK) to be airlifted. Bishop Byrne and Fr Carroll to remain. R.271225 FTMF. *Comment: See 271245 reply from Secstate computes to a response time of 0+20 operational priority out at 271225 and back via FEC with Secstate response with TOR of 271245. Must accept time of 0+20 as possible but not probable given FEC's msg. delay. 270136 Z should be ignored as impossible due to DTG conversion error. At these times the SCR 399 would have been at DND in Seoul preparing to leave with Muccio and Wright to Sihung at or before 1500. Muccio would have been available at the radio site to send his 271205 (sent 271225) and 20 minutes later at 271245 received Acheson's reply to Muccio asking for his acknowledgement. For some reason Muccio did not send an acknowledgement to Acheson. The planned move to Sihung seems to have been changed midroute by Mac Arthur's 271355. FEC follow up to KMAG wanting Sturies to get an acknowledgement from Muccio was overtaken by movement of the SCR 399 from Sihung back to DND leaving Muccio to proceed to Suwon (see 271640 KMAG to FEC returning to Seoul from Sihung and 271845 which reports Hq KA back at Seoul. 271730 gives position report of SCR 399 as enroute from Han river to DND and reports having no contact with Col Wright. See also FEC 271835 follow up for acknowledgement was overtaken by events and now constitutes an administrative nonentity which does not deserve a response from Sturies who was leading the hike to Suwon on the 28th after being up all night the 27th. FEC should have protected Sturies by initiating a message to Acheson assuring him that Muccio had not suffered the fate that worried him.*

271230 KMAG Wright to FEC Wright Gist: RE your 271150 Cannot confirm from either US or Korean sources NKA landing.

271235 FEC Almond to KMAG Wright " Request you station an officer in the Washington telephone exchange to receive and transmit telephone calls Tokyo and Seoul also that you attempt to establish telephone communication between your headquarters and telephone exchange as soon as possible in order that we may talk directly to you. We have been able to reach Washington telephone exchange successfully and consistently practically all day. Promptly advise GHQ as soon as officer has been detailed as requested" R272250 FTMF *Comment: Msg. took 10 hr 15 min getting from FEC to KMAG, the delay due undoubtedly to FEC's not having a HF radio at FEC. Similarly, KMAG's 271030 arrived some time after Almond's 271235. Had it not been subject to the delay caused by FEC having to route messages through the radios in the housing area. Almond would not have incurred embarrassment for ordering KMAG to establish telephone communication in the abandoned Banto. KMAG's HF radio had been back at DND for nearly five hours when msg. received at 2250. NKA soldiers would have been in the Banto at that hour. Almond's claim (or was it the FEC Signal officer?) that Washington Switch was in operation "practically all day" does not square with his noontime DTG of 271235 and fact that AMIK personnel left Banto at 1030 to catch the last bus for Kimpo. FEC Gen Almond was cut off at 1030 when the switchboard shut down, as KMAG's 271030 reported and "requested his instructions by radio." Contrast the KMAG critical tone of the Almond message with the KMAG supportive tone of another unidentified staff member of FEC in 271320 to the same incident described in KMAG 271030.*

271245 assumed for invalid 270136 Z FEC to KMAG pass to Ambassador msg from SECSTATE Acheson. Gist: Dissuade Muccio from endangering himself and staff. Acknowledge receipt to Acheson. FTMF *Comment: This is an alternate analysis and theory of 271205 and to the related 271245. The assigned DTG of 270136 Zebra becomes 281036 Item and unreasonable. If treated as 270136 it would work with a TOR of 271245 Item but would mean that Muccio's plan DTG of 271205 Item with a TOR of 271225 Item could not have arrived in KMAG in 20 minutes. Therefore, Acheson's concern about Muccio and staff was not a response to Muccio's plan in 271205 Item. The misuse of DTG induces much speculation in arriving at a rational chronology, especially when message routing to introduces delay. 271835 seeking an 'acknowledge receipt' is related.*

271255 KMAG Wright to FEC Wright "No info available as to arrival ten F-51 aircraft with Korean Pilots. Request info and urgently request that arrival of subject fighters in Seoul area be expedited." R271605 *Comment: The 3 hr +10 between msg sign time and msg send time may be due to relocation of chief KMAG and his SCR 399 between Seoul and Sihung. See FEC reply 272050.*

271316 Suwon Schoeller to KMAG Col Wright "Have 360 American personnel and UN personnel at Suwon broken into 12 groups of 30 each. As one plane here now loading UN personnel. Plane departed 1345 hours local." R. 271355 *Comment: I was in group #13, the last C-47 load of 30. Group #12 had long ago departed. Group 13, comprised mostly of Signal, G3 and MPs, waited for perhaps two hours for the next C47, which never came. Fighters prov-*

ing air cover disappeared. Mac Arthur's 271355 halted the evacuation of the 30 in C–47 load #13.

271320 FEC to KMAG "Re your message 271030. We are familiar with instructions you have received from DA. We have no instructions for you but assure you all possible will be done in connection with successful evacuation of all your personnel. We will appreciate regular reports from you hourly if possible for so long as available communications will permit." *Comment: this message stands in direct contrast with the critical 271235 from Almond (probably drafted by FEC Signal) on the shut down of AMIK communication while Almond was talking. The action directed by Almond was not possible to comply with and reflects a failure to comprehend the situation in Korea.*

271355 FEC MacArthur to KMAG "Remain in present location. General Church with staff will land at Suwon as early possible today. Our air will attack invaders today. Our forces are authorized to use with reservation our air and naval forces south of the 38th parallel. Be of good cheer." FTMF *Comment: Obtained missing DTG from reference in DTG 271620 as amended by remarks (italics). Person who converted DTG failed to add a day to Zebra. This message is a historical turning point for US policy regarding the Republic of Korea. It terminates the yearlong control US interests in Korea by US Department of State through Ambassador Muccio. It halts the Economic Cooperation Administration program. And it returns control of KMAG to the Far East Command. It terminates evacuation plan Cruller and set in motion the return to Korea and to KMAG of those who were evacuated just a few hours earlier.*

271412 KMAG Wright to FEC Wright G3 "Seoul area undergoing strafing attack. In view of our intended move 271500 June request immediate and adequate air coverage Seoul-Sihung-Suwon route."

271420 CinfoDA to KMAG Gist: Reminder of need for info on military situation.

271445 DTG derived from 271620 5th Air Force Partridge to

KMAG Wright Gist: Providing requested air cover for move starting 1500 hr today route Seoul—Suwon.

271502 KMAG LTC Sturies to FEC Brig. tGen. Back "AMIK communication center destroyed prior to evacuation by AMIK." *Comment: Lt Col Sturies wrote this about the time he was preparing to leave for Suwon. He was not to read Almond's 271235 until 11 hours later when he and his SCR 399 moved back to DND in Seoul. The SCR 399 went with Chief KMAG and Ambassador towards Sihung. But MacArthur message 271355 caused a return of some 30 KMAGers from Suwon to DND in Seoul.*

271620 KMAG Wright to FEC Almond "Two messages received by this group in conflict. Your message 09R DTG 270545 Zebra signed Partridge set up air cover for move this group to Suwon, (and) your message 09R DTG 270455 Zebra signed MacArthur required this group remain in place. Group now located in Sihung in conformity move Hq Korean Army at 270300 Zebra Will advise most strongly HQ KA return to Seoul and remain there. If Hq KA returns Seoul this group will conform. In any event, not felt advisable this group to separate from Hq KA. Will keep you posted." FTMF *Comment: This message is an example to all who set policy for message writers to stay in local time unless use of Zebra time is essential in operations involving multiple time zones. When the three Zebra references in this message are reconverted to Item (Korea-Japan) time it become obvious that the actor added the 9 hours correctly but forgot that Zebra is one day behind Item time. Use of Zebra time is to avoid confusion rather than provide opportunities to induce error by two needless conversions. Hence 270545/Z is 271445/I; 270455/Z is 271355/I; and 270300/Z is 271200/I (the last is not the DTG of a message)*

271625 KMAG Wright to Suwon "No Equipment will be turned over to the Koreans at Suwon. Hold all KMAG personnel on the ground pending further instructions. Advise number of em and officers remaining. Advise Ambassador to await further info from Col Wright "

271640 KMAG Wright to FEC Almond "HQ and CP Korean Army returning to Seoul at once. Will advise when CP at Seoul is open" FTMF

271640 Suwon Mahoney to KMAG "total of officers and em now at Suwon awaiting further instruction Muccio here. Transportation well in hand." *Comment: Assume msg is a reply to 271625 that fails to provide the answer. May be transcription error.*

271707 KMAG Col Wright to Suwon Mahoney "Return all officers and EM and equipment to Seoul at once and report arrival to Chief KMAG. Advise Air Force to return to base those flights no longer required. Major Wilson is driving to Suwon to explain reason for change." FTMF *Comment: reason for Wilson's travel to Suwon is probably its lack of encryption capability for the classified portion of the message.*

271730 assumed for No DTG msg KMAG SCR 399 position report. "…enroute from Han river to DND." Gist: No contact with Col Wright. *Comment: the assumed DTG is about where the SCR 399 would be if returning from Sihung. Ref: 271620.*

271835 FEC to KMAG to Sturies for Wright "Have tried repeatedly to secure info as to time of delivery of msg from Acheson to Muccio. Please advise at once." Comment: This message list does not show an acknowledgement by Muccio. Acheson's concerns overtaken by events. See comment on 271205, 271245 and 271835

271840 Suwon Mahony to KMAG Wright "Have no radio contact with plane."

271845 KMAG Wright to FEC Almond "CP Korean Army reopened Seoul 271800. KMAG CP opened same time same place"

271923 Suwon Holland to KMAG Wright Gen Church and party arrived Suwon 1920. Do you feel it safe to proceed to Seoul? If not he request you to proceed Suwon for meeting. If latter is the case come to Suwon railroad station." R. 272140 FTMF *Comment: Col Wright in Seoul since 1800 hrs with 60 KMAG personnel and SCR 399 had the task of bolstering ROKA chief of staff to have resolve to rally KA to halt or slow the NKA advance. See 280107 Col. Wright's refusal to travel to Suwon was laudable.*

271950 KMAG Wright to FEC "Unable so far to deliver your (FEC) 270430Z to president Rhee since KMAG has no radio contact with the president will continue efforts through civil communications system" FTMF *Comment: Msg DTG for TOR 271950 is used as msg sign time to replace both incorrectly derived Zebra times msg*

272023 CRAM to POUP Message encrypted *Comments: included to indicate that some encryption occurred*

272050 FEC to KMAG Wright Urmsg 270605Z. Gist: Two pilots qualified and cleared for departure. Other pilots not yet cleared. This will augment air strikes now being made on your front. R. 272050 *Comment: Compare FEC response to KMAG 271255 which was in local time. FEC's reply switched to Z tine and provides an example of confusion resulting from use of Z time when the operation is entirely within one time zone. Errors in conversions between Zebra and Item time generate confusion.*

272107 KMAG Wright to Muccio Suwon "Drumright reports that he is in Taejon and is in constant touch with the president and will remain there. President is anxious to return Seoul in view of the good news, (MacArthur's 271355 "Be of Good Cheer" message) but Drumright and I (Wright) am dissuading for the present" R. 272220.

272215 KMAG Wright to FEC "Message to President Rhee from General MacArthur DTG 271430 delivered to president 271905 via Mr. Drumright Counselor of Embassy at Taejon." FTMF

272240 Tokyo (FEC) Eberle to Church. Pass to KMAG and embassy. Ref telephone call Muccio –Almond. Plane arriving with cargo as requested at base designated by Muccio. Desire unloading by Koreans supervised by KMAG representative." TOR 280020 *Comments: Phone call Muccio –Almond indicates Muccio is at Suwon with Church because of airfield requirement and is connected into the "Mukden Cable to Tokyo at the repeater 17 miles south of Suwon. FEC's message handling time is speeding up: 1 plus 40*

Wednesday 28 June 1950

280107 KMAG Seoul Wright to KMAG Suwon Holland "Do

not feel it advisable Gen Church and party to proceed to Seoul after nightfall considering weather. Further do not feel I should leave situation here for length of time necessary for trip to Suwon in darkness. Strongly urge Gen Church and party proceed to Seoul first light on 28 June." FTMF

Comment: Reply to 271923 which asked if it was safe for Church to travel to Seoul that evening, and if it was not safe, then Church wanted Wright to do the traveling to Suwon Brig. Gen. Church seemed to think that if it was too dangerous for him to travel, it was not too dangerous for Colonel Wright.

280340 KMAG Seoul Wright to FEC " At 2 AM we evacuated from HQ and was headed for Sihung but impossible now bridge blown before we got over. We are now trying to get back to DND. Cannot locate any officers caught in traffic jam. Tanks reported to be in area." FTMF

280610 KMAG Wright to FEC Almond "At 280110 it became apparent that Korean resistance north of Seoul was crumbling rapidly. At 280700 Korean Chief of Staff announced move Korean CP to Sihung. All bridges across Han River completely blown at 280225 with only ten minutes warning to chief KMAG. This group now on north bank of Han River attempting crossings of Han River by ferry, reporting to Sihung thence Suwon. Your message 271425 Z received. Will report to Gen. Church." FTMF
Comment: Note that KMAG's SCR 399 sent this message to FEC while on north bank of Han River. Referenced 271425 Zebra converts to 282325 Item a time which is yet to occur. Neither DTG is in this message list. It seems that some person felt compelled to use the Z DTG but did not know how to convert to and from Zebra time. Was there a requirement to do so and why if all the action was to occur in Item time? Given the message's DTG 280610 Item, the sentence about the KA CP as having moved at 0700 Item time is faulty and out of context. This could have been a transcription error.

281036{270136Z}) FEC to KMAG Pass to Ambassador from Acheson Sec/ State Acknowledge receipt: Gist: Do not become a voluntary hostages. Leave Seoul to join (ROK) government before it is too late. *Comment: Time of receipt this message was*

272250 which shows delay of 10 hour 15 min between Almond sign-
ing message and receipt by KMAG radio. At this time the SCR 399
had been back in Seoul DND for five hours. The Han River bridge
explosion at 280225 would find the 399 being ferried across the river
some 4 hours later. Time of receipt 282145 {271245Z} or 11 hours 9
min to pass msg between Tokyo and Seoul radio sites.

No DTG Included in this list are three stories I assume were transmitted to FEC for forwarding to the Tokyo offices of two correspondents.
They were not included in the Full Text Message File out of concern for
copyright liability.

1) Burton Crane's story to New York Times had a DTG of
    272320 that Crane inserted. Three hours after being sent to
    FEC the radio truck was just behind the jeep carrying corre-
    spondents Burton Crane, Frank Gibney, and Keyes Beech
    when the span was dropped at 0220 on 28th June. The explo-
    sion injured Crane, Gibney and driver of the SCR 399 truck.

2) Two undated one page stories by Marguerite Higgins were
    written on Tuesday 27 June 1950. Higgins. I was in the same
    8 person skiff with Higgins that was stern paddled by the
    boatman across the Han at dawn. Unlike Higgins' version of
    events, I was unaware of any exploding mortar rounds until we
    got out of the skiff on the south shore.

Capt. Foerch states that Capt. Wells (recently deceased) told him
that he worked with Major Wilson in convincing the Han River boat
people to float the SCR 399 and PE 95 generator across the Han. Wells
said a NK tank on the north shore was firing at the things on the south
bank and put the time as around 0800 hours, or about two hours after
the crossing of the group led by Lt.Col. Sturies. Capt. Foerch who had
been at ASCOM and Inchon coordinating the Reinholt evacuation on
the 26th and at Kimpo for the Tuesday morning evacuation by C-54s
was at ROK Army HQ in Sihung (Yong Dong Po) when Wright and
Sturies were arriving at DND in Seoul at 1800 hours on the 27th.

The following 16 messages are photographs of the original 1950 tissue paper
messages that were transcribed 52 years ago from whatever handwritten form
of the message the traffic was sent or received.

TO: All Fixed Stations.

ASSUME DTG 252200

REFERENCE OUR EMER PLAN QUOTE CRULLER UNQUOTE THE US AMB HAS

ORDERED ALL DEPENDENTS TO PREPARE FOR EVACUATION PD SIGNED

MUCCIO

ASSUME DTG 260800

URGENT
/s/ SEDBERRY
G-3

TO: CINCFE

FROM: CHIEF KMAG

This message in two parts .
Part 1. Enemy tanks are advancing following points:
air strikes requested in following priorities:

(a) North of Ouijongbu area, 40 reported
tanks at (1005-1654)
(b) Munsan area : 67 reported tanks at
(980-1677)
(c) Korangpo area: 57 reported tanks at
(985-1694)

Part 2. Felt here ground support missions could
be more quickly and accurately accomplished if air support
party complete with VHF radio were provided and located in
G-3 Section Headquarters Korean Army

/s/ Wright

DTG
ASSUMED 26 1610

JUNE 1950

PRIORITY

TO: GENERAL ALMOND, CHIEF OF STAFF
INFO: DA/ GHQ

PRESENT SITUATION:

Ongjin is in enemy hands. Approximately 1700 SKSF of 17th ROT evacuated by LST 261500 June. 17th ROT lost all artillery pieces and many other weapons. Remainder of territory west of Imjin River abandoned. As planned so as to provide provide natural defense positions east of the Imjin River. 1st Division now holding along line (970-1655) - (990-1660). Estimated strength 1st Division 5000 plus 1 Battery FA. Division reserve is committed. The 7th Division zone, which, because of an early tank concentration, was recognized as being the enemy's main effort from the start is the zone now threatening Seoul. Two divisions plus 1 regimental combat team of SKSF have been committed in this zone. The enemy now occupies positions approximately six miles south of Uijongbu with an estimated strength of 3 Inf Divs and 1 tank regt committed. SKSF not presently capable of launching counterattacks that will materially affect this situation (INSERT- 7th Div strength estimated 4000 plus 2 Btry of FA) The 6th Division has lost Chunchon and is fighting in Hongchon and Kapyong. An estimated 1 Inf Div, 500 Guerrillas and 2 Bn of BOANDAI are operating against 6th Div. 6th Div strength estimated 5000. 8th Division dispositions now clearer. 10th and 21st Regiments closing into Kangnung. Estimated 2 Regts enemy advanced south from 38th north parallel in 8th Division zone. Estimated 6000 enemy has landed at points along east coast between An In Gis (1190-1668) and Juke Gun Man (1234-1585) number of landings 5. Largest group in any one landing 2600 between Kangnung and Mukho. No apparent coordination between groups. Estimated strength 8th Div 3000. Miscellaneous types small native crafts used.

Analysis of events:

Enemy tanks, longrange large caliber artillery and fighter aircraft employed in considerably greater strengths than was available to SKSF coupled with lack of decision and aggressiveness on the part of some SK units, particularly the 2nd Division, largely accounts for the events leading to the present situation. The 2nd Div Comdr was relieved, but after it was too late. South Korean stand and reaction excellent, but appearance of tank and enemy high performance aircraft, both unkowns to the SK soldier, induced unwarranted terror and contributed greatly to the rapid decline. One incident alone of this failure to provide aggressive leadership and decision at all echelons in the command is believed to be one situation that made possible the enemy's success in the Uijongbu corridor.

At 251930 June 40 enemy tanks penetrated and passed through an Inf Bn at Pochan. These tanks moved south from Pochan and remained restricted to this one narrow channelized road for several hours without infantry. This group of tanks could not have made themselves more vulnerable and yet the tanks were only slightly damaged. During the night enemy positions were consolidated and reinforced and quickly took advantage of their initial shock action.

The piecemeal employment of units added to the already critical situation. For example one division commander gave detailed instructions to a company commander to attack and destroy a hostile tank position known to contain at least 40 tanks.

South Korean forces has no comparable weapons to the long range heavy fire delivered on them in all sectors by the enemy. They have no weapons such as tanks with which they were constantly confronted. This effect is one of morale.

The regular support of high performance aircraft by the enemy induced a feeling of inferior equipment among SKSF.

Units lost much time and many opportunities because of less of contact during the night.

The premature movement of troops and the movement of these troops too close to the line restricted ability to maneuver.

Reluctance to rid army of incompetents, but rather to rotate to another job costs heavily if, and when this job becomes in operation.

Future Plans:

To place all troops in the Uijongbu area under one competent commander and launch the largest possible coordinated counterattack against this avenue od enemy's main effort.

/s/ Wright

-O- 271205/I   GR NC

TO: SECSTATE WASHDC

                                        URGENT

INFO: CINCFE TOKYO

FROM: AMERICAN AMBASSADOR

NIACT TWENTYSEVENTH COUNSELOR DRUMRIGHT ACCOMPANIED BY CMDR
SEIFFAT NAVATT LT COL EDWARDS MILATT CMA J STEWART PUBAFFAIRS
OFFICER CMA PRENDERGAST THIRD SECY CMA IVO FATIGATI CLERK CMA
BRUSCH JAS MOTOR OFFICE LEFT VIA MOTOR TEN AM TODAY TO FOLLOW
KOREAN GOVT SOUTH SOUTH PARA ITEM AM REMAINING AT ROK NATL
DEFENSE HQ ACCOMPANIED BY BERRY CLERK CMA MORGAN JAS COMOFF CMA
SMITH CMA JAS MOTOR OFF CMA MACDONALD THIRD SECY CMA EDWARDS
SECURITY CMA HOLLAND KMAG CMA AND LYNCH MILATT PD MY PARTY PLANS
 TO LEAVE WITH LAST KMAG PARTY FOR SINEUNG 1500 TODAY POSSIBLY
PROCEEDING TAEJON UNDER COVER OF DARKNESS IF SITUATION DETERIORATES
PARA ALL OTHER PERSONNEL INCLUDE 33 KMAG CMA 20 UNCOK CMA 14
CHINESE CMA 5, BRITISH PD ECA AND JAS TO BE AIRLIFTED PD IF
AIRLIFT FAILS FOR UP 150 CAN BE TRANSPORTED BY MOTOR SOUTH PARA
EXCEPTIONS TO ABOVE ARE BISHIP PATRICK BYRNE AND FATHER CARROLL
OF APOSTOLIC DEL WHO REMAINING SEOUL IN THEIR QUARTERS TIME
BEING SIGNED MUCCIO

271205/I /af JTT

TOKYO 271235/1 UNCLASSIFIED

271235

CHIEF KMAG

TO COL WRIGHT FROM GEN ALMOND REQUESTS THAT YOU STATION AN
OFFICER IN THE WASHINGTON TELEPHONE EXCHANGE TO RECEIVE AND
TRANSMIT TELEPHONE CALLS TOKYO AND SEOUL ALSO THAT YOU ATTEMPT
TO ESTABLISH TELEPHONE COMMUNICATION BETWEEN YOUR HEADQUARTERS
AND TELEPHONE EXCHANGE SOON AS POSSIBLE IN ORDER THAT WE MAY TALK
DIRECTLY TO YOU PD WE HAVE BEEN ABLE TO REACH WASHINGTON
TELEPHONE EXCHANGE SUCCESSFULLY AND CONSISTENTLY PRACTICALLY
ALL DAY PD PROMPTLY ADVISE GHQ AS SOON AS OFFICER HAS BEEN
DETAILED AS REQUESTED

R 272250/I MDF

DTG CONVERTED TO

ADA -O- 270136/E ITEM 271245

URGENT YOU PASS BT FOR AMBASSADOR WHILE DEPARTMENT DEEPLY
APPRECIATES WILLINGNESS YOU AND MEMBERS YOUR STAFF REMAIN SEOUL
IT IS FELT INADVISABLE FOR YOU OR ANY MEMBERS OF YOUR STAFF
VOLUNTARILY TO BECOME HOSTAGES AND ACCORDINGLY UNLESS THERE ARE
OVERRIDING CONSIDERATIONS NOT KNOWN HERE DEPARTMENT FEELS YOU
SHOULD ENDEAVOR LEAVE SEOUL TO JOIN GOVERNMENT BEFORE SAFE
DEPARTURE BECOMES IMPOSSIBLE SEOUL ACKNOWLEDGE RECEIPT THIS
MESSAGE SGD ACHESON

271245/T

DERIVED DTG 271355
FROM 271620

COL. WRIGHT

REMAIN IN YOUR PRESENT LOCATION. GENERAL CHURCH WITH
STAFF WILL LAND AT SUWON AS EARLY AS POSSIBLE TODAY. 27 JUN
OUR AIR WILL ATTACK INVADERS TODAY. OUR FORCES ARE
NOW AUTHORIZED TO USE WITH RESERVATION OUR AIR AND
NAVAL FORCES SOUTH OF THE 38TH PARALLEL BE OF GOOD
CHEER SGD MACARTHUR

TO: GENERAL ALMOND C/S FEC

FROM CHEIF KMAG

TWO MESSAGES RECEIVED BY THIS GROUP IN CONFLICT. UR MSG
09R DTG 270545 ZEBRA SIGNED PARTRIDGE SET UP AIR COVER
FOR MOVE THIS GROUP TO SUWON UR MSG 09R DTG 270455 ZEBRA
SIGNED MACARTHUR REQUIRED THIS GROUP REMAIN IN PLACE.
GROUP NOW LOCATED SIHUNG IN CONFORMITY MOVE HQ KOREAN ARMY
AT 270300 ZEBRA. WILL ADVISE MOST STRONGLY HQ KA RETURN
TO SEOUL AND REMAIN THERE. IF HQ KA RETURNS SEOUL THIS
GROUP WILL CONFORM. IN ANY EVENT, MOT FELT ADVISABLE
THIS GROUP TO SEPARATE FROM HQ KA. WILL KEEP YOU POSTED
SGNED WRIGHT

TOR: 271620

ADA   -P-

TO: GENERAL ALMOND C/S FEC   271640

FROM: COLONEL WRIGHT

HQ AND CP KOREAN ARMY RETURNING TO SEOUL AT ONCE.
WILL ADVISE WHEN CP AT SEOUL IS OPEN SGD WRIGHT

TOR: 271640/I   /s/ BM

         -CP-

TO: MAHONEY, SUWON   271707

RETURN ALL OFFICERS AND EM AND EQUIPMENT TO SEOUL AT
ONCE AND REPORT ARRIVAL IMMEDIATELY TO CHIEF KMAG PD
ADVISE AIR FORCE TO RETURN TO BASE THOSE FLIGHTS NO
LONGER REQUIRED PD MAJOR WILSON IS DRIVING TO SUWON
TO EXPALIN REASON FOR CHANGE

              COL WRIGHT

TOR: 271707/I BM

FROM: CHKMAG SEOUL   270510/Z   UNCLASSIFIED

CINCFE TOKYO   PRIORITY

28 1330 I

WRIQ001   PD UNABLE SO FAR TO DELIVER YOUR MESSAGE   FEC
280430 Z
DTG TWO SEVEN ZERO FOUR THREE ZERO ZEBRA TO PRESIDENT

RHEE SINCE KMAG HAS NO RADIO CONTACT WITH PRESIDENT

WILL CONTINUE EFFORTS THROUGH CIVIL COMMUNICATIONS

SYSTEM SIGNED WRIGHT

FOR: 271950/I /a/ jjt 260502

WHS WRIGHT COL GSC CHIEF OF STAFF   UNCLASSIFIED   1   1

KMAGCG   SEC 11   R.L. BUTT JR LT COL AGD

                                          ADJUTANT GENERAL

                              NR 3

TO: CINCFE

FROM: CHIEF KMAG

    MESSAGE TO PRESIDENT RHEE FROM GENERAL MACARTHUR DTG

    271430 ITEM DELIVERED TO PRESIDENT 271905 VIA MR

    DRUMWRIGHT, COUNSELLOR OF EMBASSY, AT TAEJON

                              WRIGHT

R 272215/I /a/ lj

                              271923/I   UNCLASSIFIED

APK TOKYO RELAY FROM SUWAN   -2-

CHIEF KMAG

TO WRIGHT SIGNED HOLLAND PD GEN CHURCH AND PARTY ARRIVED

SUWAN 1920 PD DO YOU FEEL IT SAFE FOR HIM TO PROCEED TO

SEOUL QUERY IF NOT HE REQUESTS YOU PROCEED SUWAN FOR

MEETING PD IF LATTER IS THE CASE COME TO SUWAN RAILROAD

STATION

R 272140/I MDP

MR 5

MAJOR HOLLAND - SUWON   *280107*

DO NOT FEEL IT ADVISABLE GEN CHURCH AND PARTY TO
PROCEED TO SEOUL AFTER NIGHTFALL CONSIDERING WEATHER
FURTHER DO NOT FEEL I SHOULD LEAVE SITUATION HERE
FOR LENGTH OF TIME NECESSARY FOR TRIP TO SUWON IN
DARKNESS. STRONGLY URGE GEN CHURCH AND PARTY PROCEED
TO SEOUL FIRST LIGHT ON 28 JUNE

                                    WRIGHT

R 280107/I

ADA   -OP-   *280340*

AT 2 AM WE EVACUATED FROM HQ AND WAS HEADED FOR SIHUNG
BUT IMPOSSIBLE NOW BRIDGE BLOWN BEFORE WE GOT OVER PD WE
ARE NOW TRYING TO GET BACK TO DMD PD CANNOT LOCATE ANY
OFFICERS CAUGHT IN TRAFFIC JAM TANKS ARE REPORTED TO BE
IN AREA

280340   - OP -   *280610*

TO GEN ALMOND CHIEF OF STAFF FEC FROM COLONEL WRIGHT
AT 280110 ITEM IT BECAME APPARENT THAT KOREAN RESISTANCE NORTH
OF SEOUL WAS CRUMBLING RAPIDLY PD AT 280700I KOREAN CHIEF OF
STAFF ANNOUNCED MOVE KOREAN CP TO SIHUNG PD ALL BRIDGES ACROSS
HAN RIVER COMPLETELY BLOWN AT 280225 WITH ONLY TEN MINUTES
WARNING TO CHIEF KMAG PD THIS GROUP NOW ON NORTH BANK HAN RIVER
ATTEMPTING CROSSINGS OF HAN RIVER BY FERRY CMA REPORTING TO
SIHUNG THENCE SUWON PD URMSG 2714256 RECEIVED PD WILL REPORT
TO GENERAL CHURCH   WRIGHT

     280610/I

Milton G. Nottingham Jr. 1950 "Sinking a ship at the breakwater would have closed the Port"
Photo courtesy of M. Nottingham

15

The Port Captains

The key to the management and coordination of the activities of any seaport is the Port Captain. He maintains lines of communications between all major elements of the port. That includes ships coming and going, the tug activity, shipping companies, warehousing, the docks and all other activities associated with loading and unloading the vessels. Without the Port Captain, the port activity would be chaotic.

The Port of Pusan   Photo by Alex Roth

Milton C. Nottingham Jr., age 30, was selected by the Department of State Foreign Service in the spring of 1949 to fill the position of Superintendent of the Port of Pusan. Milton had been raised and schooled in Baltimore and after graduating from Calvert Hall College High School in 1940 he attended the U.S. Merchant Marine Academy at Kings Point, New York and graduated there with the class of '44. He served as an officer in the Merchant Marine and the Naval Reserve during World War II and for a few more years before his assignment in Korea. He arrived in Korea in June of 1949. He was employed by the Economic Cooperation Administration (ECA) and assigned to the

Marine Branch, Transportation Division of the American Mission to Korea (AMIK). The mission of the ECA was to assist the South Koreans in rebuilding their industries, improving the economy of the country and raising their standard of living. However, the funds allotted to South Korea by the U.S. Congress were meager and only a pittance compared to the amount being spent in Europe.

Captain Nottingham was affable but authoritative and handled the many facets of the port activity with effective ease. He was also ambitious, aggressive and a hard worker. His large office on Pier One in Pusan had a window view of the harbor and was a beehive of activity day and night. In addition to the job of port coordination, he was responsible for training port personnel in the operation of the port and advising the officials of the Korea Shipping Corporation in Pusan in the operation and management of a shipping company. A formidable task for a young man of 30, but his training and experience had prepared him well. In spite of the language barrier, lack of expertise in many of the people he had to work with, and age-and-wear showing in some of the facilities, he was able to face, identify problems, and work them through to solutions. On many evenings, he would catch a catnap on the couch in his office instead of making the trek north to his house in Hialeah compound. He would be up before dawn again to the ringing of the telephones. Any seaman can tell you that ship operations have no respect for daylight versus the dark of night. He also kept abreast of the activities of the Maritime Group under Captain Forrest K. Peterson and the five ships in that group. At times problems would surface that were not formally within his scope of responsibility and realizing that they might not be attended to; he would extend himself to assist in the resolution. His satisfaction in doing things like that was seeing the resulting level of training that took place.

Nottingham: "I think that one of the most troublesome aspects of my service in Korea was the fact that so little of what we needed in the way of reference books, training manuals and supplies for the ships and other equipment was then available in the country. On the other hand, the Koreans could make almost anything in the way of machinery parts if given a prototype to copy. In the way of support, I believe that the ROK agencies and departments cooperated fully with the AMIK personnel. There may have been rare exceptions, but I doubt many. Personally, I felt that I enjoyed the full support of our government and of the Republic of Korea."

"I recall that a Japanese vessel, the M/S *Kazuria Maru*, was half submerged in Pusan Harbor. Only days before the invasion this vessel, which I had recommended be salvaged, was towed to Japan for refitting. The hull was stainless steel. The ship was returned to Korea much later and renamed the M/S *Korea*. The vessel was, for several years, the flagship of the Korean Merchant Marine."

CAPTAIN OLIVER H. RITCHIE USNR headed the Marine Branch of the American Mission in Korea, with offices in Seoul, some 350 miles to the north of Pusan.

Thomas A. King, age 29, was attached to Captain Ritchie's staff with collateral duties as the American Port Superintendent Advisor for the Port of Inchon near Seoul. Tom was born and raised in Greenwich, Connecticut and moved with his parents to Long Island New York at the age of five. He grew up in Queens and Garden City and they later moved to Forest Hills, New York. He graduated from the Merchant Marine Academy at King's Point in July 1942, and then joined United States Lines. He spent the next seven years with U.S. Lines, three of them as ship's Captain. He was First Officer of the S.S. *Washington* traversing the North Atlantic when he was called by the government to take the Korean assignment.

Tom King: "I had been 'bumped back' in 1946 or 1947 from Master to 1st Officer on U.S. Line passenger ships. Jane and I decided to marry and a shore job held attraction. The opportunity to combine a honeymoon, a shore job and service with the American Mission in Korea came along and I took it. We had a comfortable house in Korea with two Korean servants. I served under Captain Oliver Ritchie, who was the AMIK Director of Marine Transportation programs. The establishment of a Korean coastal merchant marine and, advising the Korean Marine Bureau, occupied most of our time."

Arriving in Seoul by air, via Anchorage, the Aleutians and Tokyo in March of 1949, Tom was followed by his wife Jane arriving in Korea two months later. Jane flew to San Francisco where she boarded the U.S.A.T

General Brewster, a U.S. Army Transport vessel, to Inchon and then to Seoul by bus. On board the *Brewster*, Jane shared a cabin with the Willis family; Mrs. Willis and her two children. They were joining Mr. Willis in Korea where he was a Marine Engineer assigned to the AMIK advisory group. The weather was rough and Mrs. Willis and her children were very seasick the entire crossing.

Tom and Jane had been married for only a few weeks before his departure by air for Korea. They lived in "MG2" in Seoul, which was the former Japanese Ministry of Finance Compound. Tom had two offices; his primary office in the American Embassy and a second office in the Korean Marine Bureau of the Ministry of Transportation.

At the time Tom arrived in South Korea, the six ships subsequently loaned to South Korea for training and economic assistance, were under the supervision of the U.S. Army. After transfer to the American Mission in Korea, they were sent to Japan for refurbishment. Tom boarded one of the ships in Pusan, the S.S. *Kimball R. Smith*, acting as Master with a Korean crew, and steamed the ship to Japan. He then returned by air to Seoul, Korea. Several months later when the *Kimball Smith* was repaired he flew to Japan, brought her back to Pusan and then returned again to Seoul. While under repair in Japan, the all-Korean crew had been restricted to the ship and Tom noted that the general demeanor of some of the Korean crew had changed. It had been intended that the *Smith* would proceed to Inchon towing a new Lock Gate fabricated in Pusan for the Inchon tidal basin. However, a piston in the steam Uni-flow engine had cracked and the ship limped into Pusan. A month or so after the ship's arrival in Pusan and after repair of the cracked piston, the ship was put under the command of Captain Al Meschter and proceeded in May of 1949, without the lock gate, to Inchon. The same Korean crew mutinied and took the ship to Chinnamp'o, the largest trading port on the west coast and in North Korea where Captain Meschter and Chief Engineer Al Willis were imprisoned for eighty-one days. Chinnamp'o is situated on the bank of the Taedong-gang River approximately 50 miles southwest of the North Korean capital city of P'yongyang. The river could be navigated by 2,000-ton steamships for 40 miles, and by junks for 153 miles. The kidnapping of the two Americans received some small attention in the American press.

Nottingham: "Shortly after my June 1949 arrival in Seoul, Captain Oliver C. Ritchie, Chief of the AMIK Marine Branch, asked that I go to Pusan to take up my assignment in the port. He further instructed me to move into Al Meschter's house in the Hialeah Compound in order to protect Al's personal effects, since at that time Al was still a prisoner in North Korea. Upon Al's release and return to Pusan, I moved into another house there that I shared with John Carr who was assigned to the American Consulate in Pusan. We had both a houseboy and a house girl assigned to our quarters. An amusing aside; I asked that these two young Koreans wash the windows of the house and was surprised upon my return home that same evening to find that they had taken all of the windows out of the house to wash them! Washing them in place had obviously never occurred to them. I had a jeep and driver assigned to me on a full-time basis."

Senator Tom Connolly of the Senate Foreign Relations Committee was asked in an interview published on May 5, 1950:

"Do you think the suggestion that we abandon Korea is going to be seriously considered?" The Senator replied: "I'm afraid it's going to be seriously considered because I am afraid it's going to happen whether we want it to or not. I'm for Korea. We're trying to help her. We're appropriating money now to help her. But South Korea is cut right across by this line (the 38th Parallel). North of it are the Communists with access to the mainland, and Russia is over there on the mainland. So that whenever she takes a notion she can overrun Korea just like she will probably overrun Formosa when she gets ready to do it. I hope not, of course." (From "The Korean Decision" by Glenn Paige, The Free Press, Collier-Macmillan Canada, Toronto)

Tom King: "I believe that a couple of months before the June 25th invasion by North Korea, the Secretary of State, Dean Acheson, made a statement that was considered to exclude South Korea from the defined area that the U.S. would defend. Undoubtedly, the North Koreans were aware of this and expected us to observe Acheson's omission. Further, after North Korea attacked, General MacArthur in Japan refused to send planes to evacuate Americans without fighter escorts. Acheson and General Bradley argued it out. Truman backed Bradley and authorized the fighters, which, as it turned out, were needed."

Nottingham: "The area around Seoul, including Inchon, was very near the 38th Parallel and the South Korean military forces were unable to defend that region against the overwhelming forces of the North. Therefore, the dependents of the American Embassy and AMIK personnel were promptly evacuated by ship from Inchon to Japan and were later followed by the Embassy and AMIK staff members including Captain King evacuated by air. In Pusan, the American Consulate was instructed to evacuate all U.S. personnel (women and children) in the area by sea."

"The senior military officer in the AMIK group in Pusan at that time was a Lieutenant Colonel. He immediately established a Command Post in the American Consulate building in Pusan. In the small U.S. Army cadre in Pusan at that time, there were no port (military) personnel. Accordingly, Captain Alfred T. Meschter, who was a member of the Marine Branch of AMIK and also assigned to Pusan, and I volunteered to remain with the troops and operate the port. Lieut. Colonel Rollins S. Emmerich, U.S. Commander of the Provisional Korean Military Advisory Group, immediately accepted our offer of assistance and on 28 June 1950, issued Provisional Order Number One naming his staff and designating the writer as Port Commander of Pusan and Captain Meschter, Assistant Port Commander."

HEADQUARTERS
PROVISIONAL KOREAN MILITARY ADVISORY GROUP
PUSAN, KOREA

SPECIAL ORDER   28TH June 1950

Nº. 1

The following assignments are announced effective this date.

Commanding Officer R. S. Emmerich		Lt.Col.
Executive Officer K. Guillory		Major
S-1 C.	Wells	Captain
S-2	G. Putnam	Captain
S-3	J. Morlay	Captain
S-4	H. Slater	Captain
Transp. Officer	G. Finch	Major
Provost	W. Glass	Captain
Port Commander	M. Nottingham	Civilian
Port Asst.	A. Meschter	Civilian

BY ORDER OF THE COMMANDING OFFICER:

ROLLINS S. EMMERICH
Lt. Col.Inf.
Commanding Officer

Nottingham (cont.)

"Al Meschter and I directed all operations of the Port of Pusan for the initial several days of the Korean War. This included assigning berths to the troop ships arriving from Japan, clearing piers of commercial material to free up space for military materiel and keeping the interim U.S. Forces Commander, Major General Dean, current on port operations.

Upon the arrival of the U.S. Army 2nd Transportation Port personnel from Yokohama, Japan, during the first two weeks of the war, Al Meschter and I were relieved as Port Commander and Deputy Port Commander. However, due to our experience, the 2nd Transportation Port Commander asked that we continue to direct port operations until his personnel became familiar with local conditions, and this we did for several weeks. After the evacuation from Pusan, those of us remaining behind were well aware of the possibility that the soldiers of the North would overrun the entire region. Consideration was given that, after Pusan, the next provisional capitol of the ROK might he Cheju-do. However, we were all too busy to be very concerned for our own safety. I can honestly say I never worried about it. I expected Uncle Sam would take us out of there if that became necessary."

"One of the most remarkable aspects of the Korean War was the absence of a "Fifth Column". There were a few infiltrators from the North but they were generally unsuccessful in their efforts to disrupt the United Nations Forces movements. Sabotage was almost unknown and evidenced proof of the support of the ROK government by the South Korean people and their fear of the North Koreans. Just think; if one of the rail tunnels between Seoul and Pusan had been blown up, it would have been almost impossible to supply our troops in the move north. Similarly, sinking a ship at the breakwater in the outer harbor of Pusan would have closed the major port of South Korea, upon which the UN depended, and bottled up any ships then in the port."

Ed. note: I believe that the North Koreans, deliberately and under orders, avoided taking foreigners as prisoners so as not to be burdened with them after the North Korean expected victory. They preferred instead to just frighten all the foreigners into evacuating, leaving everything intact as much as possible. From the start, North Korea did not expect the massive U.S. and U.N. invasion and recapture of South Korea.

16

Two Days of Fear

Monday, Tuesday, June 26 & 27

Marion was frightened and anticipating the worst. She was not alone with those thoughts. The guerrillas were burning the villages in the hills around us. The local police with dogs were patrolling the perimeter of our compound. There were rumors of the North Koreans making landings on the East coast just North of Pusan.

My attention was given to assuring Marion that we would get her out of there and to Japan to have our baby. I felt that I should have been at Marion's side every minute. At the same time, I felt obligated to operate the ham radio equipment in the club center. Joe and Dotty Kelly were with Marion most of Monday. I moved frequently to and from the house and clubhouse. She sat on the couch facing the front door with the loaded shotgun on her lap. Houseboy Soh stayed with her for a little while on Monday, serving her coffee and assuring her that she would be okay. "You be okay Sir! I wish you have son! It was Soh's last day with us. Miss Chun had already left Sunday night after coming in only to pick up her personal belongings. Soh would leave on the evening bus. KMAG officers called a meeting in the Quonset hut; the same one Nurse Mella's office was in, on Monday morning, the 26th. They did not seem to have a lot of information about what was happening up north. The main thrust of their words tended only to cause us more concern. They told us that we must watch for an air-attack and that if one should happen we were to lie down in the storm-sewer ditches alongside the compound streets. They also asked us to burn all of our official papers, letters of correspondence and anything that could be used to identify us should we be captured. Only the women and children would be evacuated. The men would have to stay. "We have to keep things going," was the simple explanation. When asked where the North Koreans were the response was "Don't worry, they are being fought off up north by the South Korean Army."

Then .45 caliber automatic pistols were issued to all the men and one officer used one to demonstrate the proper use of the gun. Holsters were also issued. We were to continue sandbagging the clubhouse. A vehicle convoy would be organized as soon as possible to take the women and children to American ships in the harbor. The KMAG officers repeatedly assured us that everything was "being taken care of", however, when questioned by the civilians about details they did not have answers. They appeared to be "in the dark" as much as we were. When the meeting broke up, the tension was greater than ever. We found out later in the day that the KMAG officers did know much more than they were telling us. Confiding in a few of us they told us that the guerrillas were very active in the hills just to the north and that evening we could see that more villages were burning. In one of the villages, the mayor was asked by a guerrilla band to cooperate with them, provide them food and shelter while they used the village for a base of operations. When the mayor refused they stripped his daughter and skinned her alive in the village square. The word of that event spread quickly and our Tiger Kim (not to be confused with the Tiger Kim of the North Korean People's Army) set out with his men in search of the killers. Capturing four of them, he had them beheaded for a parade in Pusan. One of the officers then produced a photo of the heads being held above buckets of kerosene in which they were being preserved. The few of us in that small meeting kept our mouths shut and we were more anxious than ever for the evacuation of the women and children.

Damn! Sitting again at the radio it suddenly dawned on me that the men left behind, including me, were intended to be the first line of defense if the enemy arrived in the compound ahead of any South Korean or American troops. I whispered to myself several times, "What the hell! What the hell! And my wife with a 12-gauge shotgun!" I prayed American troops to hurry.

The last of the dependents could not have chosen a worse time to arrive in South Korea. Mrs. Grace Stevens got off the Monday train in Pusan and she took a taxi to Hialeah Compound. Her husband Harold Stevens was at sea on one of the Baltic Coasters and, her arrival was unannounced. Under normal circumstances, she would have been greeted and escorted by Alonzo King at Kimpo airport at Seoul. She was obviously a case of nerves. Nurse Mella did her best to calm her. However, the real problem was deciding where she should stay for the night, as Mr. Stevens was not due in port until the next day. I am not sure how Marion ended up with the job of keeping Mrs. Stevens company. It may have been because Marion was alone and wanted to be with someone when Soh would leave Monday evening. A few of the women got together in Nurse Mella's office. It was decided that Marion should stay with Mrs. Stevens in the Steven's house. Harold already had most of their belongings there. Marion packed a few overnight things in a small bag and joined Mrs. Stevens. The walk to the Steven's house was only 200 yards and slightly closer to the clubhouse. The two women prepared their beds. Marion fell asleep almost immediately. Grace nervously paced the living room floor. Marion woke to a movement on her bed and switched on her small bed light. Grace was sitting on the edge of the bed and was pointing a gun at Marion. Grace was whispering in a frantic voice, "I heard a noise! Someone is out there, I heard a noise! Shhhh! Listen!" Marion asked Grace to stop waving the gun in her face and to calm down. She convinced Grace to give up the gun and Grace finally went to sleep. Both had had a long and stressful day.

At my position next to the radio, I had a view to the north and I could see a few of the men who had the fence patrol accompanied by large dogs. At night, they became only vague silhouettes and at one point, I thought I was seeing an encounter of some sort, but it was only one man relieving another. The guerrillas never did attempt to penetrate our compound.

Since there were no specific plans on what to do when and if the enemy did move in, I guess it was every man for himself. We did what we thought was necessary. I don't know what I would have done if the enemy had cornered me, shoot, run or surrender. I was not trained for hand-to-hand combat. I kept my identification in my pocket. As we were tipping the tables against the windows, it occurred to me that we had white dining table cloths if we felt a compulsion to use one to surrender.

Our identification cards were issued to us in early April.

We posted men at strategic points, at the main gate guardhouse, at the fence about every 30 degrees of the circle, at the entrance to the clubhouse, at the warehouses, and the vehicle pool. No person was allowed in or out of the compound without the Korean police guards at

AMIK Identification

the main gate recognizing them before they could pass. A dozen men were posted in the port to protect the power barge *Jacona*, the docks and the marine telegraphy station on Pier One. We had enough men to relieve each other in four-hour shifts.

6/28/50

B-26 AIRCRAFT OF THE 13TH AND 8TH BOMB SQUADRON ATTACKED THE ENEMY WITH 12 AIRCRAFT AND HAD THE FIRST FATALITIES THAT DAY. THE FIRST MISSIONS WERE FLOWN AGAINST NORTH KOREAN TROOPS IN THE HAN RIVER AREA.

The Army Lieutenant

Continued from Chapter 10

Review: Winslow arrived in Korea in September 1948 as a 21 year old Army Signal Corps 2nd Lieutenant. During his time in MacArthur's Army of Occupation, he served with the XXIV Corps' 123rd Signal Detachment and the Photo Section of the 76th Signal Service Battalion. In May 1949, he came under Department of State control by assignment to KMAG Signal as advisor to ROK Army's Signal Photo Company. He acted as KMAG Public Information Officer and operated the only US photo laboratory, projector and training film service in Korea before the war. He was a cameraman with KMAG for three months until 20 Oct 1950 then reverted to general signal duty. He departed Korea in August 1951 as a Captain. He entered Army aviation in the fall of 1954, commanded aviation units in the US, Europe, and Vietnam. He held a number of general staff jobs including another year in Korea.

Winslow's words: In early June 1950 I received reassignment orders to Maryland to the Army's only Signal Photo Company. On June 21, I took a vacation in Pusan with an Embassy friend. Captain Putnam put me up in his quarters in Hialeah compound and bunked my friend with one of his. Ever the good host, on Sunday June 25 he drove us to the station to catch the 5:30 a.m. train to Seoul after a late night of socializing at the club. We could snooze on the train to Seoul.

Our snoozing and tranquility was disturbed by an American missionary at the Taegu rail station who told us of an attack all along the 38th parallel. His story was confirmed upon arrival at Taejon by the sight of the 2nd ROK division's equipment being loaded on rail cars. KMAG advisors to the Division made it clear that those of us who predicted the North would attack the South but only after each of us had left Korea were wrong, in my case by about one week.

After a long delay south of Seoul, our train pulled into an empty main railroad station about 7 p.m. We were met by Embassy Marine guards with shotguns and given a ride to our State Dept. operated hotel.

I drove to my photo lab located in the Mitsui Building across from the Embassy. I then drove a couple miles to ROKA/KMAG Signal office where I was assigned as night duty officer. About dawn on Monday I went back to my hotel to get a few hours sleep.

Early Monday I phoned the quarters of my weekly square dance partner, who three years later became my wife. Her father said that she and her mother had left during the night for Inchon for evacuation by ship. Her father was a B&O railroader employed by the Economic Cooperation Administration (ECA) program of the Department of State to advise Korean railroad managers. He said he would soon be flying out of Kimpo. Later I bid farewell to my friend who traveled to Pusan with me. She and other employees were boarding a bus in front of the Embassy for Kimpo airport. I remember a White Russian girl who I had seen at the officers' club saying a tearful farewell to her Embassy friends. She was not being evacuated with them.

Later in the day, my two photo men (Beasley and Anderson) attempted to destroy some of the recent shipment of photo supplies. All day Monday the Embassy staff had a continuous burn of classified papers in the incinerator in the parking lot of our building, apparently allowing the crypto people to have full use of the Banto furnace. Again as the Signal Section's junior officer, I had more duty officer time that night. I could catch up on my sleep when I arrived in Japan.

On Tuesday, June 27, some 390 KMAG officers and men loaded up in a variety of vehicles for the trip to Suwon where we arrived well before noon. Kimpo was ruled out as a departure point because of increased flight time and risk of a NK fighter downing a loaded transport. We were formed into thirteen 30-person C-47 airplane loads. Fighters from Japan maintained a constant protective air cover for the departure of groups # 1 through #12. Those of us in the last group #13 signal, military police mostly-waited for some two to three hours for the air cover and a C-47 to come for us. The wait ended when we were instructed to reclaim a vehicle and return to the headquarters in Seoul.

Our convoy of vehicles carrying some 30 men re-crossed the Han River Bridge nine hours later to the cheers of Koreans who saw us go by. The mounds of explosives at four critical places on the bridge covered by rice straw matting was an ominous and silent warning to be on the south bank when the order was given to blow the only bridge over the Han south of Seoul. About 7 p.m. at ROKA/KMAG Signal Section, I lost a coin toss with Capt. Paul Wells and took the first half of signal duty officer tour. As usual for me, sleep could come later. Heavy gunfire in the north part of Seoul grew louder as the night wore on.

About 1:45 a.m. on Wednesday, June 28 a G-3 Sergeant came down to tell me that the ROKA switchboard had just shut down, and he needed to notify the sleeping men in the nearby quarters. I had a ROKA signal officer remake the connections. Meanwhile Major Greenwood of the Chief's office told me to get the two and a half ton radio truck (SCR399) headed across the bridge. After doing so, I met officers who had been awakened by the G-3 phone calls and told to get moving across the bridge. I picked up two ROKA signal officers in my jeep to join the sea of humanity in every sort of conveyance imaginable and those afoot flowing glacially to the bridge using all lanes and sidewalks. We had progressed to the point where the roadway became the bridge with sand banks on either side when, at about 2:15 a.m. a huge, yellow/orange column of flame appeared in the night sky over the bridge's south end. The explosives we saw earlier had done their job and a span of the bridge sat on the bottom of the Han.

We headed for the west sidewalk to get out of the line of direct tank fire should NKA tanks be as close as reported, that is, at the 31st traffic

Bridge with span missing. "I crossed the river in a stern-paddle boat"
Photo from Baltimore & Ohio magazine. 22nd Annual Women's Number June, 1951

circle, only a mile or two behind us. The sea of humanity seemed unre-lenting in pressing toward the Han and its blown bridge.

To investigate the possibility of driving our jeep across a railroad bridge we went west, down river, looking for the rail tracks. As we arrived at a rail station, a self-powered single car was moving on the tracks to the bridge. I gave up on the idea, as I did not want to risk a collision or get hung up on the tracks. We returned to ROKA HQ where I was not surprised to see a large group assembling. It seemed that few KMAG vehicles made it across before the explosion. (At the time, I had no idea that the ROKA Chief of Staff Chae and his KMAG advisor, Capt Hausman, traveling separately, crossed just prior to the detonation) (In Mortal Combat, Toland 1991 pg 51).

Lt. Col. Vieman, with the advice of other Americans who had hunted birds in the area and thought they knew their way around the roads on Seoul's eastern outskirts, led us on an unsuccessful (NKA reported at a key road junction) search into the night for a crossing upriver. We returned to a place on the north bank of the Han in the early morning to look for boats. I stupidly declined Major Lynnford S. Wilson's (deputy Signal advisor) invitation to go with him to find a raft to get the SCR 399 truck across. This he did. If I had my wits about me, I could have slept all the way to Suwon. At this point, my mind was barely functioning from lack of sleep. Major Wilson later told me that his radio operator Shipp (from Arkansas) was so exhausted that his hand was sending Morse code messages with a nonexistent CW key as he rode in the radio truck's cab to Suwon.

We abandoned our vehicles and found small boats to take us across at dawn. I crossed the river in a stern-paddle boat with six or eight passen-gers, one of whom was correspondent Maggie Higgins. We were under light mortar fire as we waded ashore on the south bank. The column was led by Lt Col Carl Sturies, my boss, on the long hike towards Suwon.

I had to move from the rear of this column to take these photos and I was exhausted having had only four hours sleep in Pusan on Saturday the 24th of June, three hours on the 25th, four hours on the 26th and none on the 27th.

MARCH TO SUWON Members of the Korean Military Advisory Group, withdrawing from their headquarters in Seoul on 28 June, walked over 16 miles to Suwon. Note muddy road from heavy rainfall (top photo). South Koreans fleeing from the North Korean forces (bottom photo). On 27 June, the South Korean Government moved south and enemy tanks reached the outskirts of Seoul.
Photos by F.J. Winslow

I had tossed away my heavy military still and motion picture cameras. With great effort, I made a few exposures with my Leica, one of which has appeared in histories of the early days of the war (the caption had us walking to Kimpo rather than to Suwon). By mid morning I was sleep walking at the tail of the column. Major Blanchard, KMAG's dentist, urged me on. Later in the day, vehicles carried us the final few miles to an agricultural school building at Suwon where I went into a deep sleep on a wood floor surrounded by glass display cases containing jars of specimens unknown to me.

In The Korean War No Victors, No Vanquished 1999, The University Press of Kentucky, author Stanley Sandler says the premature blowing of the Han River Bridge on June 28 almost lost the war for the ROK Army. He said the ROK government executed the Engineer who placed the charges and set them off. Oddly, Mr. Sandler had no comment on the engineer's culpability and execution. This execution apparently settled the matter in the minds of ROK government officials and in the mind of Mr. Sandler.

Contrast this "no comment" form of recording history with Mr. Sandler's curious and baseless castigation of Chief Brig. Gen. Roberts for his quote in the 5 June 1950 Time magazine. Sandler accused Roberts of conducting a campaign praising the ROK Army by saying it was the "best doggone shooting army outside the United States." As the 5 June article contains no such quote it cannot be the vehicle for Robert's "publicity campaign" nor can it be the basis for Sandler's charge that the right hand of KMAG did not know what the left was doing. Rather, Roberts and KMAG should have been lauded by Sandler for its mid June semi-annual report that warned of the coming disaster and reported having supplies for not more than 13 days. Roberts had "nothing to live down" in his retirement.

I have no doubt about who ordered the engineer to drop the span. On the morning of June 29 approximately 30 hours after the bridge explosion, Colonel Wright, Chief EMAG, wanted those of us who had been earlier trapped on the north side of the Han River to assemble under the trees at the Suwon agricultural school. Wright said Major General Chae Byong Duk, the ROK Army Chief of Staff, had something to tell us. General Chae apologized to us for his premature, and disastrous action of giving the order to detonate the span. These may not be the exact words he used but they are the essence of what he said. My reaction was that he screwed up in a very big way, but he had the strength of character to apologize. The matter was closed for me except for the lesson learned.

To my knowledge, Chae's apology under the trees has never been reported. John Toland in Mortal Combat Korea, Quill, 1991 reported that Gen Chae's jeep had crossed the bridge followed by his advisor Captain Hausman a short time prior to the explosion. As the ROKA Chief of Staff, General Chae had the singular authority and responsibility for the timing the destruction of the Han River highway bridge especially when the explosion's timing trapped his own army, not to mention me. Within a week or so, General Chae was replaced by Major General Kim Ti Kuan. Clearly, the executed ROKA Chief Engineer became the ROK government's fall guy for the catastrophe.

On June 29 and 30, I was assigned to work at the Suwon airfield to inventory Signal supplies coming from Japan on C-47s. I worked with Major Blanchard who did the same for medical supplies. Air cover for the C-47s was provided over Suwon and to the south by fighters operating from Japan that were fuel-limited to 15 minutes over Suwon. When a gap occurred in air cover, as often happened, the Yaks and IL-10s orbiting to the north of Suwon would attack the unloading C-47's. On 30 June attacks fell way off because Quad 50 Machine Guns had arrived on the airfield. These attacks did little damage but caused an extended ground time for unloading. Major damage to the airfield occurred on the 28th—bomb craters and a destroyed C-54 and P-82 Mustang.

On June 29, I asked a C-47 pilot to take my box of color slides and motion picture film that I carried from the Han River to Suwon. I asked him to get them to MacArthur's Signal photo officer in Tokyo with my request that they be mailed to my home in Maine. I had doubts that this happened because I later saw in North Korean village propaganda centers photos of an execution that looked like those I took. Upon arrival home in September 1951, I found all my photos had arrived intact. The photos I saw were taken by others at the execution who had left them in Seoul where North Koreans found them and put them to use.

Major General Chae Byong Duk—26 Sept 1949
Major General Chae Byong Duk addresses 45 officers of the
Korean Army, during ceremonies marking the opening of the new
Korean Army Infantry School. American officers seated on the
stand are left to right: Brigadier General William L. Roberts, Major
J. B. Clark, Lt. Col. B.E. Edwards and Captain J. J. Housman.
U.S. Army Photograph

On June 30 the C-47 "aerial supply train" from Japan continued, interrupted by only MacArthur's arrival at Suwon in his C-54, the Bataan, to assess the situation during a visit to his forward troops. Ever the "master of publicity" he leisurely paused, before departing Suwon, for photos much to the concern of his staff. Photographers of MacArthur appreciated his "Handshake." He used both hands when photographed greeting someone. He used his right to grasp the other's right hand and used his left hand to grab the other's right elbow to pull that person up such that they stood close together—just right for an editor to fit into one or two front-page newspaper columns.

Later in the evening as we were going to sleep we were told to quickly get on the road to Taejon, because the enemy was approaching Suwon. As we later learned-a false report. I piled into in a jeep with Capt. Wells and one or two others. Our convoy drove all night in a heavy rain. As our jeep had no top, we tried to stay warm and dry under a poncho and shelter halves. During my time at the wheel, I imagined that we had arrived in Taejon. In some small village, I turned into the gateway of a house and stopped. This woke my passengers. They told me what I suddenly knew. Taejon was still hours away.

Taejon on July 1 and 2 is where I became very aware of the Mukden Japan telephone/telegraph cable. The cable was part of the infrastructure built by the Empire of Japan both to develop its Korean Colony and to support its 1931 invasion of Manchuria and its 1937 invasion into China and expansion into SE Asia. Two telephone circuits on this little known but vital cable were terminated in the US Army/ROKA HQ building in Taejon. One was terminated in the Operations room and the other in the Signal office. In Tokyo the Signal office line terminated on a military switchboard.

The Signal office line was allotted in the evening to the ever-growing press contingent. I was given the task to manage circuit time, and to act as the first censor of the war. As the correspondents were mostly pros from the last war, I found no security problems, as one might expect in the defensive war we were waging. I read the text of the dispatches to check for revelations that would inform the enemy of our intentions. Each correspondent had 15 minutes in which to contact his office and read his story. He could get another 15 minutes by going to the rear of the queue. Wire service people liked the 15-minute allocation, but feature writers who needed more than 15 minutes did not. Beginning about 7 p.m., the process was completed in about 8 hours.

The only woman among the correspondents was Marguerite Higgins, who was in the boat with me in crossing the Han on the 28th. When she finished, she went over to where I had earlier laid out my bed on top of two desks pushed together-my bedding was a threadbare GI blanket thickly folded (to pad my sore hip and shoulder bones) and a sofa cushion for a pillow. On the blanket I had placed my worldly possessions—a musette bag, shoulder holstered 45 pistol, and an expansion folder. She pushed these items aside and went to sleep on my bed. About 45 minutes later, when I finished with the last correspondents I went over to wake her—telling her that she had occupied my bed and to get out of it. She cussed me but complied. Correspondents were asleep on the floors of the office and hallway. All but Higgins respected my bed.

A few days later Task Force Smith passed through Taejon on its way north to halt the North Korean advance. I decided to fly up to join them to take pictures. Half way there, the L-5 pilot ran into bad weather and decided to return to Taejon. I have been thankful ever since for the bad weather and the 180-degree turn. It was easy to rationalize that my job, after all, was with ROKA and not with US troops.

After some five days in Taejon ROKA/KMAG relocated to Taegu and what came to be known as the Pusan Perimeter. This time we moved during daylight hours. I was not fighting sleep while driving.

Framk Winslow continues in the Epilogue...

Seoul/Inchon Evacuation

June 25, 1950

Ship Captain Desmond Mann, with his wife Ethyl and baby Billy, age nine months, boarded the morning train in Pusan on Sunday, June 25. The baby's hernia was strangulating and they had an appointment with the doctor at the Seventh Day Adventist hospital in Seoul. They were not aware of the invasion from the north until they were half way through the eight-hour trip. They were not met at the train station in Seoul as had been arranged. They managed to get a taxi to the Hotel Kookje Sudo where they booked in at about 8 PM. From the roof of the hotel, they watched aircraft bombing the city. Captain Nelson and his wife were booked in the same hotel and they welcomed each other's company.

Unbeknown to the Manns and the Nelsons, Ambassador Muccio had decided at 11 a.m. to evacuate American women and children by one of the two ships at the port of Inchon, and had called on the Far East Command in Tokyo to prepare for additional evacuation by air. He delayed implementing the plan, however, until it became apparent that the civilians might be trapped and captured. At 11 p.m. Sunday June 25, he went on the air at the local radio station and requested that all dependents board the buses to Inchon.

At 1 A.M., Monday June 26, Ethyl and baby Billy, with some 750 other women and children, were taken by bus convoy to the Norwegian cargo ship M.V. *Reinholt* docked at Inchon. There was another Norwegian freighter in Inchon, the M.V. *Norelg*, that could have been used but it was considered too unsanitary. Therefore, the *Reinholt* was the only escape.

That same morning, Monday, June 26, Captains Mann and Nelson were told to move from the Kookje to the Banto Hotel, the American Embassy location. At the hotel desk, the clerks were reassigning the rooms by prioritizing for essential personnel and moving out long-time "non-essential" personnel. Des went up to his assigned room and knocked on the door. A tall, middle-aged man in his bathrobe answered the door. Des could see another man reclining in an easy chair. The tall man looked Des up and down and asked, "And just who are you?" Des replied, "This is my room!" The tall fellow just flicked his hand at Des and slammed the door shut.

Somewhat upset Des returned to the lobby and got the security officer to accompany him back to the room. When the man again answered the door, the security officer told him to pack up and get out. The security man left and again the tall man slammed the door. He had no intention of leaving. Des knocked again and when the man opened the door Des grabbed him by the collar of his robe and told him, "You are getting out NOW!" The two men scurried about the room, dressed, packed and left.

Now there were less than 300 civilians left in Seoul to be evacuated. Late Monday afternoon a convoy of jeeps and brightly colored orange U.N. buses was formed for the twelve-mile trip to Kimpo airfield. Mann and Nelson boarded one of the buses. Some few evacuees who had their own automobiles joined the convoy. On the way, the convoy was strafed by North Korean YAK aircraft. The leaders at the head of the convoy realized that the shells were hitting the north side of the road, so they directed the convoy to ditches on the south side of the road. A young Korean boy was caught in the line of fire and killed.

C54, Ilyushin 10 and F80 Aircraft.
Photo source: USAF Museum (Internet)

Finally arriving at Kimpo after a tense trip of two hours, the evacuees gathered inside the big brick airport terminal. They were told that six C-54 Skymaster aircraft, each with a capacity for fifty passengers, were en route from Japan, and their arrival was imminent.

Mann and Nelson, from their vantage point at a window, could see the airstrip. South Korean troops were alongside the strip skirmishing with North Korean troops and guerillas.

Four North Korean fighter aircraft buzzed the airfield and, just as they came around a second time, a few American F-80C Shooting Star fighters engaged them in combat and brought down two of them. The remaining two Ilyushin fighters quickly departed.

Mann and Nelson were ordered outside with the others and were lined up as the rescue planes landed. They watched the first, second airplanes load and take off, and they boarded the third plane.

Des Mann had advised a man loaded down with cameras to get on one of the first airplanes because the last one or two might be overcrowded and passengers might be asked to leave all luggage behind. The photographer got out with his cameras but had to leave his luggage. All six Skymasters landed safely at Fukuoka, Japan.

Evacuees boarding C54 aircraft at Kimpo airport
Photo by Desmond Mann

TOM KING

Tom King: "On June 25, 1950 the North Koreans drove across the 38th parallel. Jane and I had planned a Sunday picnic with an officer and wife of the military advisory group. Those plans were, of course, canceled. Jane was evacuated early Monday morning by ship out of Inchon together with almost 800 women and children. After much vacillation, I left Seoul Tuesday by military transport plane together with all but a skeleton staff that fled south with the American Ambassador and Korean President Syngman Rhee and his staff. Jane's ship arrived in Japan and after a few weeks, we were reunited in Tokyo."

Evacuees file
on board the
motor vessel
Reinholt at
Inchon 1950
Newspaper photo

Major Walter Greenwood was assigned to the position of Senior Advisor to the 6th Division of the Republic of Korea Army on December 23, 1948 and held that position until April of 1949. In May of 1949, he was assigned as Deputy Chief of Staff of the Korean Military Advisory Group (KMAG) and was in that position when North Korea attacked on June 25, 1950. He reported to Colonel W.H. Sterling Wright who was in overall command of KMAG.

Major Greenwood's wife of eight years, Mary Logan, and their six-year-old daughter Sallie journeyed from Huntington, West Virginia to join the Major in Seoul in April of 1949. They lived in an American-style housing area called "Camp Sobingo". The Major's office was near-by and close to the military academy.

Colonel W.H.
Sterling Wright
DOD files. KMAG IN
PEACE AND WAR
by Sawyer p119

Mary Logan's days were pretty much routine; caring for their home, shopping, attending coffee get-togethers and women's clubs. She occasionally attended dance-parties Saturday night at the Officers' Club. As Mary Logan remembers those Saturday nights today, she can hear the William Tell Overture music being played out to happy waiting dancers. She frequently entertained in her home and took lessons in Korean dance. She assisted other volunteers in lecturing young South Korean officers who were preparing to depart for schooling in the States. These lectures prepared them for the American/Korean differences in culture.

Her first concern however, was the care and nurturing of their six-year-old daughter and her adjustment to her new environment and her schooling. Sallie's teacher at the Seoul American School (17 Chon Dong), a well-educated American woman, was married to a Korean. After they were reunited in the States, Major Greenwood would tell Mary Logan that this teacher, Ann Wallace Suh from Uvalde, Texas, was dubbed "Seoul City Sue" by the Koreans. It may have happened that after the North Koreans occupied Seoul the teacher would broadcast from Radio Seoul to the retreating Americans and South Korean military much the same as "Axis Sally" and "Tokyo Rose" did to American soldiers and sailors during World War II.

In mid-June of 1950, the Greenwood's had prepared for their return to the States. Their tour of duty in Korea would soon end. Their car was shipped to San Francisco. Most of their personal belongings were crated for shipment by air and were taken to Kimpo Airport. The Greenwood's scheduled departure date was July 3, which, as it turned out, was 8 days after the invasion.

The first reports that the North Koreans had indeed attacked reached Major Greenwood before sunrise on June 25. His boss, Colonel Wright, was in Japan seeing Mrs. Wright and family off on a ship returning them to the States. Colonel Wright returned to Seoul the next day after hearing of the attack.

Continued in Chapter 17b

F-80's go into action

A daily average of nearly 100 sorties were flown by F-80 jet aircraft between June 27 and July 4. The speedy fighters were making their first appearance in combat and, while not designed for low-level operations over rough terrain, they proved to be a marked success after being fitted with extra-capacity fuel tanks giving them additional range.

Mustang fighters of the Royal Australian Air Force joined the American squadrons on July 2. Mustangs were supplied for the use of the South Korean Air Force and American personnel were assigned to assist in training Korean pilots. Ten airplanes were flown from Japan to Korea early in the campaign.

U. S. Army and Navy forces have joined the Air Force in the Korean conflict and a shift has started from a first phase of dependence on the defensive capabilities of air power to a second phase of coordinated air-ground sea operations by all three services.

F80 News article.
Stars & Stripes July, 1950

215

Major Walter Greenwood "The silence from the direction of
Washington was Impressive" Photo courtesy Greenwood collection

The Greenwood Report

Major Greenwood alerted Mary Logan about the invasion and told her to be prepared to leave sooner than planned. (Their planned departure was June 28 so most of their personal belongings were already waiting at Kimpo airport to be lifted out.) Meanwhile, after additional intelligence firmed up the earlier reports of the invasion and a short meeting with Ambassador Muccio, Major Greenwood ordered that all KMAG personnel make preparations to move south by rail and road but to hold that position until so ordered. Ambassador Muccio ordered that all American dependents evacuate by ship out of Inchon. He had, against the wishes of KMAG, intentionally delayed the evacuation all day Sunday explaining later that a premature evacuation order could have destroyed South Korean military and civilian morale.

Mary Logan Greenwood & daughter Sallie 1950 "She felt they were deserting the South Korean people" Photo courtesy Greenwood collection

Greenwood came home to dinner on the evening of the 25th to say good-bye to his wife and daughter. Under the circumstances, he would now have to stay in South Korea.

That night Mary Logan Greenwood and her daughter Sallie packed what they could carry in a couple of suitcases. Each evacuee was limited to one suitcase. Many photos, souvenirs and other personal items were left behind and, Mary Logan forgot her jewelry box. Those who had dogs for pets had to leave them behind. This would seal the animals' fate of course, as dog-meat was a Korean table delicacy. They waited on the front step for the jeep that would take them to ASCOM CITY, which was one of the collection points. A bus transported them from ASCOM CITY to the docks at Inchon. There was no panic by anyone. It was a well-ordered group that was accustomed to "Hurry up and wait". Mary Logan remembers having deep feelings of guilt as they traveled the highway to Inchon. South Korean's, mostly women, children and older men were heading south with their possessions on their backs in A-frames. She felt they were deserting the South Korean people.

The evacuation ship *M.V. Reinholt* was empty and anchored in the bay. The evacuees had to be lightered from the dock to the ship. U.S. aircraft provided cover during this operation and until the ship departed and then the U.S. Navy escorted them. Mary Logan saw her belongings, those that had been shipped to Kimpo Airport, sitting on the dock at Inchon. Someone had apparently planned to ship them on the *M.V. Reinholt* instead of by air but they missed the ship. That is the last time she would see them.

Mary Logan: "The pregnant women, those with infants and a few of the older people were given officer staterooms or crew quarters on the ship while the rest of the evacuees descended into the cargo holds. The luggage was carried into the hold by Korean workmen along with mattresses. There were volunteers to help serve food. Empty cans were put to good use as plates. Food, canned, must have come from the commissary. It tasted wonderful. We had freedom of the ship. Such patient people invaded by us women and children."

"We landed at Fukuoka. On the dock to greet us were Major General William F. Dean and the ever-ready-to-help Red Cross. Coffee, yes but I don't recall doughnuts. What a comfort."

"From there [we went] by train to Karazawa, a resort. I remember at one station stop the music being played was 'Little Red Wing'. From there [we went] to Tokyo to be with my brother who was stationed there with the U.S.Navy."

After his wife and daughter had departed Sobingo, Major Greenwood returned for one last visit to their home. He found photo albums, photos and miscellaneous personal items now scattered all across the living room floor. It was apparent that the homes had already been looted.

MAJOR GREENWOOD; "At about 0430 hours on 25 June, I received a telephone call from the KMAG Staff Duty Officer reporting the outbreak of what was apparently a fairly large fight at Kaesong. As such, affrays had been occurring with greater or lesser frequency during the fifteen months I had been Deputy Chief of Staff of KMAG I felt no particular alarm, at least over the initial report. I directed the Staff Duty Officer to contact the G2 and G3, normal procedure under such circumstances."

"Shortly after 0600, Major G. R. Sedberry, the G3 Advisor, called to tell me that the fight was breaking out all along the 38th parallel and was taking on the proportions of a major attack."

"I arose at once and went to the office, arriving there about 0700. I found Lt. Colonel William J. Mahoney, Major Sedberry and several other officers already assembled in the Chief of Staff's office."

"Major Sedberry gave me a quick summary of the information already at hand. Reports indicated major attacks in great strength all along the 38th Parallel, with a large number of tanks leading the attack, all supported with heavy artillery fire. From these early indications, it appeared likely that an all-out Communist effort was commencing. At about 0800, the Honorable John J. Muccio, U.S. Ambassador, Mr. Everett Drumwright, Counselor of Embassy and Lt. Colonel Bob Edwards, the Military Attaché, arrived. An informal staff conference took place, wherein the tactical situation was examined, and virtually everyone present gave his individual estimate of the situation. The absence of the North Korean Air Force, known to consist of 200 aircraft, caused considerable speculation. Colonel Mahoney concluded that until this air effort appeared or more information was available as to the ground situation, we would regard the attack as 'a reconnaissance in great force'."

(The following is by Major Greenwood in a separate writing):

"Re: The alleged Staff Meeting held 250800:

I do not recollect that any formal staff meeting was held. However, I do recall that at about this hour, the Honorable John J. Muccio, US Ambassador, his military Attaché, Lt. Col. Bob Edwards and Mr. Everett Drumwright, Counselor of Embassy, arrived at Hg KMAG, where an informal briefing on the tactical situation was presented by Major Sedberry, Col. Mahoney, Col. Vieman. At this time, two problems of overwhelming importance were discussed.

These were:

1. Was this North Koreans' maximum effort?

2. If so, had the time arrived to execute the longstanding plan for evacuation of dependents?

To the best of my recollection, it was concluded that sufficient evidence of an all-out effort was not yet at hand. This view was arrived at largely because the North Korean Air Force estimated at 200 combat aircraft had not yet appeared. The State Department aide was most reluctant to believe that a full-scale war was in progress. The military representatives were not so optimistic. I recall distinctly that Colonel Mahoney made the comment: 'This may be a reconnaissance in force, but I doubt it'. In any event, it was decided to alert the 2nd and 5th Divisions for movement to the Seoul area. As I recall, the 3rd Division was given the awe-inspiring task of securing Pusan, repelling possible landings on the east coast as for north as Yongdok, and securing the Pusan-Seoul railway within its sector-all this with two small regiments and primitive communications. No decision was made in regard to the evacuation of dependents, as the Ambassador expressed the belief that such a move made prematurely would have an unfortunate effect on the already jittery populace of the Seoul area, especially if the action did not evolve into a full-scale war. KMAG had never anticipated that Seoul could be held over 72 hours with the ROK forces then in being.

Consequently, we urged that the non-combatants be moved south of the HAN River without delay."

"While this informal conference was in progress, I took steps to get all KMAG personnel turned out and to their duty stations. As this was a Sunday morning, this process was not rapid. Some individuals did not get the word until they were in church at about 1100. However, it is my recollection that all senior advisors (both staff and unit) and key administrative officers were turned out by 0930."

- Officers mentioned by name are listed by the grade held at that time.

"Sometime prior to 0900, we received an urgent message from the advisors with the ROK 17th Combat Team on Ongjin reporting that they were under very heavy attack and that the regiment was about to be overrun. Air evacuation was requested. The two Army aviators, Major Lloyd Swink and Lt. Frank Brown volunteered to fly the mission in their L-5's, nearly 100 miles over open water, in foul weather, in the face of a strong enemy air force, and not knowing if they could land once they arrived over Ongjin. In the face of these hazards, they successfully evacuated the five advisors in a single trip. For their courage and skill, their country has generously awarded them Bronze Star Medals for meritorious service."

"At about 0930, we received a report that Kimpo airfield was under attack. A short time later, a couple of enemy aircraft appeared over Seoul and made a series of strafing passes, against no recognizable targets. However, some of the fire fell in the KMAG housing area, which served to irritate those of us who had our families in that compound. We now acknowledged that this was the Communist's main effort. From this point onward, my recollection of the exact time any single incident took place is likely to be in error, as virtually everything had to be done simultaneously."

"A series of situation reports to DA (Department of the Army) were initiated, to be sent every four hours. CINCFE (Commander in Chief Far East) received copies of all our outgoing summaries. An intensive effort was made to locate Colonel Wright, who was on leave in Tokyo."

"The KMAG Director of Supply**—Major T. MacConnel III, was alerted that PLAN CRULLER-the AMIK evacuation plan, would probably be put into effect in the near future."

** *The position has no counterpart in standard U.S. military organization. It was essentially the internal KMAG supply, billeting and maintenance organization.*

"About noon, Col. Wright was located and I spoke to him by telephone, giving him a limited summary of the situation. Security precluded giving him an extensive briefing. He indicated that he was returning to Seoul as quickly as possible."

"By this time, the tactical situation was unsatisfactory. The initial Communist attack had been well-planned and executed with speed and determination. The presence of so much armor had been a great shock, both physically and psychologically, to the ROKS. Information reaching KMAG Headquarters was scant and untimely. This was especially true of the information received from the east coast, where a series of small amphibious landings had generated confusion out of all proportion to the size of the enemy forces involved. The necessity for evacuating the American (and Allied) women and children was becoming increasingly urgent. However, Mr. Muccio and his State Department advisors were reluctant to commence the operation because of the probable adverse effect on the Korean populace who were already showing signs of panic. It was apparent that the continued presence of the women and children would materially impair the combat effectiveness of KMAG and I considered it of the utmost importance that they be removed as soon as possible. Sometime during the afternoon or early evening of the 25th, Mr. Muccio stated that he proposed to assemble the entire American Mission of the Embassy and surrender in a group, depending on diplomatic immunity to protect us. Such a proposal was so shockingly unrealistic that I verbally directed Major MacConnell to prepare plans for an overland motor or rail movement of the military dependents to Pusan. Admittedly, such a movement would have been hazardous and difficult. Fortunately, at about 2200 hours Mr. Muccio authorized the evacuation of women and children by any means and, without delay. Shortly after dark, the advisors to 2nd ROK Division arrived reporting their division was moving into the Yong Dong Po area. It was planned to commit this division in a major counterattack on the 26th along the axis of the Seoul-Ouijonbu Road."

"The movement of the dependents commenced at 0100 and went off rather well. We had hoped to clear the bottleneck of the Han River highway bridge prior to daylight. However, it was a good deal closer to 0900 than 0530 before the last families were out of the city. The dispersed billets in the city, combined with the normal difficulties encountered in moving large groups of females without husbandly control, hindered the process materially. However, there was no panic, and the service wives were outstanding in every way."

"Colonel Wright finally reached Seoul at 0400 on the 26th after a most arduous trip. A trip that was frequently interrupted as FEAF (Far East Air Force Command) debated the advisability of sending an unarmed aircraft into Kimpo."

"The scheduled counter-attack of the 2nd ROK Division did not come off as scheduled. Lack of time for reconnaissance and coordination with the 7th ROK Division, coupled with aggressive enemy action, produced a series of piece-meal attacks in regimental size or less. The failure of this counter-attack was most serious and portended grave consequences. Now we had at hand no other organized force of significant size that could have a substantial effect on the final outcome."

"Throughout the morning of the 26th, the tactical situation continued to deteriorate. DA (Army) and CINCFE (Far East Command) were so informed in our continuing situation reports."

"An interesting aspect of this period was the apparent lack of reaction in Washington. From the time our initial report was sent, until we abandoned Seoul on June 28th, Chief KMAG received only a single message from Department of the Army. This message, received on the 26th read: 'Do you require guidance?' Other than that, the silence from the direction of Washington was impressive."

"Based on previous information, it appeared that the loss of Korea to Communism was to be accepted in much the same manner as the loss of China had been accepted eighteen months earlier. That line of thinking consequently played a very considerable role in the recommendations subsequently presented to Chief KMAG."

"Throughout the 26th the evacuation of dependents continued. Sometime during that day, CINCFE (Far East Command) authorized

FEAF (Air Force), to provide fighter cover over the evacuation ship and COMNAVFE (Commander Naval Operations) to provide surface escort to the vessel when it cleared Korean territorial waters. These provisions were a great relief to us, although the first physical appearance of U.S. aircraft did not create a favorable impression. This occurred when an F-82 cruised over Seoul and was bounced by two YAK-3's. The F-82 went into 'high blower' and departed precipitously-hardly an inspiring spectacle."

"The tactical situation continued to deteriorate until by late afternoon of 26 June, it was apparent that Seoul could not be held for over 48 hours. It is my recollection that DA and CINCFE were so advised. (Radios should be on file with AG) Our war plans had never contemplated holding SEOUL against an all-out attack for over 72 hours."

"At 1800 I was informed by Major MacConnell that the evacuation ship was under way and all dependents in the number of 682 women and children were safe."

"During the evening of the 26th the Korean government, after some urging, elected to displace to Taejon. About the same time, Mr. Muccio announced his intention to evacuate all noncombatant male members of AMIK and certain other non-Korean personnel (United Nations Commission etc.) less the nucleus of his staff. This phase of evacuation was to be accomplished by airlift from Suwon and Kimpo. FEAF was directed by CINCFE to provide the transport lift and fighter cover."

"By this time the tactical situation was rapidly approaching the nature of a rout. 1st ROK Division was cut off and backed up against the mouth of the HAN estuary; 7th ROK, CAP Divisions and elements of the 2nd ROK were fighting uncoordinated delaying actions from the vicinity of Ouijonbu. Elements of the CAP Division were attempting to block on the axis Chunchon-Seoul. 6th ROK Division was withdrawing almost due south on the axis Chunchon-Wonju. Our information on activities on the East Coast was scant and confusing. The 8th ROK Division, consisting of only two regiments was apparently being attacked from the front (North) and by a series of small amphibious assaults that kept turning the division's east flank. In consequence, the situation was painfully confused."

"Now that the evacuation of dependents had been successfully accomplished, it was possible to return a number of officers to their advisory duties. This was particularly true of technical and administrative services personnel who had been operating the evacuation center at ASCOM City and the out-loading operations at Inchon."

"Late on the night of 26 June, Major Sedberry and I carefully re-examined the situation as we saw it. The total absence of stateside reaction, our knowledge of the U.S. position in regard to Korea, the unsatisfactory tactical situation coupled with the strength of the enemy's initial attack all combined to provide a very gloomy picture. KMAG's terms of reference contained in WARX (1 July 1949) (WAR INSTRUCTIONS) were studied but provided no indication of the course of action to be taken in event of full scale hostile invasion involving Korea only."

"Thus far, CINCFE had shown great interest only in the intelligence aspect of the operation. In fact, we had been overwhelmed with phone calls, radio messages and an abortive telecom, attempting to elicit detailed tactical information, with such questions as 'What is the color of the piping on the uniforms of the enemy tank crews?' While it was obvious what clues G2 FEC was searching for, it was equally apparent that we could not physically obtain and transmit such information."

"FECOM (Far East Command) had cooperated fully in their share of the evacuation plan. Likewise, they were preparing extensive logistical support for the ROK Army. However, days would pass before any significant quantities of supplies could be delivered to ROK Armies, even with the best of intentions."

"Finally Major Sedberry and I concluded that the most practical course of action lay in evacuating those members who could no longer effectively contribute to the combat effectiveness of the ROK Army. This included most of the technical and administrative service advisors in the northern areas and a number of tactical advisors whose units had already disintegrated, plus administrative personnel who no longer had any functions. I presented this recommendation to Colonel Wright, who withheld judgment. This was probably about midnight 25-26 June."

"I could see no point in allowing our people to be captured without the opportunity of putting up a fair fight. At that time, such an outcome appeared most likely. As the tactical situation continued to worsen throughout the night and into early morning of 27 June, I again made the same proposal. This time it was coldly rejected. I therefore started planning to redistribute those advisors who were now without employment because their units no longer existed or their peacetime functions had ceased to exist. However, these plans never progressed beyond the embryo stage as the tactical situation deteriorated more rapidly than I could issue instructions to the advisors."

"By daylight on 27 June, it was obvious that unless ROK forces in the Seoul area could withdraw across the HAN and be heavily reinforced, they would be totally gobbled up within a matter of hours."

At about this time, Chief KMAG informed me of the following plan:

The situation had reached such a state that operations of advisors below the Army level, with the exception of those with the 8th ROK Division (East Coast) and 3rd ROK (Pusan-Taegu Area) were ineffective. He proposed therefore to order out of Korea all personnel except a staff group to accompany and advise Korean Army Headquarters, as long as that Headquarters remained operative. The officers with the 3rd and 8th Divisions would remain with their units for the time being. It was planned that the group with Headquarters Korean Army would consist of approximately 33 officers and men, with their own transport and radio communications. (An SCR-399 capable of maintaining contact with General Headquarters.)"

"This plan was implemented forthwith and perhaps 400 officers and men were assembled at Suwon for airlift to Japan. Unfortunately, on Tuesday morning our radiotelephone to Tokyo had been eliminated when the Embassy switchboard had been prematurely destroyed just as I was commencing a conversation with General Almond, Deputy Chief of Staff FECOM. Thus a c/w (dots and dashes) message had to be sent informing CINCFE of our action."

"While the evacuation from Suwon was in progress, a message from CINCFE to Chief KMAG was intercepted by the station located on the field at Suwon. Col. Mahoney showed me the message which read, as I recall: 'PERSONAL MACARTHUR TO WRIGHT: HELP IS ON THE WAY. RETURN TO YOUR FORMER LOCATION. BE OF GOOD CHEER.' This message put a stop to the evacuation and approximately the one hundred officers and men who had not already been evacuated returned forthwith to Seoul. Upon my return to Seoul, Col. Wright informed me that he had received the message as he was moving both KMAG and Korean Army Headquarters south of the HAN River. Accepting the instructions literally, he had counter-marched to the original Korean Hg in the city. The unfortunate wording of this message subsequently had near catastrophic results."

"We redistributed the potential evacuees throughout the KMAG housing area and they were instructed to get some food and rest, the first opportunity anyone had had for such conveniences since they were turned out on Sunday morning, this being late Tuesday night."

"At about this same time, a radio message was received from CINCFE informing us that a survey team under the command of Brigadier General John Church was en route to Suwon by air. The mission of this team was to examine the extent to which Far East Command could provide logistical assistance to the Republic of Korea from stocks available within FECOM (The Far East Command). In addition to General Church, there were some thirteen officers representing the General Staff Section of all Technical Services of HQ Far East Command. Shortly after dark, we received a phone call from General Church at Suwon. HQ and Col. Wright had a short discussion wherein Col. Wright recommended that General Church not attempt to come to Seoul that night because of the chaotic conditions on the Seoul-Suwon Highway, coupled with the fact that the North Koreans were already fighting within the city itself. General Church accepted this recommendation. It was noted and commented upon by a number of officers that apparently the majority of the Korean Army Headquarters personnel had already abandoned the city. We could find only Vice-Minister of Defense, the Chief of Staff and Deputy Chief of the Korean Army."

"At about midnight Col. Wright instructed certain of us to return to our quarters to get a little sleep and rest and be back at Headquarters

KMAG by 0400 on the 28th. I went to my quarters, showered, had a little food and laid down to get an hour's sleep. Shortly after I got to bed, Major Sedberry called in a state of high indignation and reported that the South Koreans had announced their intention to destroy the Han River bridges without delay. At that time he was talking with General Kim Paik Ii, the Korean Deputy Chief of Staff in an effort to dissuade him from destroying the bridges until troops, equipment and supplies then clogging the streets of the city could be evacuated. I went at once to Korean Army Headquarters where I found General Kim in heated conversation with Col. Vieman (G4 Advisor) and Major Sedberry. Kim informed us that it was a decision of the Prime Minister and the Minister of Defense that the bridges must be blown forthwith."

"We were most anxious that the bridges not be blown until the enemy was actually on the approaches. This condition we felt, would not occur until after daylight, and were consequently violently opposed to premature destruction of these vital bridges. Kim then departed and we did not see him again for nearly 24 hours."

"I went at once to Col. Wright who was at his quarters. As I was leaving Korean Army Headquarters, there was an enormous blast and the bridges went up. The time was about 0135. I attempted to make my way to the crossing sites to verify they had, in fact, been destroyed although there was obviously little question. I found that the Korean authorities had blown the very large highway bridge and all of the three railroad bridges, without making any effort to halt traffic or to clear the bridges before they were destroyed. The chaos that resulted amongst the populace and the scattered troop units that were withdrawing was frightful. The main road from SEOUL to the highway bridge was jammed on all eight lanes with pedestrians, trucks, troops, artillery and all manner of vehicles. Of course, they had all stopped and not a thing was moving. It was apparent that there was no longer any means of exit across the HAN River, except by ferry. I went to Colonel Wright and so informed him. He and I made another futile effort to get to the bridge site. He directed me to assemble the 130-odd officers and men of KMAG at Korean Army Hq. We would attempt to move from the city by vehicle over bridges to the east that might still be in our hands. The assembly was accomplished in reasonably short time. Col. Wright briefed us on his plan and a motor convoy was formed up. This convoy sticks in my mind as being the most perfectly disciplined formation I have ever seen under conditions of such tension. Not a word was spoken, vehicles were spaced exactly, the rates of march maintained perfectly. All of the time this convoy was moving, the city was under heavy attack by the North Koreans. Incoming mortar and artillery fire was moving closer all the time. Fighting had already moved down to the neighborhood of the national capitol, a scant three miles from our location. Our efforts to pass over the bridges to the east of the city were abortive inasmuch as those bridges had been destroyed and we found the area already in the hands of the enemy."

"The column counter-marched, returned to the KMAG area, at which time Col. Wright dispatched a small reconnaissance party under the control of Major M.O. Sorenson to attempt to locate fords of ferry. Major Sorenson returned at about daylight, probably about five thirty, reported that there were personnel ferries in operation all along the HAN from a point east of the former highway bridge to the SOBINGO area. About that time, a Korean Lt. Colonel who spoke English rather well, Lt. Col. Lee Chi Yep, put in an appearance on foot. He had been a member of the Korean Army G4 Section and had always been highly regarded by the Americans. He was not however in good favor with the Koreans because he was regarded as being overly pro-American, a very serious offense in the eyes of the Koreans. Col. Lee announced that he would assist in ferrying of KMAG personnel. The personnel were assembled on foot to march to a ferry site. At that time, we had in the column a single SCR-399, our only communications with the outside world. Col. Wright, after insuring that all personnel were ferried across the river on Korean rafts, elected to remain with the radio vehicle and, in some manner that I have never fully understood, managed to ferry this very cumbersome vehicle and its trailer across the HAN River, which put KMAG back in communications with the outside world."

"At the same time, Col. Carl Sturies, the KMAG Signal Officer, formed up the dismounted elements of the organization and we marched overland to Anyong-Ni, a distance of about 18 miles. It is interesting to observe that this column, totally defenseless, many of us being without weapons of any sort, was never molested by any of the Koreans who had ample opportunity to gain much favor with the highly successful North Korean invaders, by scooping up a group of advisors who were already held in something less than good repute by the enemy."

"Upon arrival at Anyong-Ni, a group of vehicles were commandeered and the remainder of KMAG moved to Suwon, where we found Col. Wright had already arrived with the SCR-399 (mobile mounted short-wave radio transmitter and receiver)."

"KMAG reorganized, and without arms, food, transportation or communications equipment (other than the SCR-399), resumed its function of attempting to stiffen Korean resistance."

374th Troop Carrier Group

In 1950, James E. DeWan of Kirkwood, New York was a Private First Class with the 374th Troop Carrier Group in South Korea. He proudly submitted the following citation to the author in July of 2001.

HEADQUARTERS
FAR EAST AIR FORCES
(GENERAL ORDERS 26 November 1951 Number 554)

DISTINGUISHED UNIT CITATION

As authorized by Executive Order 9396, 22 November 1943 (Sec I, WD Bul. 22, 1943) superseding Executive Order 9075, 26 February 1942 (Sec III, WD Bul. 11, 1942), and pursuant to authority contained in General Orders Number 3, Department of the Air Force, 23 January 1951, the following unit is cited under the provisions of Air Force Regulation 35-75, 7 August 1950, in the name of the President of the United States as public evidence of deserved honor and distinction. The citation reads as follows:

The 374th Troop Carrier Group distinguished itself by outstanding gallantry and heroism while engaged in evacuation and airlift missions during the period 27 June 1950 to 15 September 1950.

The Greenwood Report

The 374th was the first unit to enter action in Korea. From a peace-time status the 374th Troop Carrier Group was called upon to immediately begin supply missions into Korea and evacuate civilians without benefit of fighter cover. On the flights into Korea, these unarmed transports carried supplies to troops of the Republic of Korea to delay the advance of the enemy. During these operations, the unarmed transports were constantly under fire, in the air and while loading and unloading on the ground. On June 28, 1950, the enemy took Kimpo Airdrome just as the last aircraft of the 374th departed. Operations were then shifted to Suwon, 24 air miles south. On 1 July 1950, the North Korean ground forces finally broke through the defense at Suwon just 20 minutes after the last carrier aircraft took off. The supplies that had been flown into the Suwon area enabled the defenders to harass the enemy until 5 July 1950. Although two aircraft were destroyed on the ground by enemy strafing, two crewmen wounded, and one aircraft severely damaged in the air by enemy fighters, the 374th Troop Carrier Group successfully evacuated over 800 United States citizens and friendly foreign nationals. On the morning of 10 August 1950, the 374th received orders to divert all aircraft to Pohang-dong for the purpose of evacuating the 35th Fighter Bomber Wing to Japan. Shortly after the evacuation began, the advancing North Korean troops fought their way to the perimeter of the airfield where they remained throughout the entire evacuation. Without regard for personal safety, the crews of the 374th Troop Carrier Group continued with evacuation for two days and two nights, during which time the aircraft and crews were constantly subject to small arms fire and throughout the nights to mortar fire as well. As a result of these hazardous operations, four aircraft were lost, six men killed and four wounded. The outstanding courage and skill exhibited by the aircrews flying unarmed aircraft, subject to enemy interception, and in landing and taking off under fire, reflect heroism and gallantry to a high degree. The tireless efforts of the ground crews in keeping the aircraft in constant operation, the exceptional flying skill of air crews, and the judgment and planning of supervisory personnel express the skill, determination and esprit de corps of the Group, which were vital factors in successfully accomplishing the evacuation and resupply of Seoul, Kimpo, and Suwon area. The diligence and devotion to duty of the entire Group resulted in 15,545 tons of critically needed war supplies flown to the front; 5,495,500 psychological warfare leaflets dropped; 26,448 Army, Navy and Air Force personnel flown from Japan to Korea, and between other points in the Far East in support of theatre operations; and the successful aerial evacuation of 7,932 sick and wounded. The achievements of the 374th Troop Carrier Group uphold the highest traditions of the military service, and reflect great credit upon themselves, the Far East Air Forces and the United States Air Force.

BY COMMAND OF LIEUTENANT GENERAL WEYLAND

OFFICIAL: S.R. BRENTNALL

Major General, USAF

Vice Commander

/s/ E.E. Toro

/t/ E.E. TORO

Colonel, USAF

Adjutant General

Seoul Survivor

By Robert Rudolph, Sr.

Reprinted from the Foreign Service Journal/July–August 1998 with permission of the author and the FS Journal

WITH NORTH KOREAN TROOPS CLOSING IN, OUR JOB WAS TO BURN THE EMBASSY CABLES, SMASH THE RADIOS, AND GET OUT FAST.

"The whole world remembers the televised image of Saigon falling in 1975— helicopters taking off from the U.S. Embassy roof, desperate crowds surging at the gate. But precious few remember the untelevised fall of Seoul, South Korea, 25 years earlier. In June 1950 Communist forces swept down from the North and we hightailed it out of there, burning embassy cables and smashing equipment with the enemy closing in. I was in that embassy. I sent out the last radio message before the power failed. This is how it went down."

DAY ONE

June 25, 1950, 8:30 a.m.

I was finishing breakfast in the dining room of the U.S. Embassy in Seoul. My job was supervisor of the Operations Unit in the Radio Teletype Section in the American Embassy. I was a 22-year-old supervising four radio operators and four Teletype operators. We communicated with the world via a duplex radio Teletype operation with the Army's Tokyo relay station. When atmospheric conditions interfered with radio Teletype signals, we exchanged messages with Tokyo using International Morse Code.

While drinking my coffee, I saw Red Mintz walking toward my table. He was the only employee scheduled to work that day in the Embassy CommCenter. I wondered why he wasn't at work downstairs.

Red said STATE (our name for the embassy cryptography section) had told him there was a flap up on the 38th parallel. The 38th was the dividing line between North and South Korea. STATE had told Red we'd probably have heavy message traffic all day. Red asked me who should be called in to work with him. Sundays in Seoul were usually boring, and handling heavy message traffic during a flap might be interesting. I decided to work with Red that day. That was the start of the most exciting 60 hours of my life.

When we walked into the CommCenter, Sgt.Brown was leaning on the counter. Brown was the military attache's cryptographer. He was writing on an enciphered message he'd prepared for transmission.

He was upgrading the message precedence to OPERATIONAL IMMEDIATE. This action violated military communications procedures. He knew it. I knew it. I didn't know why he'd made that decision but I trusted his judgment. Brown said STATE was using EMERGENCY precedence on its message to SCAP (that was Supreme Commander Allied Powers Gen. Douglas MacArthur). He believed his message would need to be OPERATIONAL IMMEDIATE to get fast handling. "What's going on, Brownie?"

"Don't you know?" he asked.

"Then I can't tell you."

Having been told that STATE had said a flap was occurring up north, I believed it. It matched the experience Red and I had had over the past two years. We thought in terms of minor military actions.

Small military firefights between North and South Korea weren't unusual on the 38th parallel. Fighting had also occurred inside South Korea. Red and I had operated an Army radio station handling messages to Republic of Korea forces fighting a rebellious ROK regiment in 1948.

While Red prepared the military attache's message, STATE called. They were sending down an EMERGENCY message to SECSTATE WASHDC. I quickly sent an EMERGENCY SUPERVISORS to Tokyo stating "CLEAR CHANNEL TO UEPSD WASHDC" (UEPSD the teletype address for messages to State).

Each relay station was supposed to take actions to speed our message to the State Department. I believed special handling actions and sparse Sunday traffic would get our message to UEPSD WASHDC in about 60 minutes. In 1950, that was lightning speed for a message going such a great distance.

We transmitted STATE's EMERGENCY message without delay. We sent it about 9:30 a.m., June 25 Korean time. We were 14 hours ahead of WASHDC, making it 7:30 p.m. Saturday, June 24, East Coast time.

We received a plain language EMERGENCY message from Under Secretary of State James Webb about 10:30 a.m. Addressed to Ambassador John Muccio, it said in part:

UNITED PRESS REPORTS 40,000 NORTH KOREAN TROOPS PLUS TANKS CROSSED THE 38TH PARALLEL AT THE ONGJIN PENINSULA AT 4 A.M. TODAY. CAN YOU CONFIRM OR DENY?

I was annoyed that our message to WASHDC had arrived after the United Press message. Our message took a lethargic 110 minutes to arrive at UEPSD. I believed it had been inept message handling at relay stations, plus message encipherment in Seoul and deciphering in WASHDC that had slowed our message delivery.

I notified STATE that an EMERGENCY message had arrived from WASHDC. Sam Berry, STATE's chief cryptographer, came to the CommCenter and read the message quickly.

"Is this what's going on, Sam?" I asked.

"Yes," he said. "It's war."

His words stunned me. I knew of course that the U.S. had a small military assistance group in South Korea, but no combat units. We had no commitment to defend the South.

By Sunday afternoon, our incoming and outgoing message traffic flow was very heavy. We added more Teletype operators to the day shift.

An air raid occurred late in the afternoon. Three beautiful propeller-driven Russian-made fighters came swooping low over the city. The sun reflected off their wings as they banked to and fro dropping leaflets along the way.

A few 50-caliber machine guns on surrounding hills fired at the North Korean fighters. Many of us, both men and women, left the 8th floor dining room and rushed to the roof to watch the show. We cheered each time South Korean machine guns fired at the planes. Then a retired colonel appeared at the rooftop fire door and said loudly: "You damned fools! What goes up must come down! Get off this roof!" We complied with the old colonel's instructions reluctantly. By this time, the constant rumble of artillery in the north could be heard when we were outdoors.

The evacuation of 2,500 Americans from South Korea began on Sunday evening. WVTP, the radio station of the American mission in Korea, began sending evacuation instructions for American mothers and their small children.

WVTP told the mothers with small children where to assemble and the amount of luggage they could bring with them. They were transported from the assembly points to Inchon and were then placed aboard a fertilizer ship that was in port.

The huge switchboard in the American embassy communicated with all U.S. and some South Korean agencies in the greater Seoul area. As a security precaution, on Sunday evening, female Korean telephone operators were replaced on the embassy switchboard by American women—just in case one of the Koreans might be a spy or saboteur. The Americans had volunteered to operate the switchboard.

Sunday night, I decided to reduce our message reference files. The message files filled a very large wheeled cart. We moved the cart to the embassy parking lot and used a thermite bomb to set it on fire. The white flames shot up 20 feet above the cart.

Smitty, our telephone lineman, was having coffee in the snack bar late that night. He said he was ready to quit repairing our telephone lines. Each bombing near Kimpo airport and the Seoul railroad station had knocked our telephone wires off the telephone poles. Smitty complained that he'd restring the wires on the poles and bombs exploding in the next air raid would knock them down again. A bomb had exploded in the street a block away from the embassy.

DAY TWO

Monday, June 26

I remained on duty during most of the night. We were now working 24 hours a day. Our peacetime incoming and outgoing message traffic had been 150,000 words a week. We were now handling 150,000 words in 24 hours and were doing so with ease.

While at breakfast in the embassy dining room, I heard aircraft dog fighting overhead. That was my first notice that the U.S. Air Force was flying cover for us.

Station WVTP began broadcasting evacuation instructions for dependent women and non-essential female employees. Evacuees were told each person could take only one suitcase.

Later in the day, we heard that the Air Force had shot down seven North Korean aircraft. The U.S. lost no aircraft in the dogfights.

That afternoon, I called home on the Korean Bureau of Communications radiotelephone system from a CommCenter phone. My call went via the RCA network in San Francisco to my parents' phone in California.

The chief telephone operator of KBC, Mrs. Lee, handled the call. Mrs. Lee was a kindly Korean-American woman from Hawaii. She had a grandmotherly attitude to those of us working in the CommCenter.

I enthusiastically described the spectacular sights and sounds to my parents. I doubt that my vivid descriptions reassured them.

The rumble of artillery from the north had grown louder as the day progressed. I decided to destroy more message files. We burned three weeks worth of messages.

Bishop Patrick Byrne, the delegate from the Vatican to the Republic of Korea, came by our CommCenter that day. We always enjoyed his visits. He liked people, had a good sense of humor and enjoyed being alive.

Celebrities and politicians may hire flacks to proclaim their so-called charisma. Bishop Byrne needed no phony buildup from flacks. When he entered a room, you were interested in seeing him and hearing what he had to say. By the time he departed a room, it had become a brighter and happier place. Bishop Byrne believed his experience in this war would be the same as what he'd encountered in World War II. In that war, the Japanese had kept him in solitary confinement for three and a half years.

His only visitors had been members of the Japanese thought police trying to find out how he learned news about the war. They never discovered his short-wave radio.

Bishop Byrne said he was going to stay with his flock in Korea.

(John Toland's book, In Mortal Combat: Korea 1950-1953, describes what may have been Patrick Byrne's last day, November 2, 1950. He and a Methodist minister were helping each other try to keep up on a 20-mile march in North Korea. He probably died shortly after that.)

By Monday evening, WVTP was issuing evacuation instructions to families with dependents. The women who'd been operating the embassy switchboard were also being evacuated. Only men would remain in Seoul after this evacuation phase.

We were now hand-delivering high precedence incoming messages to STATE. I delivered them many times because speed was important and I enjoyed walking about.

DAY THREE

Tuesday, June 27

Military Advisory Group to the Republic of Korea Headquarters sent a radio operator with a short-wave radio to our CommCenter shortly after midnight. The radio linked KMAG Headquarters with the American Embassy.

We in the Communications Branch assumed the American embassy would stay operational after the Communists captured Seoul. My boss Ira Dale and I volunteered to stay behind to provide radio Teletype communications with Tokyo. I had volunteered out of a sense of duty. I wasn't eager to be confined to the embassy grounds in a Communist city.

I was relieved when Ambassador Muccio turned down our offer. The KMAG cryptographers moved their equipment to the embassy's front parking lot using their own-armed security. I hadn't known my friends could be so steely-eyed. They stacked the crypto equipment on top of thermite bombs and then set off the bombs.

I decided to destroy all files except the current ones. KMAG let me toss our files onto their fire. The thermite bomb flames sent light reflecting off the clouds above the embassy. The Seoul Fire Department reportedly thought there was a fire. I notified all Teletype stations in the Pacific area that we had only today's message files on hand.

Ira Dale heard Ambassador Muccio would go to KMAG headquarters and move with the KMAG commander. Cryptographer Sam Berry would accompany Muccio.

Our Radio Teletype Section had a mobile radio. A truck would carry its transmitter, receiver, housing unit and generator.

This radio could provide communication to very distant places such as Tokyo. Our section had five experienced radio operators.

Ira Dale notified Ambassador Muccio of our mobile communications capability. Muccio replied that the Army would provide his communications. (The ambassador should have taken our offer: KMAG communications with Tokyo were soon overwhelmed by heavy message volume.)

Sometime before 6 a.m. we were told our Communications Branch would "kill the board" (the switchboard) at 9 a.m. We would then have 30 minutes to destroy our equipment and board a bus in the motor pool. We were given single-bladed axes or sledgehammers to use in destroying our equipment.

Buses would depart at 9:30 sharp. Anyone not aboard would be left behind. We'd be allowed to take only one suitcase each. The KMAG radio operator departed. He would operate the radio maintaining communications between KMAG and SCAP. He left the RCA transmitter and a half filled can of toddy on a CommCenter table.

Non-memorable last words

I thought about sending the last message from Seoul. A large screen would be installed high above the machinery in the Tokyo relay station and would display the words from Seoul. Important people would observe those last words, and I was the one who'd be sending them. My words would go down in history if I could send memorable last thoughts to Tokyo. I believed it had been the radio operator at Wake Island who had said, "Send us more Japs" as that island was falling. I knew the radio operator at Corregidor had sent a note to his mother as the island fell. No memorable words came to mind. I thought of asking, "Will anyone loan me some track shoes?"

As 9 a.m. neared, I talked (on the teletype) with an operator in Tokyo. Nothing dramatic came to mind so I just wrote "C U IN TOKYO." I'd missed my chance to have my words go down in history.

Sam Berry walked in just then with a 40- or 50-word enciphered EMERGENCY message to SEC-STATE WASHDC. That message tape was only about half sent when power died. It was time to start destroying communications equipment.

I dropped the message and tape into the wastebasket containing the day's message traffic. I felt bad about not getting that last message out before the power died. I could hear the sounds of the transmitters being smashed in the next room. Sledgehammers were hitting the switchboards far down the hallway. Dick Mixer, one of our CommCenter, team had started destroying the teletypes as soon as the power shut off. He went at his task enthusiastically.

I picked up my axe and smashed away. It turned out to be fun. I hit the Underwood typewriter keys and not much happened. I struck a blow at the end of the typewriter carriage. This produced a zinging sound followed by the end-of-line bell ringing as the carriage sailed into the air and onto the floor.

I had to hit the telephone several times to get good results. I smashed the Teletype in front of me. The destruction actions specified in the Teletype manual were easy to understand.

I moved over to smash the RCA transmitter the KMAG radio operator had used. Destroying such a beautiful piece of equipment bothered me. I sliced off the knobs on the front panel and smashed the dials. As I did this, the can of toddy that had been sitting on the table fell over and spread its liquid under the transmitter.

A Korean I'd never seen before had wandered in and was watching our actions. Obviously, he was going to loot things after we left. I opened up the top of the transmitter and began smashing the radio tubes. The pretty glow of the radio tubes meant the transmitter was still getting electricity but I failed to grasp that fact.

I had difficulty hitting all the tubes inside the transmitter case. The Korean looter-to-be tried to help me. He picked up the transmitter with the obvious intention of tilting it toward me so that I could more easily smash the tubes inside the case.

After picking up the transmitter, the Korean stopped smiling and just stood there quivering slightly. It was clear that the slopped toddy liquid on the bottom of the transmitter had permitted the electricity to find a new circuit through the Korean's body. I looked around for the power plug in the wall outlet. My intention was to pull the plug, but I couldn't find the outlet. The cord from the transmitter went over to the wall and behind some file cabinets. I raced over to the file cabinets and, axe in hand, began looking between them for the plug. All that time, out of the corner of my eye, I could see the Korean standing there with the transmitter in hand, quivering.

I finally spotted the power cord on the floor between two file cabinets. I chopped at the power cord with my axe. One swipe of the axe cut the power cord in two. The Korean stopped quivering, put down the transmitter and walked out of the room. He didn't smile at me as he left.

When we finished our destruction, I carried the wastebasket containing the day's messages out to front parking lot. I planned to set the wastebasket on fire with matches. I found Sgt. Brown detonating thermite bombs stacked below and on top of his cryptographic machines. I asked if I could toss my wastebasket on the fire. He said okay.

Brownie and I watched the crypto machines and my messages burning. He noticed an American missionary taking pictures of the burning crypto machines with a movie camera. Brown pulled a pistol from his holster and told the missionary to stop taking pictures. The missionary smiled triumphantly as he stopped taking pictures and turned away.

At 9:25 a.m., the Communications Branch and embassy security people boarded the buses; we were the last to leave. Koreans stood silently in the street and on the sidewalk watching our every move.

I was embarrassed by the stares of the Koreans as our convoy of buses and cars drove through Seoul. They were threatened by an invading army and we were running away.

It seemed that our evacuation of Americans was complete, but we later learned that the kindly Mrs. Lee had been left behind in Seoul. Why hadn't she listened to WVTP or called the embassy? Why hadn't one of us called her? I still think of her last reported words. She had called RCA San Francisco and said, "The bastards have left me!" She was right.

When we arrived at Kimpo Airport about 10 o'clock, we found Air Force fighters flying protective cover over us. Sometime the fighters were P-51 Mustangs, sometimes P-82 Twin Mustangs and occasional jet engine F-80 Shooting Stars.

Each time the fighters flying cover needed to return to Japan for fuel, they'd fly flat and low past us and wag their wings as they climbed away. It was their way of saying; "You're going to be without air cover for a while, so watch out!" Sometime later, a new pair of fighters would arrive to fly cover over us.

We formed in groups on the tarmac with our luggage and were issued C rations to eat.

From time to time, a C-54 Air Force transport would land and taxi up to the terminal area. A group of American evacuees would then board the aircraft and it would take off for Japan.

The only things between us and the advancing North Korean Army were a river and a few South Korean national policemen. Sometime in the afternoon, a twin-engine bomber flew toward us from the south. I was surprised to see it had the silhouette of a Douglas A-26.

Some nearby South Korean national policemen turned and began moving toward cover from a possible air raid. I shouted "Meegook, Meegook!" (American, American). The nearest policeman looked surprised. I was too. When the aircraft neared us, we saw its white U.S. stars.

This was our first indication that President Truman had committed military forces to help the South Koreans. Until then, we had assumed the U.S. wouldn't defend South Korea. I felt better. I could now look South Koreans in the eye.

By mid-afternoon the evacuation had halted. The fighter aircraft continued to fly cover over us but Air Force transports had stopped arriving. We had three planeloads of evacuees still awaiting flights to Japan.

There was much discussion about the halted airlift. We decided to try ringing an old Japanese telephone line that ran from Kimpo Airport to Fukuoka, Japan.

A telephone technician answered the phone in Japan. He transferred the call through many telephone exchanges to Far East Air Force (FEAF) Headquarters. FEAF said they'd heard that Kimpo airport had fallen to the North Koreans. The C-54 transports had been diverted to Suwon Airport about 25 miles to the south of us.

FEAF Headquarters agreed to start sending the C-54 transports to Kimpo Airport again.

FEAF Headquarters diversion of C-54s to Suwon was amateurish; it showed communications had broken down. Air Force fighters from Itazuke Air Base were flying cover over us. FEAF Headquarters should have known this.

Some of us doubted whether FEAF would send more transports to Kimpo. Ira Dale had a carryall containing food, water and a full tank of gas in the embassy motor pool. Ira, Red and I decided to go get his carryall and drive the 250 miles to Pusan far to the south.

As we walked toward the parking lot, we encountered Sgt. Brown. When he heard our plan, he recommended we not go. He said he'd received reports early that day about fighting with guerrilla forces south of Yongdungpo. That was on the route we'd be traveling to Pusan. We took Brown's advice.

Last plane out

The embassy security people asked those of us who were healthy and young to volunteer to be on the last plane out. They said we might have to travel by vehicle or on foot to Suwon Airport.

All the Communications Branch's young men volunteered to be on the "last plane." We thought we might have an adventure that we could tell our grandchildren about.

Late that afternoon, the C-54 transports began arriving once again at Kimpo. Small amounts of ammunition were unloaded from each aircraft.

A KMAG lieutenant colonel and some soldiers had arrived to pick up ammunition from the cargo aircraft. The officer said things were getting better at the front.

FEAF Headquarters instructed us to wave white towels or shirts when the last transport arrived. This was to assure the aircraft commander that the airport was still in friendly hands. We agreed to do so.

As the last C-54 aircraft arrived over Kimpo, we all waved white towels or T-shirts. I think we all felt rather foolish about doing so.

The plane landed and taxied toward the air terminal while two P-51 Mustangs continued flying cover over us. I was enjoying the drama of the last plane's arrival.

The C-54 swung into position in front of the air terminal. The cargo doors opened to reveal two crewmen holding submachine guns with ammo clips in place. They looked out at us grimly. Here was a scene we could tell our grandchildren about!

Then the crewmen put the ladder in place and four civilians appeared in the plane's doorway. They were American reporters.

Three of the reporters were men. The fourth was a pretty young woman who looked quite fetching in a white blouse and dark skirt. She was Marguerite Higgins, a reporter for The New York Herald Tribune. All the reporters got off the plane, and we learned they were staying on to cover the big story.

I felt a big sense of anti-climax. We weren't the last Americans out of Seoul after all! When the shoes of Marguerite Higgins and the male reporters touched the tarmac, all the drama of departing on the last plane had dissolved. The stories we'd be telling our future grandchildren about this day had just dropped a couple of notches on the grand scale of historical significance. We climbed aboard the aircraft quietly and soon left Kimpo Airport behind."

Ed. note: Bob Rudolph was in the Army in Seoul from about June 10, 1948 until June 21, 1949. He was the Operations Unit Supervisor, Radio teletype Section, Communications Branch, Joint Administrative Services, American Mission in Korea from June 22, 1949 until 9:30 a.m. June 27th when he departed the American Embassy, Seoul for Kimpo Airport.

Robert J. Rudolph in Seoul 1949-50 "We rushed to the roof to see the show"
Photo by R. J. Rudolph

See: Bob Rudolph in the Epilogue

S.S. "Pioneer Dale" Type C2 "He ordered his crew not to leave the ship" Photo credit: www.usmm.org Web Site

Pusan Evacuation

The cargo vessel S.S. *Pioneer Dale* departed Kobe Japan on the evening of June 21 carrying 4,000 tons of general cargo destined for South Korea, the Phillipines and Hong Kong. One of the large fleet of United States Lines passenger and cargo vessels, the *Pioneer Dale* was under the command of Captain Harold W. Lanford and carried a crew of 51. They had left New York on April 26 and after taking on cargo at Newport News, Baltimore and Charleston they transited the Panama Canal and re-fueled at San Pedro, California. They then loaded and unloaded cargo at Honolulu, Manila, Hong Kong and Yokohama before arriving at Kobe Japan on June 20. The ship was almost 2 months into a planned 4-month voyage. They had 13 more ports to call at in Asia and a planned arrival of August 24 back in New York.

On 25 June, when North Korea attacked, the S.S. *Pioneer Dale* was steaming across the Sea of Japan on a course for Pusan and its captain and crew were unaware of the invasion. The ship docked at Pier One in Pusan and commenced discharging her cargo. Captain Lanford was informed of the trouble up north. The cargo operations were postponed and Captain Lanford was requested to stand by for further orders. He was patient and understanding and ordered his crew not to leave the ship.

Meanwhile, the S.S. *Letitia Lykes*, another general cargo vessel under the U.S. flag and owned by the Lykes Steamship Lines, was ordered into the port of Pusan and assigned to pick up evacuees and transport them to Japan.

In the evening hours of Tuesday, June 27, Milton Nottingham and Al Meschter boarded the two rescue ships together.

Nottingham: "Air cover for the ships carrying evacuees was arranged by SCAJAP so it was necessary for me to instruct the ship Captains when they were to sail. As I recall the Captain of the *Letitia Lykes* was at first unwilling to enter Pusan because of the hostilities and only did so when it was demanded. I am not sure who ordered that he must come into Pusan but it was perhaps his shipping company by radio. On arrival of his ship, the Master told me that he would load the passengers and sail immediately. I told him that was not possible, as the departure of his ship must await air cover. When he protested I advised him he would sail only when I instructed him to, even if it was necessary for me to post soldiers on the bridge and in the engine room. He reluctantly agreed to wait for instructions and so the soldiers were not needed."

"After the invasion commenced, but before Seoul's capture, Bishop Patrick Joseph Byrne phoned me to indicate he intended to remain in Seoul but asked that I arrange the evacuation of the Maryknoll Sisters from Pusan if they wished to leave. Reluctantly, they did go but returned to Korea from Japan as soon thereafter as they could."

The Maryknoll sisters, (L to R, standing): Dottie Kelly, Sister Augusta, Sister Agnes Theresa (behind child dependent standing), Sister Herman Joseph, Sister Rose of Lima, Sister Alberta Marie, Jane Coburn. Seated in front: three American dependent children.

The following is taken from the book *"Her Name is Mercy"* by Maryknoll Sister Maria Del Rey. 1957 copyright by The Maryknoll Sisters of St. Dominic, Inc. Library of Congress Catalog Number 57-6074.) Cite: Maryknoll Sisters Collections; Maryknoll Mission Archives; Maryknoll, NY

Sister Augusta was a nurse from Meadville, Pennsylvania. She spent 15 years in China. She had a quick wit and ready smile.

Sister Agnes Theresa. A young doctor fresh from Maryknoll. "I'm the Grandmother doctor of Maryknoll, the first of our Sisters to practice medicine."

Sister Herman Joseph. A laboratory technician from Salem, Oregon. She was one of the corps of pre-war Korean missioners.

Sister Rose of Lima. Nurse and Pharmacist from Jersey City NJ. She could speak Korean.

Sister André. (Not in photo) She evacuated Korea from Inchon.

Sister Alberta Marie. A teacher from Detroit Michigan.

Agada, a Korean, had worked with the Sisters for many years in North Korea. She escaped over the border and got her niece Patrisya out too. They managed an orphanage in Seoul for some years. "News that the Maryknoll Sisters were to open a dispensary in Pusan filtered up to Agada in Seoul. She packed her bags and came on the run. Hardly had the Sisters landed in December 1949, when she was knocking at the door, all ready to stay forever, if needed."

Now, as the Sisters were evacuating to Japan, Agada and Patrisya would stay in the Sisters house to protect it.

"It was Nita who had helped in the short-lived dispensary operating from April until the evacuation in June. It was she and Patrisya who had brought necessary supplies like food and clothes to Hialeah where Americans were detained to await evacuation ships to Japan. It was only two days' waiting at Hialeah, but to see their beaming faces at the compound gate had been reassurance that they would return somehow."

At 11:30 PM, our convoy of 30 vehicles were in a column inside the compound guardhouse exit with their engines idling and lights out. A

KMAG officer organized the convoy and directed that only two men would be allowed on each vehicle; the driver and one-armed man. Some of these men were American KMAG; some were Korean police. Male Americans civilians were not allowed to evacuate at this time.

The women and children had been advised that they would be permitted to carry only one small bag of possessions. Marion had put on a pair of G.I. fatigues with very large pockets that extended from the waist to the knees. She stuffed the pockets with lingerie, make-up and a few apples and candy-bars. Her 8-month pregnancy protruding forward between the over-stuffed pockets; her silhouette was quite grotesque. I held her in my arms, assuring her that the ships were waiting and that she would be safe in Japan the next day.

It was tearing me apart to let her go and I dared not tell her my real fears; the biggest one being that the vehicles would be intercepted by guerrillas or North Korean troops. That the women and children would be captured. I reminded her that it would be much better to have the baby in Japan as the facilities there were so much better than those in Korea. Looking down the column of vehicles the same scene was being repeated over and over. The men holding, hugging and kissing their wives and children in tearful good-byes. One couple was on their knees facing each other, holding hands and praying. The Maryknoll Sisters were moving from vehicle to vehicle consoling and praying with each group. Nurse Barbara Mella gave tranquilizers to some women who were near hysteria.

Then it was midnight and time for the convoy to move out. There was an eerie silence after the big gates closed behind the convoy. It disappeared into the darkness quickly as they were showing no lights.

A few hours later, the drivers and men riding "shotgun" returned and excitedly reported their accomplishment over much-deserved refreshments at the bar. They said the city was blacked out but that the roads were visible in the darkness. "There was a mixture of many protestors and supporters waving signs and torches." The women and children had been boarded on the two ships without incident and the ships were already at sea and on their way to Japan.

Dotty Kelly and Marion were separated before boarding. Dotty was on the Letitia *Lykes* and Marion on the *Pioneer Dale*.

Marion: "As I stepped from the gangway to the deck of the ship I felt a hand on my shoulder and a voice said, 'Follow me young lady.' The hand was that of the Chief Engineer Arthur Quellmalz. He escorted me to his stateroom where he gave me the key. Then he closed and locked the door while instructing me to let no one into the room and not to open the door until he knocked on it in the morning. I was very tired. The bed was neatly made with fresh linen. The refrigerator was full of milk, fruit juices, fruit, cold cuts of meat and other snacks. The stateroom was large and it was neat and clean. I showered, snacked and fell asleep as soon as my head hit the pillow. I was sure that my guardian angel was looking after me. On the evening of Wednesday the 28th we arrived in Port Hakata, Japan. I woke to the sounds of the many voices on deck. Then I heard a sharp knock on the door, unlocked it and opened it. No one was there. I left the room to find people sleeping on the decks of the passageways. Going out on deck I saw most of the women and children were in a long line getting ready to disembark. It appeared that many had slept on the open decks during the crossing. I had somehow been singled out to make the crossing in comfort and I believe that Milt Nottingham was the one who had stirred my Guardian Angel. Uppermost in my mind was the men who were left behind and what would happen to them. I wondered when and where I would have my baby. On the dock at Port Hakata, the American Red Cross greeted us. They gave us a toothbrush and toothpaste then asked for a donation of twenty-five cents. We were put up in military sleeping quarters that evening and left Port Hakata on a train in the morning. After two more stops at Army facilities enroute we finally arrived at the Fujiya Hotel on Mt. Fuji; a real 'heaven on earth'."

We were all greatly relieved and turned back to the task at hand. It was four o'clock in the morning. I put my radio earphones on my head; one offset so I could hear, and dozed off with the volume up; the .45 caliber and 12-gauge shotgun at my side. Just before I dozed, I could hear the "thump thump" of the sandbags that the Koreans were still adding to our fortress.

ECA employees & KMAG personnel gather outside of the Flamingo Club "We feared for our lives" Photo by Mary Roth

19

The Waiting

Wednesday June 28

The woman and children were safely out of South Korea. Seoul was in the hands of the enemy. Our compound became both our refuge and our prison. We had plenty of food and our own water supply. We did not have to worry about losing electric power as we had our own regulated and gasoline powered generators. With the many vehicles in the car-pool, we could make a run for the port if we had to, brandishing our small arms. Much of our conversation in and around the clubhouse was about escaping should the invaders target the compound. It occurred to us that, should they decide to take the compound, we might find our-selves in a suicidal shoot-out and, in any case, we would be either killed or quickly defeated and captured. I shuddered to think of being a pris-oner of war.

Captain Putnam counsels two ECA employees "Remain calm and wait for further Instructions" Photo by Mary Roth

The men moved to and from their houses and the clubhouse, mingling in small groups, frequently playing cards again and partaking of drinks at will. The bar was now a free bar and they could fix their own highballs; select their own beer. The two female cooks had evacuated. There were only two male cooks left and they worked around the clock to feed the one hundred remaining men. The cooks welcomed help in the kitchen and there was no lack of volunteers. It seemed we had a number of hobby cooks in the group and others that jumped at the chance to keep busy. The disciplined meal schedule was no longer kept. The food was fairly good. We could raid the refrigerator at will.

It was sometime in mid-morning when we heard a barrage of gunshots. Guessing that the invaders had finally reached Hialeah, we checked our weapons while we feared for our lives. Then a KMAG officer burst through the front door and informed us that a group of KMAG men had just arrived from Taegu led by Lt. Col. Rollins Emmerich. The gunshots we heard were from Emmerich's party chasing looters out of the compound. He and a group of around 9 or 10 KMAG strode across the dance floor to our radio room and introduced themselves. We disappointed them when we told them we did not have reliable communications with our forces up north. We accepted a few messages from them for transmission to Tokyo. They stayed with us long enough to get an update on our situation and they assured us that they would be working close by. When they left, we assumed they would set up their headquarters in Pusan.

Frank and I were now busier than ever at the radio. The landlines were still working and we received sketchy reports from KMAG officers who were moving south with President Syngman Rhee and Ambassador Muccio. At the Tokyo end of our radio link, Captain Ziglinski, assisted by Major Huebler, kept MacArthur's intelligence headquarters frequently updated. 1st Lieutenant Don Dickinson and Captain Bob Slaven had also established a dedicated landline link with General Back's offices and kept him informed. Don and Bob also had a telephone link with MacArthur's intelligence people. The 71st Signal Service Group had organized monitoring teams of radio operators with their beam antennas aimed on South Korea. They were instructed to listen for any information from Korea and report it to Intelligence and General Back.

Most of the men in the compound asked us to find out how their wives and children were faring in Japan. We were not able to glean this information however as the evacuees were still in process at scattered points across Japan and our repeated requests went without response. Incoming messages far outnumbered the outgoing and we could respond to inquiries from relatives of our compound residents. We received many inquiries directly from the United States and where the inquiry was about the Seoul evacuees we could only respond that the women and children were safe in Japan. We could not report on the situation with men remaining in Seoul, except for the arrival of Emmerich and his men. We had no information regarding who might have been captured, who moved out by air and who fled south over land. When the inquiry was about personnel in Pusan we were able to give more detailed assurance, not only about the evacuation of the women and children, but also information about the safety of the men remaining in Pusan. Safety? I wondered when someone would send us a message giving us some kind of assurance.

Hialeah Compound could not have been a more perfect and well-defined target. First, it was a great circular configuration laid out on the plateau separating the mountains from the city. It could not have been a better target unless we went out there and painted a bull's-eye in the middle of it. Put yourself in the cockpit of a marauding North Korean or Russian aircraft. Would you not just cruise north out of Pusan and look for that target knowing that you could wipe out the Americans?

When you are approached by low-flying jet aircraft you have no warning until there is a sudden loud rush overhead. Our first thoughts were that enemy aircraft were about to bomb or strafe the compound. Frank and I left the radio to join the rest who had rushed outside. The jets made their pass so fast that no one saw the insignia on the wings. High in the distance there were three rapidly disappearing dots leading their contrails. Now a much slower aircraft was approaching from the East and this one was perhaps carrying a bomb. As the plane passed over-head we saw the scattered papers floating to the ground at the same time that we saw the beautiful American insignia on the wings. We waved and cheered and the pilot dipped his wings from side to side in acknowledgment. The message on the pamphlets was simple:

THE ARMED FORCES OF THE UNITED STATES ARE COMING TO THE AID OF THE REPUBLIC OF SOUTH KOREA PLEASE REMAIN CALM AND WAIT FOR FURTHER INSTRUCTIONS GENERAL DOUBLAS MACARTHUR.

The messenger plane banked and disappeared to the southeast. As wonderful as it was to receive that message, it was anti-climactic. What now? The message did not tell us that we were safe in the compound. It did not tell us that guerrillas would not break our security. It did not tell us when we would see U.S. troops or how and when we would be taken to Japan. We returned to our waiting and the radio.

JA2KK and JA2CO from HL1CD/HL1CE, "WE HAVE BEEN BUZZED BY AMERICAN JETS AND ANOTHER AIRCRAFT DROPPED PAMPHLETS FROM GENERAL MACARTHUR TELLING US THAT THE U.S. ARMED FORCES ARE COMING TO THE AID OF SOUTH KOREA"

ROGER THAT, THAT'S GREAT NEWS! NOW WE HAVE MORE TRAFFIC FOR YOU"

...and we continued message exchanges into the night; switching bands as required.

The Regimental Combat Team

Late June 1950

General MacArthur was pressing President Truman for permission to send U.S. troops into South Korea. The Joint Chiefs of Staff sent General MacArthur additional instructions. He could send his planes into North Korea to bomb purely military targets. He had to keep these planes well clear of the frontiers of Manchuria and the Soviet Union. Army ground forces, both combat and service troops, could, if it became necessary, be sent into the Pusan area to hold the port and the airfield facilities there.

June 30, 1950 President Truman ordered U.S. ground forces into Korea and authorized the bombing of North Korea by the U.S. Air Force.

July 1, 1950 General William F. Dean is U.S. Commander in Korea. The 24th Infantry Division arrived in South Korea.

General MacArthur ordered General Walker to load the MSTS (Military Sea Transportation Service) "*Sergeant Keathley*", then in Yokohama Harbor, with 105,000 rounds of 105-mm. ammunition, 265,000 rounds of 81-mm. mortars, 89,000 rounds of 60-irmi. Mortars and 2,480,000 rounds of .20-caliber carbine ammunition. He wanted the MSTS *Keathley* to reach Pusan no later than July 1.

The Joint Chiefs of Staff had not favored the use of American ground forces in Korea primarily because they knew how unprepared they were for large-scale combat.

MacArthur's immediate reactions to send supplies, these to be protected by air and naval escorts, were as far as he could go on his own authority. Certain basic decisions had to be made in Washington and the key man was President Truman.

July 2, 1950

The *MSTS Sergeant Keathley* was crewed by American civilians and arrived in Pusan with the Regional Combat Team on 2 July.

Frank relieved me at the radio. I took a jeep from the motor pool and drove down to the port to greet the ship. The tide was such that the main deck of the ship was level with the dock making it quite easy to chat eye-to-eye with the soldiers on deck. I remember asking some of them where they were from in the states. I held a conversation with a couple of them about their duties in Japan. In general terms; their response was along the lines of how much fun it was, what with all the beautiful girls, good food, bars, dance halls etc. They also admitted that they had received very little combat training, if any. My conversation with those very young boys was quite spontaneous and their words gave evidence that they simply had no idea of the seriousness of the situation. It appeared that it was just "Cowboys and Indians" to many of them. Some were cleaning their weapons. Others were shadow boxing or boxing with each other and making remarks like, "We'll wipe out those commie gooks in two weeks and go back to our girl-friends in Japan." Their remarks and attitudes were disheartening. I remember thinking that I might tell them that they were over-confident. I had second thoughts about doing that, as their confidence may have been a positive tool in what they were about to face. I had watched the wounded young-sters on Okinawa carried down out of the hills. I had watched those walking cry and hold on to each other; trying to comfort each other. As I walked back to my jeep, I remember wishing for a fast arrival of more experienced and mature troops. I couldn't help but wonder what was going to happen to these innocent and foolhardy young men. Finally, as they met the enemy up north, they were all but completely annihilated; so it was reported.

I was not aware at that time that most or all of the KMAG officers and enlisted men, who had evacuated Seoul/Kimpo by air to Japan, were also on board the ship and being returned to duty in South Korea.

The signalmen arriving on the *Keathley* appeared to be well trained. They followed me to Hialeah compound to relieve our amateur radio communication station. They obviously knew their equipment and procedures well as in short time they were communicating with a truck that was moving south from the Suwon perimeter. They had trucks loaded with power supplies and transmitters. They operated from inside the vehicles. I offered them my radio log, which they accepted but they later just trashed it. I dismantled our ham radios while listening to them in very formal military communication; "This is Able Able Two" exchanging reports and orders and the ever-present sign-off with a simple "OUT" which I never did care for. In our amateur operations we were much more informal with a sign-off of something like; "JA2KK, this is HL1CE, signing off after a very enjoyable contact. We appreciate your help and hope to talk with you again soon." Not just, "OUT". The military does not have time for these social and gracious words. Their military jargon and procedures were not completely foreign to me; but most of it went right over my head. Seems everything had a code word so their exchanges were not very descriptive. The word "deploy" was used often. I felt comforted in believing that, if I couldn't understand what they were talking about, there was small chance that the enemy could. They sort of scoffed at the amateur radio operation I had. When I offered to leave my equipment behind a mature Sergeant simply said, "Don't need it son, thanks anyway." Frank Crosby had already pulled his equipment out and left with it. I loaded my radios into the jeep. I would bunk on board the *William Lester* for the duration.

The troops made themselves comfortable in house 306. There were just too many of them in one house. I had spent a restless night on board ship and decided in the morning to return to house 306 to retrieve a few things I had hidden in the attic space. Cigarettes and booze mostly. The cache was no longer there. There must have been as many as 50 troops in the house. Their boots still laced tight, they had carried in a lot of mud. The place was a mess and I was very happy that they were there. It meant that I could leave South Korea as soon as it was decided how we would leave. The troops had a lot of words for me, e.g., "Hey Man, where's your 'oooooniform?' ' Where's the bar?' 'You got any women round here?' etc. I laughed, drank and smoked with them. They were about to be ordered north.

The *Keathley's* vehicles, arms and ammunition were loaded into rail-road cars for delivery to the front. Most every vehicle in Hialeah compound motor pool was also loaded on the northbound train.

Train leaving Pusan with cargo of military vehicles
U.S. Army Photo

American soldiers were assigned to guard the precious cargo. One of these soldiers, a dog lover, observed a native scene that he should never have seen. The train jerked to a stop in the countryside for some reason and the soldier's railroad car was immediately above the back yard of a Korean family's home. The Korean family, husband, wife and two small children, were busy at a perfectly normal Korean chore. They were preparing to butcher a dog but first they had to tenderize the meat in traditional Korean style. The dog was tethered tightly between two posts while the family paddled the dog. The soldier watched in disbelief for a few minutes and then, he "lost it!" He raised his rifle and killed all four members of the family and the suffering dog. He was arrested by his military superiors on the train and subsequently shipped off to Honolulu where it was later reported that he was court-martialed.

The Airplane Crash

The 71st Signal Service Battalion in Tokyo advised me by radio on 28 June that a C54 Skymaster was enroute to Pusan to relieve our amateur radio operations. The aircraft carried all the elements of a complete military radio communications station and the signalmen to operate it. There were four officers and fifteen enlisted men on board the huge aircraft as they circled the Pusan area for their landing approach. Their first approach had to be aborted because there was a large piece of machinery on the only runway. The machinery had been placed there earlier to prevent North Korean aircraft from using the field. On making their second approach while the machinery was being removed from the airfield, the C54 ran into the side of a mountain 85 miles north of Pusan.

Bob Slaven: "The signal section, in MacArthur's headquarters, under Brigadier General George I. Back, was embarrassed to be caught with their pants down, not having any communication with Korea. That's when you and I got into the act with ham radio. I was given a direct phone line to MacArthur's headquarters to pass along info from you, or to you. I recall one message for you to give to some Major, who was apparently one of the few U.S. Army people still in Korea. He was told to put obstructions on the airfield to prevent an aerial invasion from the North. Our battalion had emergency radio teams set up for just such an occasion and they were immediately flown to Korea but the plane crashed, killing all hands, the first U.S. casualties of the war. So, I was given the job of training new teams."

Word of the crash reached us quickly via the South Korean police. Frank Crosby, with his camera bags draped over his shoulder, left with the police in their jeep. Somewhere down the road, they commandeered a large truck and several Korean volunteers and headed for the small village nearest the crash scene. En route and after arriving at the village, more volunteers and trucks joined the effort. Now numbering about fifty, they started the trek up the mountainside and reached the crash site after approximately two hours. The aircraft was demolished; pieces of the plane and lifeless bodies spread over approximately three acres.

The volunteers were told how to check each body for signs of life and to check for identification dog tags before moving a body to the village. There were no survivors.

In the village, the bodies were checked again for identification and were loaded onto the trucks. The villagers built a small altar, which they decorated with South Korean and American flags. Every town village along the 85-mile route to Pusan had honor guard lining the roadway. Peasants left their fields to bow to the trucks carrying the bodies.

When Frank returned I noticed specks of blood on his shoes and pants cuffs. He was very quiet for the next two days before I debriefed him. I never did see the results of his photography.

The dog tags and bodies were turned over to the Korean Military Advisory Group.

C-54 SKYMASTER Source: http://www.rob/clubkawasaki.com/js19.jpg

S. Koreans Honor Dead

International News Service

SOMEWHERE IN KOREA. July 7—The bodies of the 23 Americans killed in the crash of a C-54 transport plane were honored by every Korean village through which they were carried by burial parties.

Every town village along 85 miles route had honor guard lining the roadway. Peasants even left fields to bow to trucks which carried bodies.

In the village where the bodies were first brought for identification and to be put on trucks, Koreans built a small altar which they decorated with Korean and American flags.

South Koreans
Honor Dead
International News
Service July 7, 1950

CASUALTY LIST

It was a typically American set of names. There was a Tomlinson, a Kiezanowski, a Morrissey, a Rolek, a Brown and a Selig. They came from all over the country: Westfield, Mass.; Oakland, Calif.; Warren, Ark.; Kalamazoo, Mich.; Aitkin, Minn.; Clearwater, Fla.; Baltimore.

There were 15 in all, four officers and eleven enlisted men, on the first casualty list issued by the Army. The men were lost in the crash of a transport en route to Korea.

Casualty List
Time Magazine July 10, 1950 1st page

263

U.S. Reveals Casualties

Kyodo-AP

WASHINGTON, July 3— The Army Sunday announced its first official casualty list of the Korean campaign.

It named 11 officers and men missing after the crash of a transport plane carrying them from Japan to South Korea.

The announcement gave no details except to report that the plane is believed to have been lost while attempting to land.

Among the casualties were the following with dependents residing in Japan:

First Lt. Louis G. Selig, First Lt. Roy T. Riggs and Sergeant Alex Rolek.

U.S. Reveals Casualties
Kyodo-AP Press July 3, 1950

IN MEMORIAM

1st Lt. Roy J. Riggs

1st Lt. Louis G. Selig

2nd Lt. Edward M. Crays

2nd Lt. Charles R. Tomlinson

Sgt. Boyd W. Elam

Sgt. Alex Rolek

Cpl. John C. Brown

Cpl. Elmer E. Hardy

Cpl. Edmond A. Kiezanowski

Cpl. Richard E. Millis

Cpl. Raymond G. Morrissey

Cpl. Ernest L. Pitre

Pfc. Stanley A. Gogoj

Pfc. Emerson P. Huff Jr.

Pfc. Dale L. Magers

Pfc. Myron P. Marble

Pfc. Edward Peska

Pfc. Peter Ternes

A memorial service was held in the 71st Signal Service Battalion Chapel in Tokyo at 1500 hours Sunday July 16, 1950. Chaplain Stemple led the service.

ANOTHER TRY

Shortly after the ill-fated C-54 took off for Pusan, another C-54 with a second communications team was made ready to fly into Suwon, just south of Seoul. The 71st Signal Service Battalion personnel on board included one Private Frederick J. Walsh and a radio operator called

FIRST AMERICAN CASUALTY—Sunday's SGS carried a photo of the parents of Pvt. Frederick J. Walsh, looking at his photo after the Army announced he was the first American war casualty. Here, Walsh gets the Purple Heart from Lt. Col. John Johnson, who commands the 71st Signal Service Battalion. Col. Neal C. Johnson and Brig. Gen. George I. Back, FEC Signal officer, are shown (left to right, rear) looking on. (U.S. Army Photo)

First American casualty news article with caption.

U.S. Army Photo

"Smitty" who was an acquaintance of Robert J. Rudolph, author of "Seoul Survivor" (Chapter 17C).

Shortly after the flight touched down at Suwon, the field was under enemy attack and Pvt. Fred Walsh was wounded. He was sent back to Japan on the next outbound flight. This author surmises from the scant evidence available in other writings that this same C-54 may have been destroyed shortly after landing.

Rudolph: "Smitty said the North Koreans listened to the airfield communicating with aircraft coming in. He said they would wait until they knew a transport had landed and would time their air raids to hit the transports on the ground. He said he was caught in an open field between his SCR-399 Radio Set and the river (or stream). He had just bathed and put on clean underwear and fatigues. He was walking across the open field when here came an enemy aircraft. He said he hit the ground and as the aircraft strafed him, he learned the meaning of the phrase: 'Keep a tight a—hole'. He said he had to go back to the river to bathe and put on his old underwear and fatigues."

Coffee on the Ceiling

Robert M. Simmons (WWII Veteran): "C87-converted B24's were replaced by C-54, a DC4 cargo version during April 1943. This was a more comfortable flying aircraft although not very speedy. Behind the cockpit was a crew compartment complete with two bunks. Another compartment containing four gas tanks each holding 250 gallons of fuel. The remaining section was for cargo and or passengers who sat on drop-down bench-seats along each side. The toilet was at the very rear of the compartment.

"A problem developed shortly after the C54 was put into service. All four engines would stop and because the altitude was only 7 or 8 thousand feet, it would cause you to get a little excited. The reason for the low altitude was that the cabins were not pressurized. For higher altitudes, oxygen masks were required. The reason for the engine stoppage was leaky cross-feed valves. The routine procedure was to use wing tank fuel until reaching cruising altitude. Then one of the cabin tanks was switched over and all four engines were fed gas from this tank. When the fuel level dropped to about 50 gallons three of the four engines were switched to another of the cabin tanks. The remaining engine would run on the original tank until it used up all the fuel and was then switched over to join the other three engines. Because of the leaky cross-feed valves air would get into all four engines causing them to cough sputter and stop. The crew would turn on booster pumps and that would clear the problem. But, on one occasion we dropped to about 1000 feet above water before all engines would start up. I experienced this thrill once flying just south of Greenland and a second time flying from Scotland to Africa when we were just passing the Bay of Biscay. We discussed flying east to Portugal and being interned for the rest of the war. The Portuguese were reported to be excellent hosts and Americans were not detained for very long. I totaled 2511 hours of flying time and 200 one-way trips across the North and South Atlantic. I went out on a pilot training flight once out of LaGuardia. After they got it airborne, they were practicing shutting down engines. With a shut down on one side, I got a little nervous. Then they practiced stalls. The old bucket of bolts started to shake and shiver. I remember one trip into Casablanca when prior to landing we lost all hydraulic pressure so we had no brakes except for the emergency air brakes. We circled and waited for daylight then buzzed the field to take a look at the runway. Fortunately, it was a nice long runway and when we landed, we didn't need brakes.

We picked up a C54 at the Azores Islands that had been in severe turbulence, which turned it upside down. We flew that aircraft to Goose Bay and then to LaGuardia. Coffee grounds were still on the ceiling of the cockpit."

A WWI Battleship, the "Regina Margherita"
www.battleships-cruisers.co.uk

Power Ship "Jacona" rests at Sasebo after evacuation tow.
Photo by author

The Power Ships

The U.S. Government contracted with a company in Hawaii to supply the ports of Inchon and Pusan with much needed additional electric power. The Hawaiian company supplied an old World War 1 battleship to fill the requirement at Pusan.

The ship had been completely stripped, reducing it to nothing more than a large barge without any means of self-propulsion.

The mammoth engine and generators in the engine room had been completely overhauled for the Korean task. A small galley and sleeping quarters remained intact to accommodate the crew of Hawaiians who maintained the machinery. The ports of Inchon and Pusan received many hundreds of kilowatts of much needed power. The power barge in Inchon was dubbed the *Electra* and the one in Pusan the *Jacona*. The *Electra* at Inchon was a barge with a large housing.

At both Pusan and Inchon, these power-supplying vessels were permanently moored at docks close to the other harbor facilities and their

Power barge "Electra" at Inchon
Photo by Frank Winslow

crews could easily go to and from shore. The Hawaiians on the *Jacona* would frequently take the bus out to the Flamingo Club at Hialeah compound. Very large and tan fellows; they for some reason kept very much to themselves and always around the bar. When they finally came under the influence of all the liquor they consumed they would entertain us with the Hawaiian war chant and other Hawaiian songs.

The day after the invasion the power barge *Electra* had been scuttled to prevent its use by the invaders. The big cables that carried electric power into Inchon were disconnected, dropped into the water, and the old ship sank slowly into the mud at the bottom of the harbor.

By July 15, all but a few of us had already been evacuated from Pusan. The North Korean troops had moved steadily south and by July 20 were between Taejon and Pusan. The odds seemed to be in favor of the North Koreans sweeping into Pusan and taking us prisoner. We decided to use one of our own training ships, the S.S. *William Lester*, as our escape vehicle while at the same time towing the *Jacona* to Japan. It took two days to make up a towing bridle. The size of the old WWI

The "Electra," scuttled to avoid use by enemy
Photo by Frank Winslow

battleship *Jacona* dwarfed the *William Lester* as it was moved into position to secure the towline.

The *Jacona* had been tied up to its pier for four years and now, with her mooring lines and electric cables disconnected, the ship was free to move. I was on the bridge of the *Lester*, looking aft, watching the towline and bridle tighten between our stern and the bow of the *Jacona*. The *Jacona* lurched hard to starboard as she was pulled away from the dock, then she rolled enough to port so that you could see the build-up of barnacles below her waterline. A few of the Hawaiian electricians who had maintained the power ship were on board to make good their escape. The weather was excellent as we pulled out of the harbor. People on shore applauded our departure. I wondered if they knew they had just

Captain Nelson's Radio Receivers. Photo by author

lost one-third of the city's electricity. I stood on the bridge wing as we moved out to sea. As the movement of the ship created a welcome breeze, I felt a great sense of relief and anticipation. I was up most of the night keeping in touch with the men on the *Jacona* on our walkie-talkies. Captain Kitts was in command of the *Lester* and her tow and Murphy was in the engine room. A few of our men were stationed at the bow to watch the bridle and towline. The *Jacona* was now just a big quiet hunk of steel with engines dead and the rudder set at zero-zero degrees; straight ahead. We would be in Sasebo Japan the next morning. We had no idea of what we would do from there but trusted that the authorities would get us transportation to where our wives were being housed in Japan. I had two of Captain Nelson's ham radio receivers on board and he would pick them up in Japan. For our amateur antique radio readers the receiver on top is a National Model NC-155. The unit next to the typewriter is a National NC-57.

"HMS Belfast." "I pulled the canvas cover off our port wing blinker light" Photo by author

Sasebo, Fujiya & Tokyo

July 14, 1950

South Korean President Syngman Rhee wrote a letter to General MacArthur:

"Dear General MacArthur:

In view of the common military effort of the United Nations on behalf of the Republic of Korea, in which all military forces, land, sea and air, of all the United Nations fighting in or near Korea have been placed under your operational command, and in which you have been designated Supreme commander United Nations Forces, I am happy to assign to you command authority over all land, sea, and air forces of the Republic of Korea during the period of the continuation of the present state of hostilities, such command to be exercised either by you personally or by such military commander or commanders to whom you may delegate the exercise of this authority within Korea or in adjacent seas.

The Korean Army will be proud to serve under your command, and the Korean people and Government will be equally proud and encouraged to have the overall direction of our combined combat effort in the hands of so famous and distinguished a soldier who also in her person possesses the delegated military authority of all the United Nations who have joined together to resist this infamous communist assault on the independence and integrity of our beloved land.

With continued highest and warmest feelings of personal regard,

Sincerely yours,

Syngman Rhee

As we approached Sasebo, we were challenged by a U.S. Navy ship using blinker light. In dots and dashes, the message was simply "WHAT SHIP?" I pulled the canvas cover off of our port wing blinker light and replied "*U.S. SHIP WILLIAM LESTER* AMERICAN CREW EVACUATING PUSAN WITH POWER BARGE IN TOW" Navy ship: "ROGER -WAIT" It was a long wait. The Navy ship never did answer. I thought my message was very clear. Perhaps it was so out of the ordinary that they couldn't find anyone who knew how to respond. Either that or we guessed that their response would be to visit our ship after it was anchored.

Captain Kitts had slowed the *Lester* and the towed *Jacona* to a stop in the middle of the harbor, carefully avoiding a collision between the two vessels. There were a dozen or more military ships in the harbor and I snapped photos of several. The light cruiser USS. *Juneau* was among them. Also; the British destroyer HMS *Black Swan*, British heavy cruiser HMS *Belfast* and a Japanese hospital ship, the S.S. *Takasago Maru*. It was comforting to be in their company but it would have been would have been much more comforting had they made their appearance in Pusan and earlier.

The Japanese hospital ship "Takasago Maru"
Photo by author

On a pre-arranged hand-signal from Captain Kitts, the men on the bow of the *Jacona* dropped her anchor. Then, Kitts anchored the *Lester*. The towline was dropped from the *Jacona* and we picked it up with the *Lester's* stern winch. Two jets flew over us a half dozen times during these operations. U.S. Navy launches finally arrived alongside both of our ships and all of the two crews were ferried ashore. Captain Kitts formally turned over command of the vessels to the Navy. The next morning the "Star and Stripes" military newspaper gave full credit to the U.S. Navy for saving the *Lester* and the *Jacona* from the North Korean advance threatening Pusan. We just smiled. This credit stealing happened frequently.

July 28 Captain Kitts, Engineer Murphy and I boarded the train for Tokyo. Much to our disappointment, there were no sleeper cars in the train and we slept off and on sitting straight up on wooden seats. We transferred to another rail line in Tokyo where we had our first good meal in several days. The last leg of our journey terminated at Miyanoshita and the Fujiya Hotel.

The Fujiya was the very first resort hotel in Japan and had been introducing the tradition and culture of Japan to foreign visitors since 1878. The beauty of the hotel and surroundings are almost indescribable. Some 33 years after our stay there a New York Times April 17, 1983 article by one William Hamilton states in part: "The Fujiya's rooms in the Flower Palace, the older part of the hotel, are pleasant spaces with high ceilings. Furnished thoughtfully for the fastidious traveler in several once-modern styles, they contain a vanity table, bureau, desk, good reading lights, a walk-in closet, comfortable armchairs, restful beds and surprisingly, a good bridge table that proves useful for afternoon green tea. Massage is available in one's room by appointment."

The guest rooms were named after flowers and at the desk, I was told that Marion was in the Moonflower room. When she opened the door we fell into each other's arms and there were tears of happiness. Marion told me of her train ride from Port Hakata after she left the S.S. *Pioneer Dale*. After the Red Cross offered her a comb, toothpaste and a toothbrush, which she declined, they asked her for twenty-five cents. She had no money. She boarded the waiting train with the others. Her train's first stop was at Hiroshima and a U.S. Army post where they were taken to a military hospital. She was assisted to a surgery room and onto a large stainless steel table. The doctor examined her and gave her a clean bill of health then gave her a sheet and a blanket and told her to stay on the table. He told her he would close the room and she would not be disturbed there. She was exhausted and slept well. In the morning, the women bathed in the post's communal shower, which she didn't care for at all, as she was accustomed to absolute privacy when bathing. To put it in Marion's own words, "I couldn't believe I was carrying a baby and bathing with a dozen or more naked women who were escaping from war in a foreign country."

The next day the manager of a department store in Hiroshima opened his store to the women. They were told they could take any clothing that they and the children needed. The generous manager was

Fujiya Hotel at Miyanoshita
Photo source: 1950 Souvenir postcard

sure to receive positive and valuable advertising for this kind deed. Marion picked out underwear, a maternity dress, stockings and shoes.

The women and children were next transported by train to Camp Shimodayama where they again had to go through physical examinations. They ate and slept well before the final leg of the trip to Mt.Fuji.

I related to her everything that had happened after she left Pusan. Holding each other, we napped for a couple of hours in the large comfortable bed. We ordered coffee to the room. The view from the Moonflower room was spectacular. We toured the grounds holding hands and talked at length about the baby. Marion was now in her ninth month.

We took a cable-car ride up to the higher reaches of Mount Fuji and that proved quite frightening for Marion. The idea of being suspended at great heights by cable was not her idea of fun. I am not sure whether that experience had anything to do with it but she was suddenly anxious to get to Tokyo and closer to the hospital where she would have the baby.

I told Chief Dempsey that evening at dinner that Marion felt like leaving. He said he had been requested to escort us to Tokyo when ready. Apparently, he was an old-timer around Tokyo and could guide us to our assigned quarters there and give us instructions on how to get around.

Before leaving the hotel, I called Captain Joe Ziglinski, one of the radiomen who answered our distress calls from Korea. I told him that we were leaving the Fujiya Hotel and would put up in an apartment in Tokyo from where I would call him in the next few days. He said he would call the other radiomen, arrange a time and place to get together. We boarded the train at Miyanoshita and settled back for the long ride.

Marion and Chief Dempsey wait for train to Tokyo
Photo by author

On the way, the train made several stops. It was very hot and we were very thirsty. We bought ice cream being hawked by a vendor strolling alongside the open windows of the rail cars. That was a mistake. The "ice cream" was in a little sliding carton like a matchbox and looked and tasted like frozen sugar-water. Now we were even more thirsty. I spotted a vendor with bottled water and left the train to get some. I had to run after the departing train and leaped on just as the last car reached the end of the platform. Chief Dempsey explained that the Japanese passengers always carried their own supply of food and water. A few hours later, we arrived at Tokyo Central station. Dempsey hailed a taxi and spoke to the driver in Japanese. After a hair-rising ride through heavy and dangerous traffic, we arrived at the Mantetsu Apartments. A ten-story building, it had been an annex to the American Embassy before it was converted to housing for American transient personnel.

Apartment number 222 had been reserved for us and we were settled again in comfortable privacy. Room 222 had all the amenities. The bedroom, dining and living rooms were actually one very large room. No walls. Large windows at the living room end provided ample light and a good view of MacArthur's residence, conspicuously white about a mile away. Adjacent to a full bath there was a small kitchenette that we seldom used except for morning coffee. We could order food and drinks to the room.

Mantetsu Apartments
Photo by author

Two views of room 222 Photos by author

Captain Jay and Jane Kressen were also residents of the Mantetsu. We spent some evenings together playing Bingo in a large meeting hall within the building. One morning we asked our driver to drop us off near the Imperial Palace. I had picked up an inexpensive Kodak camera and wanted to try it. On the way, I was able to snap a photo of General Douglas MacArthur exiting the Daichi building, his Far East headquarters.

General MacArthur exiting Daichi building Photo by author

The Ernie Pyle Theatre in Tokyo was showing a first rate movie that we had not seen so we called for a car from the car-pool to take us over there. The theater had been renamed for the star war reporter, Ernie Pyle, who was killed by Japanese machine-gun fire on the small island of Ie Shima in April 1945. On our first visit to the theatre, an American soldier told us not to venture far from the theatre as an area close by had a reputation for crime and prostitution. When we came out of the theater, it was dark and it appeared that prostitutes were lingering under the lamplight immediately across the street. There were a couple of G.I.'s with them and apparently in serious negotiation. I wondered how soon these men might be in South Korea. The pregnant farm-girl at my side had never seen women soliciting men and wondered why it was necessary. I tried, unsuccessfully, to put some meaning to it in words. Sometimes it's better for a sailor to just keep his mouth shut. Our scheduled driver from the car-pool finally showed up and the subject was dropped.

FOUR'S A CROWD in "Champagne for Caesar," the new comedy at the Ernie Pyle Theatre. The four: Barbara Britton, Vincent Price, Ronald Colman and, in the foreground, Caesar the parrot.

Ernie Pyle Theatre
Stars & Stripes July 1950

The Mantetsu apartments were not without regal and pretentious atmosphere. A crew of Japanese maintenance people were constantly cleaning, scrubbing and polishing. There was a garden-like atmosphere everywhere in the building but it was the formal dining room on the third floor where this ambiance was most evident. We approached the room the first time for breakfast. The Maitre-d', in black and white tuxedo, tight cumber-bun and bow tie, greeted us stiffly with a smile. At the same time, I could see that he was gazing at our attire. We were dressed informally and he spent a few moments looking at his appointment pad. Over his shoulder, I could see that the dining room was at near full capacity with all of its occupants in somewhat formal dress. Neckties all. I thought that perhaps he was going to turn us away. I think it helped that Marion was pregnant. He seated us near the entrance at a small table for two, holding Marion's chair out first and then mine. Another penguin filled the crystal water glasses and gave us over-sized menus. There were large beautiful bouquets of flowers everywhere and soft background music filled the room. The tablecloth was of rich and stiff white linen and the utensils were real silver. We spoke in whispers. A third black and white "penguin" took our orders. We had both decided to start with orange juice and a bowl of dry cereal. The cereal was still wrapped in its small box and we opened them at the same time. We had uncapped the refuge of at least a hundred moths the size of small flies. Did you ever get the giggles? I mean really hysterical and uncontrollable giggles. The contrast of our surroundings and escape of the moths struck us slowly at first. The first sign of our reaction came with suppressed laughter but soon turned to audible giggles. Then our laughter became an uproar of hilarious laughter and, try as we may, we couldn't stifle our outbursts. Some of the moths flew to the ceiling and others circled our table where, by now, two "penguins" were trying to stand between the staring patrons and us. The maitre d' was polite at first and asked us to be quiet as we were surely disturbing the other guests. Just at that, time a moth landed on the end of my nose and Marion was again out of control. Her next laugh bordered on sounding like a scream. Tears were streaming down her cheeks. The maitre d' asked us to "please leave", and we did, still laughing. We had been summarily evicted from the royal palace but I wouldn't trade that experience for anything. When we came to our senses we agreed that the primary reason for our eviction was the embarrassment it caused the establishment. Moths in the cereal. I don't believe the Mantetsu ever served another box.

When we returned to our room there was a message to call Joe Ziglinski. I returned his call and he invited us to the Signal Officer's Club for drinks and dinner on Saturday.

Shopping in Tokyo was simply a delightful adventure through a maze of silks, embroideries, porcelains, ivory, fine china, jewelry, electric appliances, radios etc. Japan was recovering quickly from the devastation of World War II and we found an unexpected abundance of goods of all kinds. On our first trip to the department stores, Marion's choice was a setting of Noritake china. Mine was an eight-millimeter movie camera. I would take movies after the baby's arrival. We kept shopping trips short since the baby was expected at any time. On a subsequent trip, we agreed on a pair of hand-painted silks.

Our driver was not scheduled to pick us up for another hour or so and we wanted to see a few shops on the Ginza. We flagged down a taxi and during our trip, I noticed the driver of another taxi stopped at curbside and was stoking a charcoal fire in the trunk of his vehicle. When we left our own taxi I made it a point to look at the trunk and, sure enough, the trunk lid had been removed and there was a combination of glowing wood and charcoal fueling his engine. I had not noticed any difference in acceleration or speed during our ride. Our ride was at pretty slow speeds however and I guessed that at higher rates of desired acceleration the required power might not be there. In later studies, I learned that charcoal had been employed to fuel vehicles in Europe for many years. Had I known this in the early 1940's I may have tried to convert my engine to a charcoal burner during the gasoline-rationing period.

Still another shopping trip presented a nice surprise. Marion was looking for a dress that she could wear after the blessed event. I tried to avoid the lady's lingerie department while she was busy going through the dress racks. She turned to go between two of them. At the same time Marion reached for a dress, a hand came through from the other side of the rack and reached for the same dress. They nearly collided and laughed together. The two women chatted for a while about clothing, weather etcetera. A clerk approached and asked, "Mrs. MacArthur, may I help you?"

Marion was somewhat astonished that she had been conversing with the wife of the Supreme Commander and said that if she had known who it was she perhaps would have not been able to speak. Jean MacArthur told the clerk she did not need assistance and continued to chat with Marion. I had heard the clerk address Mrs. M and kept my distance while they finished their chitchat. MacArthur's young son, Arthur, was with her.

We arrived at the 71st Signal Service Battalion Officers' Club at the appointed time and found our hosts gathered at a small shelter gazebo near the club entrance. Capt. Bob Slaven, Lt. Don Dickinson and Capt. Joe Ziglinski introduced their wives to Marion and me. We had fun conversing and taking photos for a while before going into the club for drinks and dinner.

More talk and laughter over our drinks. Bob Slaven gave me his chit-book so I could visit the bar at will. There are still tickets in the book totaling $1.10 (Year 2002).

The Radiomen and their wives, standing left to right:
Betty Ziglinski, Marion Maurstad, the author, Ruth Slaven, Anne
Dickinson. Squatting in front (L to R): Bob Slaven, Joe Ziglinski,
Don Dickinson Photos by author

Captain Slaven's chit book

We had a great time together and we were reluctant to part quickly so we agreed to have coffee at Joe's home the next day.

Don Dickinson, Bob Slaven and their wives joined us at the Ziglinski residence where we had a nice luncheon with more pleasant talk and picture taking. Joe climbed his antenna tower for one of the pictures. We took a

Joe Ziglinski JA2KK on his antenna tower
Photo by author

picture of Joe's radio station and Bob and Don had brought along snap-shots of their stations. (See Chapter 14).

It was August 25 and in our anxiety to see our first child the clock seemed very slow. Two weeks overdue, the birth was imminent, so we no longer ventured far from the apartment building. We were given many ideas about bringing on labor pains one of which was for Marion to have a strong gin and tonic and walk for a mile. We went to the bar and ordered the drink. There were a few couples at the bar and the women were discussing their pregnancies. Marion asked one of the women when her baby was due. The woman said, "I'm not pregnant!" As they continued to converse; the same woman said she had experienced a false pregnancy. Marion responded, "Oh, my dog went through that!" Realizing that she had just stacked one faux pas on top the other; Marion ordered a second drink. I walked with her for about a mile and she was exhausted when we retired for the night.

She woke up in the middle of the night with labor pains. Half asleep myself, I dared to ask her how long it was between pains. Her reply was: "Get the ambulance, NOW!" I dialed; we dressed, and headed for the building exit. The ambulance had responded very quickly and pulled up in front of the building. The driver, alone, asked Marion how she was doing. He was guiding her to the extended cot at the rear of the ambulance. Marion said, "Oh, I can't lay down, I would rather sit up front." As she was settled into the front seat, there was no room for me. The driver turned to me and said, "Sir, you will have to ride on the cot in back." So there we were, roaring to the hospital with the siren whining and with me in the patient position. As the driver braked at the emergency entrance to the hospital, the back doors were pulled open by two fast-moving attendants. They pulled the cot out and prepared to carry me in. Marion was already out of the vehicle and walking in the front entrance when I caught up with her.

She asked me, "Are you going to make it Sir?" We laughed and parted as nurses guided her down the hall and I went to the registration desk. Most of the paperwork had already been completed in over-the-phone conversation the previous week and only a few more details and signatures were required.

I went to her assigned room and as I approached it her doctor met me and said it would be a few more hours. He said everything looked normal and he expected a normal birth. I visited with Marion for a few minutes and then went to the waiting room. There were a half dozen or more people in the waiting room and I introduced myself to them all. They had been engaged in conversation about the celebrity in the hospital. Randolph Churchill, the son of the Prime Minister Winston Churchill was a patient after being wounded in South Korea. He was a journalist and reporter covering the Korean situation.

I tired quickly and snoozed where I sat. When I woke a little later, I inquired at the desk but the baby had still not arrived. I realized that I forgot to bring my new camera with me. Guess I didn't have the same priorities as Frank Crosby. I went to the chapel and prayed for Marion and the baby.

Tokyo General Hospital was managed by the U.S. Army. Acquired by the occupation military the hospital had an adequate staff of doctors, nurses, attendants and other required staff. The Japanese name of the hospital was "Toranomon". Translated to English it meant "Tiger's Gate." Many of the staff were American doctors and nurses and the rest were Japanese.

At daylight, I was walking the halls trying to kill time. I roamed to the back of the building and saw that the back parking lot was filled with large tents. Each tent had a large red cross on its top and ambulances were coming and going. The wounded were being received in a steady stream and doctors and nurses were very busy going to and from the tents and the hospital. I felt a pang of guilt. The same men who came to fight for us in Korea were lying wounded in hospital tents while my wife and Randolph Churchill enjoyed the comfort of the hospital.

Tokyo General Hospital Toranomon (Tiger's Gate)
Photo by author

The nurses drew blood from all hospital patients on a daily basis to keep up with the blood required by the wounded. That included Mr. Churchill since he was recovering and it would include Marion once the baby was born.

MADE IN OCCUPIED JAPAN

Announcing THE 1950 MODEL

The 1950 Model Design & copy by author

Murray Raymond Maurstad was born that morning, August 26, at 8:58 A.M. He weighed in at 7 lbs 7 oz and 22 inches in length. I cried with Marion as she held the new member of our family. Mother and baby were in the hospital for seven days, customary in those times. We would have to wait six weeks before the baby could travel so we took up apartment life once more.

Earthquakes are a common occurrence in Japan and we were to experience a rather strong one. We were sound asleep in the early hours of morning when we woke to a shaking bed. Baby Murray was asleep in his bassinet. The bassinet started to roll across the room as the slight shaking increased to a severe level. I crawled across the floor with Marion and helped her onto the couch. I put the baby in her arms. I grabbed the arms of the couch, one in each hand, arms outstretched. I put my chest over her body and the baby to protect them. The couch began to slide. The building was now swaying. The lamps toppled off the table next to the bed. The fan and the ashtray stand fell to the floor. The window drapes began to sway and the view out the window was deceiving. The sway of our building made it appear that it was the entire city that was moving. I realized that the building could topple. I prayed to God that we would survive this. Had we come all this way only to perish in an earthquake? Then, after a minute or two there was silence. A long silence followed by voices in the hallway. Someone shouted, "stay off the elevators!" Then a loud knock at our door and the demand was repeated, "stay off the elevators!" Someone was moving with that message from door to door. I thought of after-shakes that often come after the main quake and convinced

Marion that we should move to the first floor. More than anything else was my fear of the building coming down with us in the rubble. We would have to take the stairs down nine stories, a rough decent for Marion and for me holding the baby. Reaching the lobby we found that most of the guests were already outside, some awe-struck while experienced old-timers were calm. There were no following tremors and after thirty minutes, everyone was encouraged to re-enter the building. Some did, some waited longer. The elevators were tested by maintenance and found safe.

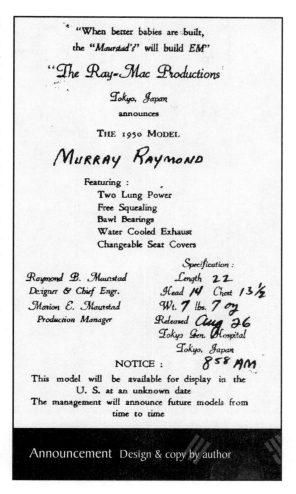

"When better babies are built, the "*Maurstad's*" will build EM"

"The Ray-Mac Productions

Tokyo, Japan

announces

THE 1950 MODEL

MURRAY RAYMOND

Featuring :
Two Lung Power
Free Squealing
Bawl Bearings
Water Cooled Exhaust
Changeable Seat Covers

Raymond B. Maurstad
Designer & Chief Engr.
Marion E. Maurstad
Production Manager

Specification :
Length 22
Head 14 Chest 13½
Wt. 7 lbs. 7 oz
Released Aug 26
Tokyo Gen. Hospital
Tokyo, Japan

NOTICE : 858 AM

This model will be available for display in the U. S. at an unknown date
The management will announce future models from time to time

Announcement Design & copy by author

More bingo was in order and one evening we won a Noritake tea service set. More shopping too. We spent many hours on the roof of the building. In the August heat, we could find a cool breeze up there and expose the baby to some sunshine.

Captain Jim Scanlin picked us up on a sunny day and took us to Tachikawa Air Force Base where his sister lived with her Air Force husband. We had a pleasant visit. We toured the base and saw the awesome strength of the many aircraft. The runways were very active with aircraft leaving for their runs over Korea and returning flights carried the dead

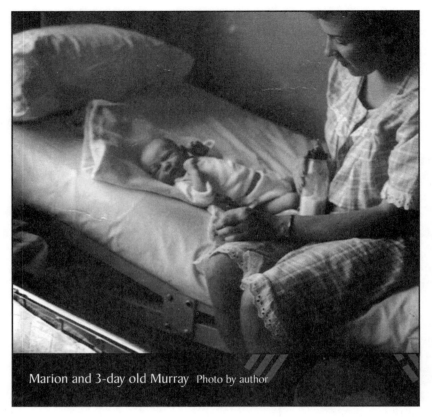

Marion and 3-day old Murray Photo by author

and wounded. I enjoyed driving golf balls at a driving range close by. Baby Murray began to show the first signs of colic that day and we left early for the return trip to the apartments.

We registered Murray's birth at the American Embassy. Failure to do this could deny his U.S. citizenship later. A rule of law provided that at age 18 he could opt for either Japanese or U.S. citizenship. We waited for six weeks before we were allowed to fly out of Japan.

We had an eventful flight home. We were five rows back from the flight deck. The first four rows of seats on the starboard (right) side had been removed to make room for our 600 pounds of luggage. I found it very comfortable to cross the Pacific with my belongings within sight at all times. Murray's colic condition had worsened and his very loud crying became a source of irritation for the other passengers. Before leaving Tokyo the doctor had anticipated that the colic problem might erupt in flight and gave us a small bottle of Belladonna (Tincture of Opium) with instructions to give Murray a teaspoonful to quiet him. The doctor told us it would relieve the pain at the source of the colic. We followed instructions and gave baby Murray the teaspoon dose while he was screaming and had his mouth wide open. He stopped and went to silent sleep so fast we thought we had killed him. We took turns listening to his heart and were relieved to hear it beating normally. He was really just sound asleep and slept for the next six hours. We dared not to give him any more of the medicine and instead endured his crying spells with the rest of the passengers. We later learned that the Belladonna medicine was three or four times the strength that it should have been. Someone had erred in preparing it.

The flight home took us through the island of Shemya for refueling, and then Anchorage and Edmonton, Canada and we finally landed at Minneapolis. The total time of the flight was thirty-four hours including the stops. Murray's grandfather, Henry Carlson, met our flight with a rented pickup truck. The airline allowed him to drive onto the ramp to transfer our load from the aircraft.

I drove; Marion took the middle seat. Henry held the baby riding on the passenger side. Murray filled his diapers and Henry remarked, "It's good to have you kids home." We finished the last couple of miles to Northeast Minneapolis with the windows open.

Colonel Walter Greenwood and Mary Logan
Greenwood 1984. Photo by Mary Logan Greenwood

Epilogue

Walter & Mary Logan Greenwood

Mary Logan Greenwood and daughter Sallie spent a couple of weeks in Japan and then flew to San Francisco. They picked up their car in San Francisco and drove cross-country to Huntington, West Virginia.

Walter remained in Korea until March of 1951 and then returned home. He subsequently had assignments at Ft. Bragg, Ft. Knox, Norfolk, Virginia and in Germany. In Stuttgart, Germany for four years, he commanded the 11th Armored Cavalry and was Assistant Chief of Staff in G2, Seventh Army. Mary Logan and Sallie were with him on these assignments. They came home when the Berlin wall went up, (1961). They then went to the National War College in Washington D.C., the Dept of the Army and Joint Chiefs of staff. Walter retired from the Army as a Colonel in 1970 after 30 years of service. He was the recipient of the Legion of Merit (Oak Leaf Cluster), the Bronze Star Medal, the Joint Services Commendation Medal and the Army Commendation Medal.

Sallie Greenwood.
Photo by Mary Logan Greenwood

Their son, Walter Merritt, was born in Fayetteville and at age 15 he was a student at Episcopal High School in Alexandria, Virginia. Sallie went to University of Maryland and at age 27 she was employed by the National Geographic Society

Walter Greenwood was assistant to the Dean of Cleveland-Marshall College of

Law, Cleveland State University, 1970 up until his retirement in 1981. He passed away in 1991, a victim of cancer.

Desmond & Ethyl Mann

After the close call, evacuating Kimpo Airfield the aircraft landed safely at Fukuoka, Japan. Des and the other evacuees were put on trains and were distributed to various locations in Japan. Here are Des's own words:

"The group I was in was sent up to Osaka. After a fifteen-hour train ride they put us in the 1st Cavalry barracks. The next morning I was wandering around the camp and heard my name on the loudspeaker. It was the Red Cross calling; Ethyl had arrived at Fukuoka on board the *Reinholt*.

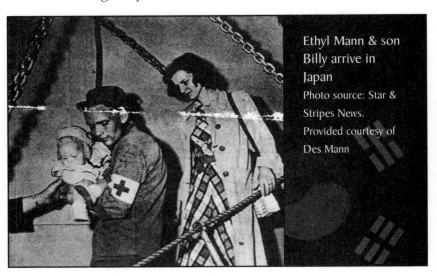

Ethyl Mann & son Billy arrive in Japan
Photo source: Star & Stripes News.
Provided courtesy of Des Mann

They put her on the phone. The baby's hernia had strangulated. They put Ethyl in the hospital with the baby and an Army Colonel pediatric surgeon operated and fixed the problem. An Army Major gave me travel orders to fly to Fukuoka. I was in a small four-seater to Nagoya with one other passenger. There was only one parachute and I gave it to the other passenger, as I wouldn't use it anyway. Nagoya to Sasebo was on an Air Rescue aircraft. Troops were boarding the same aircraft and my casual dress with a flashy sport-jacket attracted their attention: 'What are you doing here?' After explaining that I was a ship

Evacuees leave the ship "Reinholt"
Photo source: Stars & Stripes News Provided courtesy of Des Mann

captain and giving them an idea of what I had just been through they settled back; apparently accepting that I was making my contribution in to the effort."

"At Fukuoka, I stayed at the hospital with Ethyl and Billy. I got there Friday morning just after the operation. On Sunday we left for Atami (an Army R&R Hotel), a 24 hour ride with the baby but he was doing fine. We had no sooner arrived there around July 4 when I received a message to proceed to Sasebo to join one of our ships. I just ignored it. A Lieutenant signed that first message. The next message was more dramatic and signed by a Captain. A Major signed the third one. Finally, I was called to the front desk of the hotel where the hotel manager told me, 'If you don't got down there to Sasebo as ordered we will have to check you out of the hotel.' I headed for Sasebo."

"When the train arrived at Osaka we were switched to a sleeper car. I put my bag inside my assigned berth and a WAC (Woman, Military) came in with baggage and claimed the room was hers. An MP (Military Police) happened to be passing by and asked what the problem was.

After explaining, he asked both of us for our travel orders. After looking them over he said 'yours are signed by a General, hers by a Colonel.' He told the WAC that she would have to remove her bag and find other space on the train."

"The train arrived in Sasebo about two in the morning and it took a little while to locate the small shipyard and the ship. Nelson was there! Now I began to understand where the pressure to join the ship might have originated. I woke him up and after chatting a while I headed for the Engine Room for a routine check before retiring. A bearing had just been replaced on the generator and a Japanese Engineer had two thermometers on the bearing to check any heat build up. I went to sleep for an hour or so when a Navy man woke me and asked if I was the Chief Engineer. I told him that I was the advisor to the Chief Engineer. After I got my shirt and pants on he went with me to the Chief Engineer and then two more Navy men led him off the ship. The Navy man said, 'This ship is supposed to lead a convoy to Korea but the ship has been sabotaged!'

"I said that I had seen an Engineer working on the generator when I boarded and believed that if the generator had overheated it may been because the Engineer fell asleep. The Navy man said that I was wanted in the Commander's office immediately! He was demanding with a stern military stance. I told him he should take it easy. 'I'm a civilian!' Nelson and I went with the Navy man to the Commander's office. After his secretary announced who we were the Commander's face turned red and then . . . redder. He started to stammer and say something . . . I interrupted, 'we are civilians. This Navy man here claims there has been sabotage and there was no sabotage.' He almost spat back 'But the ship can't sail!' I assured him that the ship could sail without a problem. 'Hell', I told him, 'we have sailed these tubs in Korea by candle-light.' The Commander had cooled down some and he started comparing our official military (U.S. Naval Reserve) serial numbers to his own. Nelson's numbers were lower than the Commander's were and now the Commander was not only calm but also showing us respect. Rank was everything! The next morning we sailed for Korea with trucks, landing nets and a few hundred troops on deck. We led a convoy of 10 small ships in a 12-hour run to Pusan. After off-loading, we returned to Sasebo and were preparing to make another trip but it was canceled as bigger ships were now coming in to do the job. Therefore, we tied up our ship in Sasebo and we took the train back up to the Fujiya hotel where we spent a nice ten days of rest and relaxation. We were with our families again. The government would not release the men. They flew most of the women and children home but Ethyl and Billy were put on board a C4 Troopship; one of the President series. Harold Stevens' wife Grace and two children were also on board. The ship ran into a typhoon and though Grace had been told to stay in her cabin, she took the two kids to the dining room where a piano broke loose. The piano slid across the deck of the dining room into Grace and broke her leg. Harold sued the government when he got back to New York but he lost the case."

"The men were finally released and flew back. I was on the dock in San Francisco to greet Ethyl and Billy on their debarkation."

Ethyl & Desmond
Mann—1993
Courtesy: Ethyl Mann

Photo of Josselyn &
Francis J. Winslow
Photo courtesy:
Josselyn Winslow

Frank Winslow: "During July and August 1950 I moved between KMAG detachments at ROKA corps and divisions. Those months were memorable. In July, I had repeated bouts with dysentery and my weight went down to an estimated 120 to 115 pounds (no scales anywhere to check.). The Eighth Army Photo Officer, Major Ed Schreiber, contrived a trip for me to Tokyo for a week to sleep and eat in late July. During August Cpl. Anderson, my photographer, broke bones of his foot when the jeep I was driving slid sideways off the road during an air strike. He was evacuated and not replaced. All our exposed film went to Tokyo via the Eighth Army photo officer. Later I was able to view some of my motion pictures in a format similar to the old newsreels of pre-television days. MacArthur's headquarters edited, numbered, and dated and circulated them weekly within Eighth Army. Eventually I saw most of my still shots (35 mm and 4x5)."

"When MacArthur's Inchon landing in September caused the NKA in the Pusan Perimeter to retreat, Sgt. Kim, my ROKA assigned interpreter and I joined up with ROKA I Corps and its Capitol and 3rd Divisions as they pursued the retreating NKA up the East coast. I photographed KMAG advisors with their ROKA units and took the often-used pictures of the 38th parallel first crossing by ROKA on the East coast on 1 October."

"To learn where, when, and with whom I was with during those days I found my copy of motion picture caption cards dated from 1 August to 19 October 1950. I exposed sixty-three 100-ft. rolls of 35 mm motion picture film. The 100-ft. rolls were cut from out-dated 1000-ft rolls of film in lengths ranging from 90 to 110-ft."

"I took the only still and motion pictures at Hamhung of some 300 North Korean men and women killed by North Korean captors by drowning in a jail well and by suffocation in nearby caves. North Korean relatives were present to identify the bodies. The killing took place just prior to arrival of ROKA forces in the area. The still photos of this sort from all sources were released in August 1953 to newspapers nationwide to show the barbarous and inhuman methods communists used in Korea to dispose of their prisoners, whether Koreans or Americans."

"With the approach of winter and having no compelling desire to go north to the Yalu with the ROKA I Corps, Sgt. Kim and I, with our

Captured communist-led North Korean soldiers, guarded by ROK Military Police, remove the bodies of the 65 political prisoners of the North Korean Army, which were dumped into wells in the city of Hamhung, North Korea. (130 miles north of 38th parallel) U.S. Army photo by F.J. Winslow.

half-ton truck, caught a 45 minute flight from Wonsan to Seoul on a C-119 'flying boxcar.' For a while, I considered pilots' offers to take us to their home base in Japan from which we could catch another hop back to Seoul. I did not relish explaining to authorities in Japan why we were AWOL in an island country with a truck from the Korean War Zone. On 20 Oct., we drove our truck off the airplane at Kimpo and in another 45 minutes arrived at ROKA/KMAG signal in Seoul. If the C-119 flight had not been available, we might not have ever arrived in Seoul on a direct drive over the mountains between Wonson and Seoul. Our stay in Seoul was rather brief because of the Chinese entry into the war caused us to move south for the winter."

(Bodies of 12 women) Awaiting identification by friends and relatives are the bodies of about 12 women, some of the 65 political prisoners of the Communist-led North Korean Army which were found dumped down wells in Hamhung, North Korea. U.S. Army photo by F.J. Winslow.

(The Caves) The bodies of 300 political prisoners killed by the Communist-led North Korean Army are removed from the caves where they were found, to await identification. They died of suffocation after being forced into the caves, which were subsequently sealed off, just outside of Hamhung, North Korea.
U.S. Army photo by F.J. Winslow

(Body identification) Korean women weep as they identify their men.
U.S. Army photo by F.J. Winslow

"My stint as a cameraman covering ROKA ended in October 1950 upon return to KMAG in Seoul. There I went into general duty Signal work to meet the expanding communications with division advisors. One exception was to arrange with Eighth Army for ROKA photographers to be at the second meeting (10 July 51) of the peace talks at Kaesong. We expected the talks to be concluded quickly. Instead, they were subsequently moved to Panmunjom to become indeterminate truce talks. I accompanied the ROKA photographers and took my Leica along for old times sake. We saw two faces of military communists: North Korean generals in fancy colorful Soviet style uniforms and Chinese of all ranks in the same drab, shapeless, dust colored uniforms. The red star of communism is the common badge."

Frank Winslow had just one employer in his lifetime: the US Army for thirty-one years. Work in a photo lab while in high school launched him into 5 years of military photography. He was an instructor at the Army Air Corps School of Photography and he taught air photomap making. After OCS (Officer Candidate School) he became a Signal Photo officer and arrived in Korea in October 1948. As a captain, he went into Army aviation in 1954 qualifying in both fixed and rotary wing aircraft. He commanded aviation units specializing in communications, electronic and aerial photography. As a Signal Corps major, he commanded an Infantry division aviation company of fifty aircraft, seventy officers and two hundred enlisted men. He served a fourth year in Korea in logistics and a tour in Vietnam. He served nine years in Germany and 17 years in USA.

Josselyn Bennett returned from Korea in July 1950 with her mother, Dorothy. Josselyn completed college in 1951. She and Frank wed two years later. They raised, in short order, a daughter and five sons. They had 24 street addresses. Their four oldest children graduated from Heidelberg American High School in Germany with ceremonies held in the historic Heidelberg Castle.

In the first year of his retirement, Frank and Josselyn took two of their teenage sons and traveled for a year. They camped their way around Europe in a German car and caravan on both sides of the Iron Curtain and in North Africa. Letters from a son living at home with his grandmother while attending college reported that Dorothy's symptoms of Alzheimer disease were making living with her very difficult.

Dementia in their family determined how they would occupy their retirement years. The family living at home were Dorothy's caregivers from 1977 to 1983. Dorothy spent her final two years; of the ten years, she had dementia, in a nursing home. She died at age 80. Harold died at age 61.

Frank and Josselyn organized a support group of dementia family members in 1980 and three years later incorporated the Alzheimer Society of Washington. The society conducts periodic dementia training for professional and family caregivers. In 1981, they began the long trips to the State Capital to educate the state legislators and the state bureaucracy on dementia. Josselyn continues this advocacy but after nineteen years, Frank withdrew from the advocacy in Olympia to support Josselyn on occasions. Josselyn continues on as a full time unpaid executive director of the society. Several years ago Frank and Josselyn met with other independent Alzheimer organizations to form a national organization. Frank did the work needed to incorporate the organization and obtain its tax-exempt status.

Frank is at the age where records of all sorts, especially photographic, must be compiled to produce and preserve the family history. Part of search for information was their visit to Seoul to attend the 25 June 2000 50th anniversary of the attack by North Korea on the Republic of Korea. In a visit to the Korean War Museum, he was pleased to show Josselyn a number of his photographs in the exhibit. But the exhibit's disappointment for them was its failure to indicate the part America played in the building of the Republic of Korea in the years prior to the 25 June 1950 attack.

Given today's mention in the news of US advisors, military and civilian, going to the aid of foreign countries around the world, Frank and Josselyn hope that the newcomers will learn from our nation's mistakes. But human nature being as it is, they doubt it.

The Bennett Family

The attack on South Korea by the North Koreans activated a U.S. plan to evacuate all U.S. Government personnel from Korea. Korea was excluded from the U.S. Mutual Security zone in the Far East until President Truman decided on Tuesday, 27 June, to include it. Dorothy and Josselyn were among some 600 women and children and a few men, all westerners, who sailed on 26 June from Inchon on the Norwegian freighter MV *Reinholt* to Japan.

Josselyn: "After the war began, when my family and I were evacuated to Japan, we began a waiting game. The Army moved us from the heat of Tokyo to Karazawa, a lovely Japanese resort town. Then the Army decided it needed to have my father return to help with the Korean railroad. He and his friend, Paul Oakes, would be expected to stay in Korea until the Army Transportation Corps got things in hand. Other families were being sent back to the States on any and all available ships but Mother and I decided to stay in Japan during the summer of 1950 in hopes that my father would be finished with his wartime tour in Korea and be able to go back to the States with us. However, by August the Army said that they wanted all of the families that had been evacuated from Korea to continue on to the States. We also knew that I could not wait any longer if I was to be back for the start of my college year in September."

"We got word to report to Yokohama to board the *President Wilson*. As it turned out, the *President Wilson* was a very different kind of ship from the Army Transport we had traveled on to Korea. The *Wilson* was a luxury ship with all the comforts of home—and a few more—a floating hotel with spacious dining rooms and sumptuous food. The majority of people were traveling for pleasure and expected to be pampered. But, there were several women, including my mother and me, who were former evacuees."

"Shortly after we left port we ran into the edge of a typhoon. The Wilson heaved and pitched. I remember heading 'like a drunken sailor' down the passageway, rather bouncing off one side of the corridor and then the other. Very few passengers made it to the dining room for a couple of days, but those of us who did learned to eat with our feet wrapped around the table legs so that we would not tip over or slide away with the ship's wild rolls. After the storm was over the rest of the passengers joined the few hearty ones who had weathered the storm and ship life returned to normal. Passengers were assigned to tables so that they could get to know the other travelers, including a group of Army officers from the Philippines who were on their way to Infantry School at Fort Benning, Georgia."

"In August of 1950, just a year after we had said farewell to San Francisco, we returned to the States. We boarded a train to take us back to Ohio. Mother and I had an overnight stop in Chicago and stayed at the Palmer House Hotel. I remember that a big convention of cigar smoking men was in town. A group of them were sitting in the dining room at the table next to mother and me. One fellow asked in an overly friendly way where we were from. Mother smiled and said 'Korea!' With the Korean war in all the newspaper headlines that gave those partying fellows a real chuckle."

"When we got back to Columbus, to my grandmother's house, a reporter came to interview us about life in Korea and the war. Then I returned to school and life as a student. It seemed as if Korea had just been a year's fairy tale—a trip back in time to a land from a history book."

"Meanwhile, mother was waiting and worrying about my dad. He wrote regularly and kept us up with his travels. Finally, at Christmas, we got the word that he was no longer needed by the Army Transportation Corps, and would be returning to the States soon. He arrived at the airport in early January wearing a Russian-style fur hat and vest. Our Korean saga was over."

"As I said earlier, Lieutenant Frank Winslow was my regular Friday night square dancing partner. In addition, since he was the KMAG Photo Officer he ran the photo lab where Army film was processed. He mentioned one time that it was interesting to develop film and make the prints. A couple of us told him we would like to learn more about the process so he invited us to his photo lab for a few evenings of instruction. We learned a bit about developing pictures and about printing them. During that time, I noticed how serious he was. In the spirit of fun, the other student and I printed a large sign which said, 'Ye Old Photo Shoppe' and posted it one night above the Army photo lab door. I got a call the next morning. Frank had arrived early for work—and was able to take down the sign before he got into serious trouble. Fortunately for my future he was still willing to be my Friday night square dancing partner."

"We dated regularly through the year—on Friday nights, however, both of us had other regular Saturday night dates. By the time I left Korea, I had gotten to know Frank quite well-just as a friend. He seemed like a nice guy, but quite serious."

"When I got back in school I asked to stay with my class. I used the credits I had earned at the two Korean Universities and took a maximum number of class hours to keep my standing; I wanted to graduate with my class."

"Despite the busy class schedule in February I found time to buy a silly card with a photo theme that said, 'Dear Valentine I would like to get you into a dark room and—open the card to read—Sneak out!' That tickled my funny bone and I decided to send it to my friend, Frank Winslow. I am not sure what he thought when he received the crazy Valentine in the middle of the Korean War, but he sent a note back."

"Come June I was delighted to be graduating and just wanted to be finished with school. Although I didn't understand why, my parents told me to order several graduation announcements. The folks arrived for graduation. I was packing and trying to get out of the dorm. Mother asked what she could do to help. I handed her my address book and said, 'Since you wanted me to order all of these announcements, why don't you address them and send them out?' It was a month or so later, when I received a letter from Frank congratulating me on my graduation and saying that he would be coming back to the States in September. I wrote back and asked him to stop by Ohio on his way home to Maine. He did stop for a quick visit, and he agreed to come back to Ohio in November. It was during that November visit that we realized we had grown to be more than just friends."

Harold was evacuated on 27 June by air to Japan and a week later he flew back to Korea to continue assisting Koreans in railroad management. 1950 June to August Dorothy and Josselyn waited at the US Army operated Hotel Mampei at Karizawa for transportation to USA. 1950 August 11 Dorothy and Josselyn left Yokohama for San Francisco on President Lines' S.S. *Wilson*. 1950 December Harold returned from Korea, rejoined the B&O, and moved the family to Flushing, Ohio (near Wheeling). 1951 Josselyn, age 21, graduated Western College at Oxford, Ohio with a Bachelor of Arts degree in Sociology. June 1962 Harold retired from the railroad. 1963, Harold died in Ashley, Ohio at age 61 on 8 September. He was buried in the Ashley cemetery plot. Dorothy's ashes were added in 1985.

Bob Rudolph departed from Korea twice in the summer of 1950. The first time was from Kimpo Airport on June 27. The second departure was from the Pusan Perimeter on September 10.

On June 27th, the C-54 transport he had boarded and the two P-51 fighter escorts made the trip from Kimpo to Southern Japan without incident. His group was then moved to an Army recreation center in Kyoto. Meanwhile, members of the Communications Branch

Robert J. Rudolph, his wife Mary Anne, daughter Nancy & grandson Ethan. Photo courtesy R.J.Rudolph

from Seoul volunteered to go to Pusan and help the Army by doing communications work for them. Bob was the first State Department communications employee allowed to make the trip to Pusan. He reported to the GHQ Long Lines Officer in Charge and volunteered to work where he was most needed.

Still annoyed at not having used historic last words in sending the last message from Seoul, he asked to be the sender of the last message if Pusan fell. The OIC agreed that he could do that. It was July 22 and at that time, the left flank of the American front line was hanging in the air. The North Koreans advancing on Pusan from the west could have outflanked our line. Bob was confident that if Pusan fell he would think of historic last words to send and would then somehow get across the 120 miles of sea to Japan. (Ah! the confidence of youth!). He worked as a Message Center Supervisor for the GHQ Long Lines in Pusan working a seven-day week, twelve-hour day schedule from July 22, 1950 until his departure from Pusan on September 10. Just before he left Pusan,

Marines were loading aboard Landing Ship Tanks nosed up on the shore next to the docks in Pusan Harbor.

When Bob Rudolph's terminal leave with the State Department Foreign Service ended in October 1950, he was attending Fresno State College on the GI Bill. It was there that he met a pretty girl named Mary Anne Bliss and married her in 1952. They now have one son, two daughters and one grandson. Upon receiving his B.A. degree at Fresno State in 1953, Bob accepted a Western Union job in Portland, Oregon.

After graduating from Fresno State his education was mostly confined to military training. Courses completed were:

- Engineer Officers Basic Course

- Infantry Officer Career Course

- Nuclear Weapons Employment Officer Course

- Command & General Staff Course

- Army Counter-Terrorism Course and,

- Industrial College of the Armed Forces Course

After enlisting in the Oregon Army National Guard in 1954, he was commissioned in 1955. After later taking a job in Spokane, Washington, he was hired as a full time training officer of the Washington Army National Guard in 1960. Over the next 22 years, he worked at eight different jobs. The three most interesting jobs were that of training officer of an infantry unit, commandant of an officer candidate and NCO academy, and as Plans, Operations and Military Support Officer in the state military headquarters. The Military Support part of the previously listed job at times had some heavy demands on his time and attention. For instance, the Mt. St. Helens volcano in Washington State became active in 1980 and then controlled his life for a year and a half.

The first major eruption of Mt. St. Helens on May 18, 1980 was cataclysmic. It was more catastrophic than pre-eruption briefings received from geologists had led them to expect. There was a second major eruption on May 25, 1980 followed by major eruptions in June, July and later in the year. No one could accurately predict a volcanic eruption in advance of the event. At the start of their experience, Bob and his co-workers even had to learn how to tell whether initial volcanic activity was the start of a major eruption. They initially activated their response mechanisms each time they learned that the volcano was emitting a plume into the air. It omitted small plumes often. Many of them were just made of steam. Experience soon told them that if the cloud was not at 45,000 feet and climbing 30 minutes after the report of a plume, then it was not a major eruption. The FAA radar at Portland International Airport became skilled in deciding whether a plume contained ash or just steam. They also learned how to predict with fair to good accuracy where most of the ash would fall if a major eruption were to occur.

Bob Rudolph continues: "I've written or helped to write two studies that were of some importance. In the National Guard Bureau Counter-Terrorism Study in 1979, I was one of four writers. The study's purpose was to answer the question: What shall be the role of the National Guard in Counter-Terrorism operations? The second study, in 1982-83, was my 43,000 word study of evacuations of major populations in times of disaster that was prepared for the Washington State Department of Emergency Management."

"My hobby is photography. My specialty is landscape photography."

"I look back upon my adventures with mixed emotions. I had started out as an unworldly young man from dusty and boring little California towns. My adventures permitted me to see some places of beauty and other places afflicted with great poverty. I observed people who were inspiring to me in later years and a couple of people who are best forgotten."

"I believe the Yosu Mutiny on October 19 1948 marked the opening phase of the Korean War. An intensive Communist guerrilla war in South Korea had started. I was one of three high-speed CW radio operators pulled from my regular radio operator job. We were suddenly assigned to a CW radio station in Seoul and began communicating with a CW radio station moving with ROK forces chasing, finding and fighting the mutineers. Sergeant Canning, Red Mintz and I operated that radio station 10 to 14 days in October (and early November) 1948. Some of the mutineers escaped to become guerrillas in the Kiri-san Mountains. They fought ROK forces until May 1950. That guerrilla

United States Department of State

Washington, D.C. 20520
October 18, 2000

Mr. Robert J. Rudolph
c/o David J. De La Cruz
15450 Oak Hills Drive
Salinas, CA 93907-1118

Dear Mr. Rudolph:

It has come to my attention that your valiant efforts at
the onset of the Korean War were not appropriately
recognized. Although long overdue, I would like to offer
my belated personal appreciation for your heroic efforts
during this period.

Your role in transmitting vital information to Department
of State officials was an integral part of the Department's
success in meeting the demands of the ensuing war. I
enjoyed the opportunity to read your account of the June
1950 events in the July-August issue of the Foreign Service
Journal. I found your article inspiring.

On October 13, I had the privilege of swearing in a new
group of Foreign and Civil Service employees. I stressed
that they are joining an institution with a long, proud
tradition of service to America - a tradition embodied by
your heroic service. I am proud to be a member of an
institution that included people such as you.

We are grateful for your selfless actions and your skill
under pressure during the three evacuations required to
ensure the safety of American citizens. Your efforts were
invaluable in securing sensitive U.S. Government documents
prior to departure.

It is my honor to commend your extraordinary contributions
during these times of great hazard for our country's
representatives abroad.

Sincere

Marc Grossman

State Department letter of commendation
Source: U.S. Dept. of State

warfare interfered with the conduct of important steps in ROK Army training during a critical time period."

"I wonder why the North Korean Communist guerrilla operations in South Korea were kept from the news media and even from many of us working in the American Mission in Korea? Surely, the ROK Army's more than 500 separate counter-guerrilla fights from July to December 1949, for instance, were known to the North Korean government. If the intensive Communist guerrilla operations were known to the enemy, why weren't they made known to us?"

"I'm pleased to have been on duty as Operations Unit Supervisor in the Radio Teletype Section in Seoul, Korea from 8:30 a.m. June 25 to 9:30 a.m. June 27, 1950. I'm proud of the professional ease the employees of the radio Teletype operations unit displayed in handling the very heavy message traffic load at that time."
"I'm also pleased to have been allowed to work for GHQ Long Lines Group in the Pusan Perimeter in the summer of 1950."

"I am still appalled by the fact that some Army units were not physically and technically prepared for war upon their arrival in Korea in July 1950. Is today's Army preparing to fight in war when artillery and mortars at Ft. Lewis only fire about twice in a year and Army helicopters are rarely heard or seen in the air? Has the money needed to purchase fuel, ammunition and spare parts been squandered on social programs disguised as military projects? I am worried about the Army. I just want it to be trained and able to fight a war and win."

Ed note: Bob Rudolph retired as a Lieutenant Colonel in 1982

Robert K. Slaven & wife "Rudy"

You will remember that 34-year old 1st Lieutenant Bob Slaven was in the "Train Wreck" Chapter One and was also, from Japan, one of the first to respond to the radio distress calls from Pusan. Here is some "before and after Korea" background on Bob Slaven, in his own words month of May 2002:

"Ever since being a kid I wanted to go to the U.S. Naval Academy at Annapolis, Maryland. I went to a Navy prep school near Annapolis. I passed all the exams but flunked the physical because of poor eyes. (Our oldest son is an Annapolis graduate and is now a retired Navy Captain.) Being young and foolish, I wanted to go to sea so I put in a couple of years in the Merchant Marine as an Ordinary Seaman and enjoyed every minute of it. In 1936 I missed my ship (a tanker) and knowing that the Army had a number of ships, including troop ships, cable ships etc., I let a recruiting Sergeant sign me up, hoping to get on one of those ships. Instead, because I passed a code aptitude test I ended up in the Signal Corps which in retrospect wasn't too bad. I made Sergeant in Panama in 1936 with a signal intelligence unit. I had already passed through the canal six times with Grace Lines Steamship Company. Our commanding officer was a brand new 2nd Lieutenant fresh from West Point. Later, in Korea, I met him again as a full Colonel and he helped me get gasoline for our power units. After the war, we entertained him at our signal club in Tokyo. I was in and out of several Army signal schools, including radar, was radio operator in 1st Corps area (New England). I became a 'ninety-day wonder' right after the attack on Pearl Harbor. I had radar units in the Pacific Northwest and Florida. I shipped to England in 1943, had a brief stint with the Royal Air Force then crossed the English Channel a week or so after D-Day with British equipment and trucks (excuse me...lorries) right-hand drive and all. Then, served in France, Luxemburg (Battle of the Bulge) Germany and Austria. Received five battle stars on ETO (European Theater of Operations) ribbon and Bronze Star. On return to the U.S. I ran an Army radar school, attended Staff & Command College in Fort Leavenworth. I went cross-country with new equipment demonstration teams. Shipped to Korea in 1948 and to Japan a year or two later, then back to Korea again for the Inchon landings. I got another Bronze Star in North Korea (called Oak Leaf Cluster to medal.) I still have a tender right foot thanks to frostbite. On return to the U.S. I again ran an Army radio school for a while. In 1953, I returned to Germany on a classified mission that I wish I could tell you about but it is still classified. Visited Italy, Greece, Turkey, Saudi Arabia, Eritrea, Egypt, Crete and other North African countries, mostly in broken-down C-47s. Promoted to Major and returned to the U.S. in 1956 to be Post Signal Officer of Aberdeen Proving Grounds. It was near enough to Annapolis so we could visit our son at the Naval Academy. He graduated the same year that I retired, 1958. I was left on reserve status for some years of course. In the fall of 1958, we bought the 'Stone House', an 1820 granite building in Blue Hill, Maine with five bedrooms. It became our much beloved home for the next 42 years. It cost all of $9000 and we threw in another 500 bucks for a lot of old oak furniture. Of course, we had to put on a new roof, add storm windows, dig a well, improve the septic system, build a garage, install central heat, (it has five open fireplaces.

Ruth & Bob Slaven—1995 Photo courtesy of Bob Slaven

two of which are in bedrooms), renew the wiring, etc. etc. All of the joys of fixing up an old house. Because of its massive granite construction, at one time a granite quarry building, it is carried on the town records as an air-raid shelter. We sold it in year 2000 for $375,000 and moved into a retirement center. Meanwhile, I skippered a twin-screw yacht, bringing it back and forth from the Chesapeake to Maine waters. I managed a yacht club, sailed to Bermuda, ran a boat yard for many years, owned three power boats and two sail boats, one of them a classic. Delivered boats down the coast became Rear Commodore of the local yacht club, belong to Navy League and two Historical Societies and was trustee of the local Academy and Hospital. I occasionally put my ham radio on the air. Most of my contacts are with hams in Europe because we are on the east side of a hill and my signal doesn't get out well to the west."

"The stone house has a certifiable ghost that we have experienced."

(L to R) Rear Admiral (USMS) Joseph D. Steward, Superintendent
of the Academy, Milton G. Nottingham Jr., & Dean of the
Academy, Warren Mazik.
Photo courtesy Milton Nottingham Jr.

Milton G. Nottingham Jr.

When Milton Nottingham left Korea in the Spring of 1951 he was
offered his choice of going to Manila as the Administrative Officer of
the American Embassy or returning to Washington D.C. as a transportation officer with the ECA and its successor agencies. He chose the
latter to remain in the transportation field. After three years with the
ECA/MSA, he left the government to become a ship-chartering broker
with a local firm and ten years later he opened his own office. He is now
semi-retired as the Chairman of the Board of Directors of two small
ship brokerage firms: Pacific Cargoes, Inc., and International Services
Corporation with offices in Washington D.C. A Master Mariner and a
Commander, USNR (Ret.) he is an active participant in many maritime
professional and charitable organizations including the U.S.Merchant
Marine Academy Alumni Association where he is past National

President, the United Seamen's Service (past Director), the American Merchant Marine Museum, the National Maritime Historical Society and the Pan American Society of Naval Engineers. He is a former member of the U.S Maritime Administrator's Advisory Board of the National Bank of Washington. An experienced arbitrator with particular expertise in maritime disputes and a member of the American Arbitration Association and the Society of Maritime Arbitrators. He was named a Knight of the Sovereign Military Order of Malta in 1984 and is a Rear Admiral in the U.S. Maritime Service, the training organization of the U.S. Merchant Marine. He was presented with an Honorary Doctor of Science degree by the Academy in June 2001.

Thomas A. King

"After being reunited with Jane in Tokyo I was assigned to the staff of the 1st Amphibious Force (Admiral Doyle) in the Daichi building where General MacArthur had his offices. We were planning the landing of the 1st Cavalry Division at Inchon. I interpreted aerial photos as they were brought in and we planned where in Inchon harbor the troops would land. I was to return on one of the first LST landing craft either as a reactivated naval reserve officer or as a civilian advisor-I preferred the latter. The strength of the North Koreans was badly underestimated; they captured all West Coast ports, so the 1st Cavalry landed instead at Pohang on the East Coast. They were unopposed. The American forces retreated to the Pusan perimeter. Since I then considered myself out of a job, I resigned and returned with Jane to the U.S. We flew home on a chartered PanAm aircraft. We went on to New York City where I went to work for a tramp/bulk operator called Triton Shipping as something between Operations Assistant and Operations Manager. Within a year, I was offered a position with the Maritime Administration, a U.S. Government agency. That agency was deeply involved with breaking out World War II laid-up ships and assigning them to commercial shipping companies as agents for the government and operation in the Korean military sealift as well as support for foreign shipments to other countries. I spent seven years in Washington with a four and one-half month assignment as Director of NSA operations (National Security Administration) in New Delhi, India. Our general agency ships were

carrying grain to India and I acted as 'owners representative'."
"In 1958 I was transferred to New Orleans as Gulf Coast Director for
MARAD. (Maritime Administration) There we had two reserve fleets
of laid-up ships, at Mobile and Beaumont, 4 subsidized owners of
U.S. flag commercial ships and a substantial staff of engineers, opera-
tions, auditors and maintenance staff."

"In 1965 I was transferred to New York City as Eastern Region
Director of MARAD. My responsibilities were an expanded version of
the New Orleans duties. While serving as Eastern Region Director, I
was detailed in 1977 as Acting Superintendent of the U.S. Merchant
Marine Academy at Kings Point, New York. After four months, I
returned to my duties as Eastern Region Director. Then, in 1980, I was
permanently assigned as Superintendent of the U.S. Merchant Marine
Academy. In 1987, I retired from government. Later I took a position
with USMMA Alumni, a non-profit organization and retired a second
time in 1991."

*Ed: The Kings had two sons, one born in 1953, the other in 1955. Tom and
Jane King settled in Florida.*

Joseph & Dottie Kelly

After Joe's wife, Dottie departed Pusan on board the S.S. *Letitia Lykes*
the night of June 27; Joe departed a week later on a Greek Freighter
with a number of other male civilians landing at Fukuoka, Japan. Joe
and Dottie made their way across Japan separately and were reunited at
the Fujiya Hotel two weeks later. After staying at the Fujiya for a few
weeks, they departed for the U.S. on the USAT *President Cleveland*.
They were met and welcomed in San Francisco by John Connolly, a
former member our group who had left Korea earlier in the year. They
departed for their home in New Jersey in August 1950.

Joe was rehired by the U.S. Army's Picatinny Arsenal located in
Dover, New Jersey, where he had been employed previously as a teenager during WWII. He remained at the Arsenal (which later became
Headquarters, U.S. Army Munitions Command) in various administrative capacities, until his retirement from Federal Civilian Service in 1982.

During his last assignment, Joe served as Chief of Protocol where he became expert on overall Department of Defense protocol as related to U.S. Military and VIP civilian visitors and foreign dignitaries. Joe originated the Protocol Office in 1960 supervising a staff primarily concerned with high level visitors, conference management, ceremonies, ammo demonstrations, R&D Facility tours and the rendition of military honors when appropriate.

Joseph & Dorothy Kelly (1999)
Photo courtesy of Dorothy Kelly

After his retirement, Joe entered the field of real estate and later managed the Picatinny Arsenal Golf Club before retiring to Florida in 1989. Since he is an avid golf enthusiast, Joe has continued to pursue his passion by working at several of the local country clubs.

Not to be discounted; Dottie has been an active partner carving out a career as on Office Manager and Accountant for several large commercial concerns and, for twenty years, as a Church Secretary for Parish Affairs. Since moving to Florida, Dottie is engaged in a new career as a Travel Agent for Fun Tours, specializing in-group travel.

Dottie and Joe celebrated their 50th wedding anniversary in November 1999.

LT. COL. Joseph H. Ziglinski

Joe Ziglinski received the Bronze Star for his efforts in maintaining critical communication circuits between General MacArthur's headquarters in Tokyo and US forces in Korea during the opening days of the Korean War.

After his Japan tour, Joe went on to be Secretary of the Signal School at For Monmouth N.J. and that is where Tom was born. Then

Joe returned to Japan. His wife Betty (Elizabeth) with young Tom followed in 1955. Joe retired from active duty in 1963 after serving several tours at the Pentagon as a civilian working as Chief Engineer of MARS (Military Affiliated Radio Service) for another 15 years. During the Korean War Joe got interested in hypnosis and became a professional hypnotist teaching for many years in the Washington D.C. area. He had many interesting hypnosis events including murder investigations, sports hypnosis and a pioneering effort to hypnotize the deaf. Joe's wife Betty (Elizabeth) passed away at age 81 on July 22, 1966 at the Walter Reed Army Medical Center in Washington D.C. She is buried in Arlington National Cemetery.

I received the following e-mail in July 2001 from Joe's son Tom:

"Ray, I am sorry to tell you that my father, Lt. Col. Joseph H. Ziglinski, passed away at Marion, IL VA Medical Center on July 4, 2001. He was battling a lung infection that just seemed to wear him down. His funeral will be at the Ft Myer Chapel followed by a military funeral in Arlington National Cemetery on August 6 at 12:45 PM. Just before he died, I had been busy cleaning out and selling his home in Virginia. He had lots and lots of radio equipment. I also did make contact with Bob Slaven about 3 months ago. We talked for a while about his time in the 71st Signal Service Battalion. It was very interesting but I haven't had the chance to make contact again. Anyway, I hope all is well with you. Take care."

Tom Ziglinski

Alex & Mary Roth

In June 25, 1950, the S.S. *Elisha Whitney*, with Captain Alexander Roth on board as Master, was docked in Osaka, Japan discharging cargo. Alex heard of the outbreak of war in Korea over the Armed Forces Radio station. He was the only non-Korean on board at the time.

His Chief Engineer, Milo Atkinson, who had injured his knee returned to San Francisco, had never been replaced. His Radio Officer, Frank Compton, had been put on another ship with no replacement. The other four ships were in Pusan.

Lt.Col.Joseph Ziglinski and his son Tom
Photo courtesy of Tom Ziglinski

Alex's mind raced. "Is Mary safe? What will happen next? Should I discontinue discharging cargo and return to Pusan immediately? Should I go ashore and try to contact Mary?" Then, to concern him even further, Alex saw the ultimate goal of developing a Maritime Academy in Pusan fade from view. That would have to wait for future years and could possibly be invoked? He had graduated with the first class to graduate from the Kings Point Merchant Marine Academy in 1942 and took his first ship out of Galveston that same year.

Subsequently he had served as Deck Officer on Grace Line vessels until 1945 when he was given his own command on a Norton Lilly Company vessel. From then on, he was master of six more ships with only one break from sea duty to attend Advanced Naval Training with the United States Maritime Service. He was a full Commander in the USMS. Given his schooling and sea experience Alex felt he was more than qualified to lead the effort to develop a Korean Merchant Marine Academy. Alex and Mary Elizabeth Mehaffey wed on April 20, 1946 in St. Peter's Episcopal Church, Salisbury, Maryland.

Now in Osaka, Alex went ashore and made several attempts to connect with some in Pusan but was unsuccessful. He had no way of knowing that Mary would soon be in Osaka with their daughter Susan. Mary and the other Americans at Hialeah were informed that they would be evacuated with their children to Japan. They would have to wait for the

S.S. "Elisha Whitney" docked at Osaka. Photo by Alex Roth

women and children from Chinhae and the surrounding countryside to be brought to Hialeah and evacuated with them. They were told that they would be allowed to carry only one suitcase per person. Mary: "Since Susan was so young, I knew I would have to carry her if she got tired. So one small suitcase was all I could handle."

Back in October 1949, Alex flew from Salisbury, Maryland to San Francisco California for a December 2 briefing with Pacific Far East Lines (PFEL), the

Kings Point graduate
Alexander Roth Jr., Class of '42
Photo courtesy: Mary Roth

steamship company acting as agent for the Marine Division of the Economic Cooperation Administration (ECA). Alex departed San Francisco by plane on December 3 and arrived in Japan December 5. His assigned vessel, the S.S. *Elisha Whitney*, departed Yokohama January 15, 1950 and arrived in Pusan South Korea on January 17.

Mary: (In an interview January 15, 2002) "I flew with two and a half year old Susan from Salisbury Maryland to San Francisco in mid-March 1950. On March 15, we boarded a freighter, the S.S. *Edward Luckenbach* with other Korea-bound wives and two of their children. The ship arrived Pusan on April 23rd and Alex was waiting on the dock."

Mary continues: "Daily life on Hialeah compound consisted mainly of taking care of Susan and seeing that the Korean house help did their house chores. I also began teaching them how to prepare American foods. There was a playground on Hialeah in the housing area that the children enjoyed. The PX (Post Exchange) and the Commissary were in one small room in the Flamingo Club and held only the necessities. I remember soaking any local vegetables or fruits (ones with no rind) in potassium permanganate or boiling them for at least twenty minutes, as human excrement was used for fertilizer in South Korea.

The S.S. "Edward Luckenback" arriving Pusan (That heavy smoke is coming from the tugboat)
Photo by Alex Roth.

A person could never forget the honey buckets!"

"I don't remember any school in the compound. Our daughter Susan was only two and a half years old. The only school-age children in our Maritime Group were Audrey Kitts' 10-year old son and 8-year old daughter and she was schooling them herself at home."

"As a former school teacher with valid credentials and experience, I was approached in late May to set up a school on the compound for 1950-1951. It was arranged for me to travel to Seoul the first week in July to order the necessary textbooks and materials. Unfortunately, the outbreak of war ended those plans." "We lived in House #326 and Captain Meschter lived across the street."

"Chief Engineer Willis and his family were two houses down from us. The Kitts family lived on the other side of us. The houses had a living room with dining area, kitchen, two bedrooms and bath. The basic pieces of furniture were included.

"The coal and wood-fired kitchen stove was a real challenge, as I liked to cook and bake. Alex ordered an oven for me from Sears which

#326 Hialeah-Roth Residence   Photo by Mary Roth

I never got to use as it arrived only a day or two before the North invaded. I often wondered afterwards if the Koreans ever figured out what it was or how to use it."

The Living Room in the Roth Residence
Photo by Mary Roth

"I went shopping in the city only one time, as seeing half-naked children with chapped faces and runny noses playing the streets upset me."

"I would go to the Flamingo Club only when Alex was in port, which wasn't often, or when invited to a party there. It was the one place besides your home where you knew it was safe to eat as the food was properly prepared."

"During my two-month sojourn on Hialeah Compound there was only one unforgettable experience. One Sunday I was invited to a neighbor's house for a cocktail party and dinner afterward at the club. I had given Susan her dinner and put her to bed before I left. The houseboy was to stay with her while I was gone. I made sure he understood where I would be if he needed to contact me. When I decided to check on Susan before going on to the club for the dinner party, she was standing at the living room window crying. She was all alone! No houseboy? I never had a houseboy again. I had two women instead and it worked out very well."

Mary Roth
in Hialeah
Residence (1950)
Photo by Alex Roth

"We had only begun to get settled before the North attached South Korea. I was worried about Alex, his being the only non-Korean on board his ship. I was reminded of what happened in 1949 when the S.S. *Kimball Smith*, one of the six ships loaned to the South Koreans under the Army, was seized by North Korean communists who were on board as part of the crew. They took the ship to North Korea where the American Captain (Meschter) and American Chief Engineer (Willis) were imprisoned for three months before they were released."

"We were driven at midnight from Hialeah Compound to the Pusan dock. There we boarded the U.S. Lines freighter S.S. *Pioneer Dale* with women and children all over the deck. The ship waited for daylight before departing for Fukuoka, Japan. I'll never forget walking down the gangplank, carrying a sleeping Susan and our one suitcase, and the sailor who came hurrying up the gangplank to help me."

"Another welcome sight was the Red Cross people on the dock, waiting to help us in any way they could. We were permitted to send one message to a relative in the United States, telling of our safe arrival in Japan."

"We were taken from Fukuoka to Hakata where we stayed overnight. Then by bus to Camp Shimodayama at Osaka were we stayed in the Army barrack. There I was able to contact the Red Cross about Alex and the *Elisha Whitney* and learned that he and his ship were in Osaka. He was able to see us before we left for Atami where we stayed for about two weeks. We left Atami by train around the middle of July for the famed Fujiya Hotel in Miyanoshita, Hakone National Park. What a beautiful place with the scenic lakes and mountains surrounding the hotel! We celebrated Susan's third birthday early so he could be part of it."

"On August 11 we board the USNS *General Heintzelman* for departure that day. Susan had another birthday party on her natal day, August 13, on the ship which all of the children on board enjoyed. A day or two later we ran into a typhoon with really rough weather conditions. Mrs. Willis, one our group from Pusan, had taken her two small children to an announced Catholic Mass where she was injured by unsecured furniture. After that occurred we were confined to our staterooms and told to remain in our bunks for safety. Food and drink were brought to our cabins until the rough seas had subsided. On our arrival in California, Susan and I visited my sister and her family in San Mateo before flying home to Salisbury, Maryland."

"Alex stayed on the *Elisha Whitney* which was taken over by the U.S. Army. In early July 1950, the ship loaded with ammunition sailed in

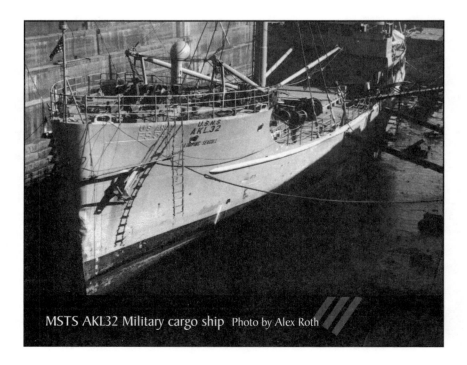

MSTS AKL32 Military cargo ship   Photo by Alex Roth

convoy to Pusan. While there he was able to go out to Hialeah Compound to our house were everything was gone. Even the light fixtures were ripped from the walls."

"As a Lieutenant Commander in the U.S. Naval Reserve and possessing an unlimited Master's License, Alex's services were needed by MSTS (Military Sea Transport Service). He was released from his AMIK-ECA State Department contract the end of August by Capt. Forrest Peterson, the Maritime Group project manager."

"On Sept. 1, 1950 he joined MSTS *WESPAC* as Captain of the AKL32, whose mission was the delivery of general military cargoes, (ammunition, mines, rockets, fuel tanks, etc.) From Japan to Korea."

On Sept. 30, 1951, his contract with MSTS ended. Susan and Mary were waiting form him on his arrival at Moffett Field, California in early October.

Alex Roth & The Korea Maritime University

Between 1951 and 1953 Alex Roth took command of three more ships. The S.S. *Russell A. Alger* for Pacific Far East Lines the S.S. *Amersea* and the S.S. *Amerocean* for the Blackchester Steamship Company. In 1953, he was with the U.S. Navy Training and U.S.M.S. Loran and Radar School.

On March 30, 1954, Alex received his appointment from UNKRA (United Nations Korea Reconstruction Agency) to the Pusan Maritime School as "Education Officer, Nautical Science, Category 4." When he arrived in Pusan in July 1954 he learned that his duties were much more extensive. His title was "Project Officer (Project 9, 72)" which involved:

- The building of a Merchant Marine Academy on Cho-do Island which formed the southwest side of Pusan Harbor.

- Building an access road to the academy.

- Finance Officer

- Purchasing Officer.

Alexander Roth Jr., Education Officer
Photo by Alex Roth

- Advisor to Pusan Marine Bureau—harbormaster.

- Advisor to Ministry of Transportation on re-writing of Republic of Korea (ROK) Navigation Laws.

- Setting up and writing examinations for Third, Second, Chief Mate & Master licenses.

- Starting a Correspondence Course Institute for afloat personnel.

A formidable challenge for the average teacher but well within the voracious appetite that Alex had for developing Korean maritime academia. He set about to do all that was expected of him. This time Mary and Susan were not permitted to accompany Alex to Korea.

On August 8, Alex took photos of the construction site and pieced the photos together for a panoramic view.

Panoramic view of the construction site—August 8, 1954
Photos by Alex.Roth Jr.

AMIK Maritime Group Mission Accomplished

KOREA MARITIME UNIVERSITY
http://www.kmaritime.ac.kr/kmu_e/index.html

Maritime Sciences

History: The College of Maritime Sciences had its beginnings in the Korea Merchant Marine Academy which was the first of its kind established in Korea. On November 5, 1945, Korea Merchant Marine Academy was founded to ensure that such people are available to the nation as merchant marine officers and as leaders in the sea transportation field who will meet the challenges of the present and the future, and along with it the Departments of Nautical Science and Marine Engineering were created. On March 1, 1992, the Departments of Nautical Science and Marine Engineering were reorganized into the College of Maritime Sciences. At present the College of Maritime Sciences consists of four divisions and one department; Division of Maritime Transportation Science, Division of Marine System Engineering, Division of Ship Operation Systems Engineering, Division of Mechatronics Engineering, and Department of Maritime Police Science, with 1,529 students and 57 full-time professors.

Profile: The purpose of the College of Maritime Sciences is to provide students with sound theories and technologies required in marine science and marine engineering. The College offers well-organized curriculums and facilities including sea training systems (Marine Simulation Research and Training Center, training ships *Hanbada* and *Hannara*, etc) to furnish students with outstanding leadership and team skills which are indispensable for successful professionals in the maritime field. Every student of the College receives a four-year scholarship and also comfortable quarters, uniforms, and well-balanced meals are provided for all students at government expense. Graduates of the College have gained employment within a wide range of careers at sea or on land. Graduates serve as officers in the merchant marine and Korean Navy and also are employed in maritime-related fields, transportation industry, public sector, business management, and related industries, both shore side and at sea.

Ocean Science & Technology

Founded in 1999, mainly with the previously established departments of Engineering College, the College of Ocean Science and Technology, has been dedicated to advancing the knowledge, utilization and conservation of the ocean and its resources. Our goal is to educate well-rounded specialists who have the broad vision and interdisciplinary background necessary to address interrelated problems that face marine and coastal environments.

The College of Ocean Science and Technology has the research vessel, *Hae Yang Ho*, which supports maritime experimental programs based on the KMU curricula.

There are as of now, 26 full-time professors and 1100 students belonging to the College. We are planning to replenish more full-time faculty members in the near future.

Engineering

The College of Engineering aims to foster professionals who will be able to make substantial contributions to the development of the information and high-tech society in the 21st century. Accordingly, the College provides the educational environment so that students can prepare themselves to meet the new world-level standards. Each division and department provides well-organized and future-oriented curricula, which reflect the demand of industries. High-quality and motivated graduates will play a creative role in the development of related industries.

International Studies

Today's world attempts to form the new world order to realize common goals of mankind, and every country makes unlimited competition for maximum benefits. Recently, these changes have been made more speedily in the ocean and international fields. The new slogans of the 21th century are 'globalization' and 'national development through the sea'. Therefore, the 21st century is called 'the new era of globalization' and ' the new maritime era'.

The objective of The College of International Studies is to educate the specialized persons to work in the maritime and international fields. For this goal, this college has many departments and divisions such as the fields of 'International Trade, Commerce and Economics', 'Maritime Management', 'Maritime Law and Public Administration', 'English' and 'International Area Studies'. Our college consists of three divisions and five departments.

Our college selects the new entrant students free of departments and divisions and then within one semester allocates the students into each department and division, based on the students' aptitudes and academic records.

This process of student selection is in line with the demands of students, rather than suppliers of education. We are providing many policies for students such as 'dual major systems' and 'minimum major credit evaluation systems'.

Colleges

Maritime Sciences

- Division of Maritime Transportation Science
- Division of Marine System Engineering
- Division of Ship Operation Systems Engineering
- Division of Mechatronics Engineering
- Department of Maritime Police Science

Ocean Science /Technology

- Division of Ocean System Engineering
- Division of Ocean Development Engineering
- Division of Ocean Science
- Division of Architecture and Ocean Space
- Department of Maritime Physical Education

Engineering

- Division of Mechanical and Information Engineering
- Division of Civil and Environmental System Engineering
- Division of Radio and Information Communication Engineering
- Division of Mechanical and Material Engineering
- Department of Applied   Science
- Division of Electrical and Electronics Engineering

International Studies

- Division of International Trade and Economics
- Division of Shipping Management Division of Law
- Division of International Commerce & Maritime Administration
- Department of English

- Department of East Asian
- Department of European Studies

Graduate School

Classes

- Maritime Transportation Science
- Marine Engineering
- Ship Operation Engineering
- Marine Police Science
- Mechanical Engineering
- Marine Systems Engineering
- Electronics & Communication Engineering
- Ocean Development Engineering
- Logistics Engineering
- Control & Instrumentation Engineering
- Material Engineering
- Refrigeration & Air-Conditioning Engineering
- Electrical Engineering
- Radio Science & Engineering
- Civil and Environment Engineering
- Computer Engineering
- Architectural Engineering
- Mechanical and Vehicle Engineering
- Applied Mathematics
- Shipping Management
- Maritime Law

- International Trade
- English Language and Literature
- East Asian Studies

Master Courses

- Maritime Transportation Science
- Marine Engineering
- Ship Operation Engineering
- Mechanical Engineering
- Marine Systems Engineering
- Electronics & Communication Engineering
- Ocean Development Engineering
- Logistics Engineering
- Control & Instrument Engineering
- Material Engineering
- Refrigeration & Air-Conditioning Engineering
- Electrical Engineering
- Radio Science & Engineering
- Civil and Environment Engineering
- Computer Engineering
- Shipping Management
- Maritime Law
- International Trade
- Cooperative Study (KIMM)

Maritime Industrial Studies

- Maritime Transportation Science
- Engine System Engineering
- Ship Operating System Engineering
- Logistics Engineering
- Mechanical System Engineering
- Naval Architecture, Ocean & Architectural Engineering
- Electric, Electronics, & Control Engineering
- Electrics Electronics
- Civil & Environmental Engineering
- Maritime Management
- Maritime Law
- Maritime Administration
- Advanced Management Program

Research Institutes

The Research Institute of Maritime Industry was established in 1981 and reorganized in 1990 to contribute to the development of the maritime industry, maritime education and applied technology. The RIMI was a core leader in establishing KMU. The RIMI is a superior Institute that has been designated by the Ministry of Education in 2000 to receive 200 million won to purchase experimental laboratory equipment.

The Research Institute of Industrial Technology (RIIT) established in 1991 aims at the development of advanced technologies related to engineering industries and at progress in collaboration with the government, institutes or industries. Unified with the Research Institute of Basic Sciences, the Center for Logistics Studies, the Radio and Communication Research Institute and the Research Institute of Port and Harbor in May 2000, RIIT has its research capability of 103 professors and three full-time research professors and research facilities in nine Divisions and the Consortium Center for the Development of Technology. Its main activities include conducting joint research, organizing seminars and conferences on related subjects, producing publications and providing consultation.

The Research Institute of Marine Basic Sciences was established in 1981. The Research Institute of Marine Science and the Institute of Corrosion and Corrosion Control were founded in 1991. They were integrated and reconstructed as the Research Institute of Marine Science and Technology in May 2000. The specialized research institute has been recognized as a leader in basic research and applied technology of marine science.

The Institute of International Affairs (IIMA) was newly established in May 2000 through merging of the existing three institutes such as Marine Transportation Institute, Research Institute of Marine Culture and Center for Social Science Research. The Institute focuses on the studies regarding Shipping and Port Management, Maritime Law and Public Administration, Sea Sightseeing and Venture Business, International Trade and Finance, Regional Affairs and Culture.

Marine Equipment Research Institute (MERI) was established in 1994 to serve a diverse marine equipment research community. MERI is a specialized organization responsible for enhancing basic research activities on advanced marine equipment and promoting joint research activities and cooperation between KMU and industries. MERI has successfully carried out the Navigation and Telecommunication Project, which developed eleven kinds of navigation and telecommunication equipment.

The International Maritime Information Research Center (IMIRC) is the specialized Information Research Center of Korea Maritime University, which was established in, May 2000 on the basis of "A Study Group on IMO", founded in October 1995. The Center is conducting the research and projects essential to promote the quality of intramural research institutes and national shipping industries through collection, investigation, analysis, publication, distribution, of International trend and information related to IMO, ILO and other maritime agencies.

The Marine Simulation Training and Research Center (MSTAR) offers an active computerized simulated training program consisting of Ship Handling Simulation (SHS), Engine Handling Simulation (EHS), Global Maritime Distress and Safety Simulation (GMDSS). With simulator, many types of situations may be done allow users to apply their knowledge in a very real environment but not place individuals in any danger. The Center has been one of the most widely visited facilities at KMU since its opening on 18th March, 1999.

The Business Incubator Center, designated by the Small & Medium Business Administration as an incubating business for the foundation of ventures in October 2000, was founded as part of the governmental policy to foster small- and medium-sized ventures in March 2001. The center will support and provide advice and consultation on founding companies and their management for those who want to establish them. Especially, the center will offer the KMU owned infrastructure, manpower and facilities, to the new founders who have new ideas and the state-of-the-art technology related to the advanced shipbuilding and marine equipments, automat zed equipments of navigation, engine, and marine telecommunication, and intelligent systems of shipping and logistics. The center has twenty incubation rooms.

Alex Roth (continued)

When UNKRA moved its headquarters to Seoul in 1955, Alex converted one of the larger residences on Hialeah Compound into an UNKRA Club. He also became President of the Pusan Masonic Club, which sponsored an orphanage with a small clinic. As the needs of the clinic increased, the club decided to build the Pusan Children's Charity Hospital, which was supported by a Washington D.C. registered organization.

In June 1956, the Korean Merchant Marine Academy (later renamed Korea Maritime University) was turned over to South Korea. Alex terminated his contract as of July 31, 1956. He was honored with a full-scale parade of the cadets and presented with a gold Academy Crest ring. A Special Medal was cast for him from the Pusan Ministry of Transportation. There was a Kaesong party hosted by the academy staff, as well as one hosted by the Ministry of Education Inspectors and Pusan City officials. The Pusan Children's Charity Hospital board and personnel gave a farewell dinner party.

In Seoul, the Ministry of Transportation and the Ministry of Education gave a western style banquet in the official Government Entertainment Pavilion which was attended by

Lieutenant General Coulter (ret.), Agent General of UNKRA and other UNKRA officials. At this affair Alex was presented with a Bureau of Marine Republic of Korea unlimited Master License number BM001 by the Minister of Transportation. It is the only one ever given to a foreigner. The license had no expiration date.

The following speech by Lt.General John B. Coulter, Agent General of UNKRA:

"There is a great satisfaction in being present for these ceremonies today, for the completion of a new Merchant Marine Academy for the Republic of Korea marks the fulfillment of a long dream."

"I knew that from the earliest days of liberation, the country has sought to build up its merchant fleet. It has tried valiantly to train more officers to sail ships that will mean economic lifeline between this peninsula and distant countries."

"But there has been many hardships. I have been told that when liberation came, there were few experienced Korean ship's officers; few instructors who can train a new generation of students in the craft of seamanship; no suitable training facilities; not even any up-to-date text books."

"Three years ago, the head of the Merchant Marine Academy described the situation in a letter to the United Nation Korean Reconstruction Agency. He made this statement: 'No one will deny the fact that our country, surrounded by sea, will prosper only by marine transportation, superior ships and mariners are most important'"

"Now, in the academy that we see today, the Republic of Korea has a suitable training ground for the mariners it needs."

"Only one and a half year ago, this site was a quiet stretch of hilly farmland, given over to vegetables and foothills timber. Now we see modern buildings, lecture rooms, laboratories, and dormitories forming a complete educational institution ready to train hundreds of young men for maritime duties at sea, in commercial shipping firms and government offices."

"How did this transformation come about? The answer is: International teamwork of the highest order."

"The team that built this Merchant Marine Academy has had many members. Government representatives supervised construction and that, I know, meant a night-and-day job. UNKRA specialists worked with them, providing the benefits of international experience. Korean contractors and scores of individuals including women workers stuck to their tasks, in good weather and bad, to finish them on time. The City of Pusan an access road, cutting it across hills and paddies to permit tons of supplies to be trucked from the docks to the site."

"And a special tribute should go to the academy officials who kept the former school together at its makeshift, temporary quarters while giving constant help in preparations for the new institution. The United Nations Korean Reconstruction Agency has been privileged to serve with the team in a number of ways. Its assignment was to provide construction materials in the planning and building of the academy, bring in teaching equipment and supplies and give technical assistance in developing a curriculum to meet present-day needs."

"To carry out the first part of its task, UNKRA imported, among other things, more than 2,000 tons of cement, 250 tons of steel and a quarter of a million board feet of lumber. It also brought in more than 4,000 books, equipment for a complete machine shop and hundreds of pieces of apparatus to fit out scientific laboratories."

"A mere group of buildings is not, of course, an educational institution. The heart of any school must always be the training it gives and the faculty that provides it. Consequently, while physical walls of these buildings were rising, UNKRA advisors were working side by side with the academy staff to devise the best possible training courses and the most effective training techniques."

"Even with all the limitations that have hampered this school in the past, it has sent many graduated into officers' posts in the merchant fleet and responsible positions ashore. Now, with its broadened curriculum and its new physical plant, the academy can be expected to play an even more vital role in the nation's expanding maritime operations."

"Mr. President, I know how deeply interested you have been in this project. It gives me a great pleasure to present to the government of the Republic of Korea a new Merchant Marine Academy. May it stand as a proud and lasting symbol of the international partnership that built it."

After a two-year assignment in South Korea, in early August 1956 Alex returned home via San Francisco to his wife and daughter in Salisbury, Maryland for a long awaited vacation.

The last week in August, Alex was invited to the U.S. Merchant Marine Academy at Kings Point, New York for a special ceremony. The Republic of Korea Ambassador to the U.S. and the Vice-Minister of Transportation were there to present scrolls and citations from the Republic of Korea to various individuals at Kings Point who had assisted the ROK academy.

Mary & Alex Roth celebrate reunion.

From September 1956 to April 1960 Alex served as Master of S.S. *Hawaii Bear*, S.S. *Canada Bear*, S.S. *Indian Bear* and the S.S. *Surprise* for Pacific Far East Lines. The S.S. *P&T* Adventurer for Pope & Talbot and the S.S. *Hawaiian Fisherman* for Matson Lines.

In June 1957, Alex's wife and nine-year old daughter moved from Salisbury, Maryland to San Mateo, California. In October 1958, Mary gave birth to their daughter Jennifer and asked Alex to get a shore job in the shipping industry.

July 1960 Alex signed a 2-year contract with Getz Brothers, a San Francisco transportation company, as their Shipping Department Manager on the island of Guam. In the next month, his wife and two daughters joined him there.

April 1962 to January 1967 Getz Brothers, who did business there as E.J. Griffiths Company transferred Alex to Okinawa as Transportation Division Manager (Shipping, Household Van and Moving & Travel Department).

January 1967 to January 1970, Alex was moved back to Guam and held the same position he had on Okinawa.

In January 1970, Alex was asked to go to Seoul, Korea to open a Getz Bros. Transportation Divisions. He agreed to do that so if his family were given their two months home leave in the states early before proceeding to Korea. This would give Mary the opportunity to acquire winter clothing and to get acclimated to the cold climate. (Guam has a tropical climate all year long.) The home leave request was granted for January 25 to March 25.

March 27, 1870 to June 8, 1974, Alex served as General Manager of Getz Bros. Transportation Division in Seoul, Korea.

June 8, 1974 to August 9, 1974, Alex and family went on home leave in the states. Before leaving, Korea Alex was asked to go back to Guam as Transportation Division Manager after home leave.

August 9, 1974 Alex, wife Mary and daughter Jennifer arrived back on Guam. One of the worst typhoons to hit Guam (Pamela May 20th 1976) did extensive damage to the company house, household van warehouse and the travel office. Jennifer's graduation from George Washington High School was held seven days later outside the school on the football field.

March 1977 Alex retired from Getz Bros. He and Mary, who was a teacher with the Dept. of Education, decided to remain on Guam. They bought a house in the village of Dededo.

Epilogue

October 1977 the Port Authority of Guam (PAG) gave Alex a contract as a consultant. He served in several administrative positions including Assistant Harbor Master.

March 1988 Alex took leave from PAG for personal reasons. He was involved in a Guam Community College (GCC) Maritime Education project. This necessitates a visit to the U.S. Merchant Marine Academy at Kings Point, New York concerning maritime study courses. He wrote two six-week study courses (Introduction to Marine Transportation and Marine Insurance) and taught the courses at Guam Community College.

December 1990 the Port Authority of Guam asked Alex to return to the port as Marine Traffic Controller.

Mary Roth: "A surprise event occurred while Alex was still at the port. On December 6, 1995, the Korea Maritime University training ship T.S. *Hanara* arrived on its yearly visit to Guam. Alex and I were invited to attend a reception on board ship at 7 P.M. that evening. In addition to the Korean crew and cadets, there was a large number of Korean businessmen and their wives from the Guam community in attendance. The Korean Consul General and his wife also attended and paid their respects. The ship's captain, Lee Deok-Su, told us that the reception was being held in Alex's honor, celebrating the 40th Anniversary of the founding of the Korean Merchant Marine Academy in 1955."

"Alex was introduced as 'The Father of the Korean Merchant Marine Academy' and presented with a commemorative book on the history of the academy and its development into the Korea Maritime University."

"The only English in the whole book is Alex's speech at the dedication of the academy in Pusan in 1955. He was also presented with a framed painting of the ship *Hanara* and two sets of Korean etched silver chopsticks. A special Korean buffet dinner and a tour of the ship concluded this memorable evening."

(Ed. by author): The Captain of the training ship, now Professor Deok-Su Lee, wrote to me from KMU on February 8, 2002:

Training Ship "Hanara" & Captain Lee Deok-Su.
Photo courtesy of Korea Maritime University

Alex Roth & Ship Captain
Lee Deok-Su
Photo courtesy of Korea
Maritime University

"Dear Mr. Raymond B. Maurstad,

I am Professor Deok-Su Lee of Korea Maritime University. I was the master of the training ship *Hanara* when the ship visited Guam on December 1995.

I am sorry for my late informing about the visiting voyage of our training ship. Here I give you the short story of visiting voyage of training ship with attached some pictures.

The voyage of T/S *Hannara* started at November 13, 1995 and ended on December 16, 1995. The track route of that voyage was Pusan-Singapore-Manila-Guam-Kagoshima (Japan)-Pusan. It was the 2nd routine oversea navigation training service of that year with total of 150 cadets and about 50 crews including some faculty members. At that voyage, we added a special visit to Guam, as you know, because we wanted to meet Capt. Roth and his wife. Below is the summary of visiting voyage.

Dec. 6th, 1995

09:40hrs - The T/S *Hannara* arrived at Guam and alongside her starboard at V-6 pier of Guam.

14:00-16:00 – Captain, Chief officer and 3rd officer went to USCG, Port Authority to pay courtesy call.

17:00-22:00 – Held on board reception party at the poop deck of T/S *Hannara*. About 70 Korean residents and Korean consular officials came on board to take part in the reception party. Capt. Roth and his wife also came on board. During the reception party, I introduced Capt. Alexander Roth to all participators with some explanation about his important role and meritorious services during his stay in our University as an advisor on around 1956, at the early stage of our university. And I delivered a book of "The 50 years history of Korea Maritime University' to him with a picture frame of T/S *Hannara*. The book is total 900 pages but all text is Korean alphabet only. At the page 105, 3 pages of the writing which Capt. Roth had contributed to our school magazine of 1956 inserted.

Capt. Roth also had a speech to the participators of that party as a return courtesy and he gave me a frame with historic picture of his belongings. The picture was a memorial shoot of him with all faculty members at the early times of our university. I brought the picture and delivered to the president of university at arrival with the details of our party story.

This is my information which I can give you about the voyage of *Hannara* at 1995.

I hope the above information can give you some helps and if you have another question, please give me details which you want to know.

Please give my best regards to Ms. Mary Roth and her family. Also, I hope you to complete the manuscripts as scheduled.

Kind regards,

Professor Captain Deok Su Lee

Korea Maritime University"

September 1996 Alex submitted a letter of resignation to PAG, as his health was deteriorating.

April 28, 2001 Alex died in his sleep at home on Melissa Lane in Dededo, Guam. He was 83 years old. He and his wife Mary had just celebrated their 50th wedding anniversary on April 20.

Alex (age 81) & Mary (age 77) in 1998.
Photo by Mary Roth

May 12, 2001 a memorial service was held at the Lutheran Church of Guam in Aniqua. His ashes were interred at Wicomico Memorial Park—Cremation Gardens, Salisbury, Maryland.

Ray & Marion Maurstad

By Deborah Lynn Merten

On return to Minneapolis after the Korean assignment, Ray tried again to break from the sea, this time working as a meat cutter in a slaughterhouse in South St. Paul and as a deckhand on a Great Lakes ore boat for one winter voyage. He decided chipping ice on an open deck with fifty-knot winds was not his "cup of tea" and he returned to the salt water out of New York. As his aircraft circled over New York City Ray looked down on the tops of skyscrapers and visualized himself a corporate officer with a large manufacturing company. This vision of himself as a "big wheel" was

Ray & Marion Maurstad—2002

etched in his mind with such great importance that he thought about it almost daily for the next ten years.

He upgraded his Federal Communications Telegraph ticket to First Class and his U.S. Maritime Service rating was advanced to Lieutenant J.G.

Ray and Marion, with baby Murray, bought their first home at Westbury on Long Island, New York in the spring of 1952. This kept the coastal waters close at hand and Ray was busy hauling oil between ports in the Gulf of Mexico and the Eastern Seaboard. Deborah Lynn Maurstad was born in Brooklyn on December 15, 1951. A bumper sugar crop in Cuba in 1952 afforded steady work for a year bringing molasses out of Cuba to the alcohol plants near Philadelphia. Mitchell Allan was born in East Meadow, Long Island April 13, 1953.

Another interesting assignment took Ray to the Greenland ports of Narsarsuaq, Sondre-Stromfjord and Thule on board the S.S. *San Mateo Victory*. Interesting because they had to break ice with the bow of the ship for 14 hours to get into one of those ports.

He was involved with scouting at the Boy Scouts Nassau County Council Long Island and was advisor to an Explorer Post. He took eight canoes and twelve 14-year old Explorer Scouts on a two-week wilderness journey in Canada. He says, "Those boys grew up overnight."

He took a position with ServoMechanisms Inc. in Westbury, New York testing aircraft control servomotors. The job lasted eight months before Ray once more succumbed to foreign intrigue and an offer to sail to Africa on the S.S. *African Dawn* for Farrell Lines out of New York. After a year on the *African Dawn*, Ray started a well-earned vacation at home. One week into his vacation, he received an emergency call to relieve a Radio Officer who had fallen ill on the tanker S.S. *Robert E. Hopkins*. He joined the Hopkins in New Jersey and anticipated only one round trip to Texas. He was asked to take a second trip and on July 25, 1956 the Italian luxury liner S.S. *Andrea Doria* and the Swedish liner MS *Stockholm* collided near Nantucket. Ray was the first radioman to respond to the distress calls from both vessels and the Hopkins was the fourth ship alongside the sinking *Andrea Doria*. While the French liner *Ile de France*, the MS *Stockholm* and the Navy transport *Pvt. William H. Thomas* removed most of the passengers from the *Doria*, a lifeboat from the Hopkins rescued the last man to leave the ship. Fifty-one dead or missing, over 2000 were saved. (See the Website at **http://www.andreadoria.org**) Ray finished the voyage and returned to his vacation at home.

After another year on the *African Dawn* Ray qualified for a position with Press Wireless, a world wide wireless communications company headquartered in New York City with a large transmitter site at Hicksville, Long Island, New York and very close to Ray and Marion's new home at Westbury. The station was eventually moved east thirty miles to Centereach, Long Island. The job was both challenging and interesting and Ray made good use of the longer commute time by operating his amateur radio from his car. It was now apparent the he had finally broken the spell of the sea.

In mid-summer 1960, Marion had her own lure to attend. She became fascinated with TV commercials that boasted the great weather and living in Arizona, the "Land of the Sun".

Always a sun worshipper, she talked of moving there every day. In June of 1960, they sold their home and drove to Scottsdale, Arizona where they rented a bungalow. Ray found work with KOOL CBS Television at their studio in downtown Phoenix and at their transmitters on South Mountain. Unable to make it on the low pay Ray took a second job at KBUZ Radio in Mesa as a disc jockey. These hours turned out to be too much of a grind and Marion had not anticipated the extreme heat, dust devils, scorpions and horny toads. In August, they packed up and returned to their home state of Minnesota where they rented the first floor of an old duplex in northeast Minneapolis. Ray's brother-in-law, Floyd Oehler, told Ray about an interesting project at Remington Rand UNIVAC, the typewriter company that had recently gone into the computer business. The project was the design and manufacture of antenna coupling devices for Boeing and Hughes aircraft and Ray quickly found a position there as Manager of Production Engineering. He found many problems and their solutions. One success followed another and it wasn't long before Ray was picked up by the computer side of the house. Before leaving Antenna Coupler manufacturing Ray was asked by Fred Hargesheimer, of World War II Papua, New Guinea fame, to go to the Gillette Hospital for Crippled Children in St. Paul and negotiate some space in the hospital where an amateur radio station could be installed. Space was found and a marketing manager, H.A. "Mick" Alsop, joined Ray in the radio project. They erected a tower and a large beam antenna. Funds were found to purchase a state-of-the-art transmitter and receiving station. Radio theory and code classes were conducted by both Mick and Ray and the handicapped patients were soon on the air. They chatted over the radio with Barry Goldwater who was sitting at home on the eve of the presidential election. Extra equipment was purchased and bed-ridden patients were sent home with a bedside radio station. When Ray and Mick had to leave the radio project it was continued under the supervision of George Selin, another Univac employee. Recognizing his ability to motivate and organize people Ray was given a Program Manager position guiding the design and manufacture of a major computer system. After coordinating that product to its successful placement with customers, he was asked to take over the troubled Federal Aviation Agency computer program. Installed systems at Leesburg, Virginia, Indianapolis Indiana, Oberlin, Ohio and Nashua, New Hampshire were failing and the core of the problem was the printer being utilized in the system. The problems required updating of other parts of the system. The print problems were soon solved and the systems updated. In recognition of another success, Ray was given a new computer system Program Manager position.

Ray and Marion bought their second new home in Blaine, Minnesota, just north of Minneapolis.

He attended the Extension Division of the University of Minnesota for four years and studied Industrial Engineering, Mathematics and Aviation. He decided not to fly after getting his certificate but he was able to put the Engineering and Mathematics studies to good use in his future work with UNIVAC. Matthew Adam Maurstad was born in Minneapolis on September 6, 1963.

A major reorganization of the company that split the domestic and international operations launched Ray into his long held vision that some day he would have an important level of command in a large organization. His first assignment was to dissolve the old Remington Rand style of order services and Ray became the Manager of the Worldwide Export Department for Sperry UNIVAC. The success of this department resulted in the placement of a greatly increased number of computer systems around the world. The old and outdated Field Engineering was not ready for the sudden and mounting work of installation and maintenance and new problems were being encountered in the newest systems. Ray was asked to leave the Export Department to take over Worldwide Field Engineering. He was promoted to Director and he moved his office to headquarters in Blue Bell, Pennsylvania.

One of his first moves was to take over the UNIVAC Field Engineering Training Center in Zurich, Switzerland and call a conference of Field Directors from every one of the 13 European subsidiaries. Marion joined him in Switzerland for a few weeks.

The Directors from the Far East and Australia were also asked to attend the conference. Ray proposed a complete reorganization of the field engineers reporting on a dotted line to his own offices in Switzerland and Pennsylvania along with some urgently required common activities and goals. New rules were set, fast reaction technical teams were formed and a greatly motivated field organization went to

The author addresses Worldwide Field Engineering Directors in Switzerland. "Our people have the talent. They need stability of organization and focus to solve the system problems and, we will solve them."

work with refreshed and accomplishing attitudes. The newest computer systems being installed were carefully tracked for performance and maintainability. A marketing conference was called for and all European marketing directors were asked to gather in Barcelona, Spain. Ray met them there along with one of his technical assistants. They had prepared a very large chart displaying the performance and problem reduction in the last 100 systems installed. Ray finished his presentation to a standing applause from the attendees who were greatly relieved to receive such good news.

Ray was asked to move to the next area of concern. Worldwide inventories of spare parts were bulging and much of the inventory was obsolete. Accenting the inventory problems was a demand for quantities of parts far in excess of what was required to maintain the systems but the Field Managers perceived high cost power supply and assembly requirements as "insurance" or "just in case" items which the company could ill-afford to stock in every location. After establishing strategic placement of these items to be shared, it was time to organize a worldwide distribution system. Ray assembled a team, established a worldwide distribution center in Elk Grove next to Chicago's Ohare Airport. Daily flights carried required parts to stocking point all over the world via Schiphol Airport in the Netherlands. Ray hired a young Englishman by the name of Michael Ostick to assist him in establishing the European central and then brought him into Ohare to oversee the worldwide system. The physical and staffing organization took place as planned and anticipated economies were realized. It was time for Ray to move to the next trouble spot.

All the attention given to the international installed base left the domestic base of installations in some varying degrees of disrepair but most of the problems were encountered in bringing up newly installed systems. Customer complaints were mounting and the complaints were not being adequately responded to at the local (division and branch) level. The Sperry UNIVAC President asked Ray to find the solutions but limited his resources to one office, reasonable communications facilities, one assistant and a secretary.

Ray set up a Customer Satisfaction Control office in the Blue Bell, Pennsylvania headquarters. Four telephone lines with six instruments, and four telex (teletypewriter) machines were installed. Ray hired a technical man from Europe and a good secretary. They set up a "Fastboard" at one end of the conference room and systems complaints were displayed on the board by customer. Every Monday morning all headquarters Vice-Presidents were required to attend the control room meeting. The power to react was in the room as customer complaints were aired. The allocation of the resources necessary to solve the problems was direct and positive and unhappy customers were rapidly changed to satisfied customers. Ray was asked to turn the activity over to W. A. "Pete" Manskar, another capable manager as he again was needed elsewhere.

Sperry's typewriter plant in s'Hertegenbosch, The Netherlands, was producing single element typewriters for the worldwide market. The Italian government was bringing a great deal of pressure on Sperry management to manufacture product in Italy inasmuch as Sperry was enjoying a profitable market there. The single element typewriter * became a candidate to be shared with the Netherlands plant at 'sHertegenbosch (called Den Bosch for brevity). The entire typewriter effort in Sperry was under the guidance of Vice President E.C. "Tommy" Thompson. A closed Remington shaver manufacturing plant near Naples was the candidate location to be activated. Ray was coupled with a Sperry manufacturing manager from the south of England who had considerable experience in the Remington shaver and typewriter activities and together, they set about to transfer part of the Den Bosch capability to Naples. The old shaver plant became a producer of typewriters and the Italian government was satisfied. During one of his visits to the Naples plant he asked Marion to join him and they spent Easter together on the Isle of Capri.

The single element typewriter was developed by IBM Corporation. To settle a lawsuit between IBM and Sperry, IBM gave only a single element typewriter to Sperry with the stipulation that if Sperry could successfully copy the machine for their own production; they could produce and market the machine worldwide.

Now it was 1980 and the winds of political war were blowing throughout the Sperry management. Ray was overlooked in a major reorganization. The handwriting was on the wall and Ray knew it was time to return to the "green green grass of home", their children and grandchildren.

After accepting a position in Software Systems Management in Minnesota. Ray came into his Blue Bell office on a weekend and wrote across the large chalkboard, "I DID IT MY WAY", then packed some miscellaneous things in his briefcase and quietly left headquarters. Now

Marion Maurstad—1971

Ray Maurstad—1971

he and Marion could go back to where their relatives and children were living, go fishing with old friends and leave the hectic corporate life behind. Up until this time Ray's mentors in Sperry UNIVAC were A.B. Bert Meuleners and Paul J. Spillane.

Marion took up an artist's life, joined a writer's club, took up lap swimming, practiced Yoga and kept busy. Ray got involved in Manufacturing Program Management and customer satisfaction activities again but he did not enjoy his work as he once did. He fished the lakes in the wilds of Canada and on Lake Michigan off the Wisconsin shore with great success. He was more comfortable with a home life.

The Burroughs Corporation swept up Sperry Corporation in a hostile take over in the 1980's and by 1989 Ray said yes to a retirement offer. Within two weeks, he was back at sea as Radio Officer on board Texaco tankers hauling jet fuel from California to Alaska and Hawaii.

Marion was his shipmate on one of the Hawaiian trips. He finally did quit the sea in 1996. He was then 68 years old. Back to fishing, gardening and writing until surgery for prostate cancer and a stroke during that procedure slowed him down considerably and virtually ended his fishing in far away places. Now at 74, a calm afternoon on a local lake satisfies his marine urges and appetite for fish.

General Douglas MacArthur

On April 19, 1951, General Douglas MacArthur gave the following speech to Congress:

"Mr. President, Mr. Speaker and distinguished members of the Congress. I stand on this rostrum with a deep humility and great pride—humility in the wake of these great American architects of our history who have stood here before me, pride in the reflection that this forum of legislative debate represents human liberty in the purest form yet devised. Here are centered the hopes and aspirations of faith of the entire human race. I do not stand here as an advocate for any partisan cause for the issues are fundamental and reach quite beyond the realm of partisan consideration. They must be resolved on the highest plane of human interest if our course is to prove sound and our future protected. I trust, therefore, that you will do me the justice of receiving that which I have to say as solely expressing the considered viewpoint of a fellow American. I address you with neither rancor nor bitterness in the failing twilight of life with but one purpose in mind—to serve my country. The issues are global and so interlocked that to consider the problems of one sector, oblivious to those of another, is but to court disaster for the whole. While Asia is commonly referred to as the gateway to Europe, it is no less true that Europe is the gateway to Asia. And the broad influence of the one cannot fail to have its impact on the other. There are those who claim our strength is inadequate to protect on both fronts—that we cannot divide our effort. I can think of no greater expression of defeatism. If a potential enemy can divide his strength on two fronts it is for us to counter the effort. The Communist threat is a global one. Its successful advance in one sector threatens the destruction of every other sector. You cannot appease or otherwise surrender to Communism in Asia without simultaneously undermining our efforts to halt its advance in Europe. Beyond pointing out these simple truisms, I shall confine my discussion to the general arena of Asia. Before one may objectively assess the situation now existing there, he must comprehend something of Asia's past and the revolutionary changes which have marked her course up to the present. Long exploited by the so-called Colonial Powers, with little opportunity to achieve any degree of social justice, individual dignity or a higher standard of life such as guided our own noble administration of the Philippines, the people of Asia found their opportunity in the war just past to throw off the shackles of colonialism and now see the dawn of new opportunity, a heretofore unfelt dignity and the self-respect of political freedom. Mustering half of the earth's population and 60% of its natural resources, these peoples are rapidly consolidating a new force, both moral and material, with which to raise the living standard and erect adaptations of the design of modern progress to their own distinct cultural environments. Whether one adheres to the concept of colonization or not, this is the direction of Asian progress and it may not be stopped. It is a corollary to the shift of the world economic frontiers, as the whole epicenter of world affairs rotates back toward the area whence it started. In this situation, it becomes vital that our own country orient its policies in consonance with this basic evolutionary condition rather than pursue a course blind to the reality that the colonial era is now past and the Asian peoples covet the right to shape their own free destiny. What they seek now is friendly guidance, understanding and support, not imperious direction; the dignity of equality, not the shame of subjugation. Their pre-war standard of life, pitifully low, is infinitely lower now in the devastation left in war's wake. World ideologies play little part in Asian thinking and are little understood. What the peoples strive for is the opportunity for a little more food in their stomachs, a little better clothing on their backs, a little firmer roof over their heads, and the realization of the normal nationalistic urge for political freedom. These political-social conditions have but an indirect bearing upon our own national security, but form a backdrop to contemporary planning which must be thoughtfully considered if we are to avoid the pitfalls of unrealism. Of more direct and immediate bearing upon our national security are the changes wrought in the strategic potential of the Pacific Ocean in the course of the past war. Prior thereto, the Western strategic frontier of the United

States lay on the littoral line of the Americas with an exposed island salient extending out through Hawaii, Midway and Guam to the Philippines. That salient proved not an outpost of strength but an avenue of weakness along which the enemy could and did attack. The Pacific was a potential area of advance for any predatory force intent upon striking at the bordering land areas. All this was changed by our pacific victory. Our strategic frontier then shifted to embrace the entire Pacific Ocean which became a vast moat to protect us as long as we held it. Indeed, it acts as a protective shield for all of the Americas and all free lands of the Pacific Ocean area. We control it to the shores of Asia by a chain of islands extending in an arc from the Aleutians to the Mariannas held by us and our free allies. From this island chain, we can dominate with sea and air power every Asiatic port from Vladivostok to Singapore and prevent hostile movement into the Pacific. Any predatory attack from Asia must be an amphibious effort. No amphibious force can be successful without control of the sea-lanes and the air over those lanes to its avenue of advance. With naval and air supremacy and modest ground elements to defend bases, any major attack from continental Asia toward us or our friends of the Pacific would be doomed to failure. Under such conditions, the Pacific no longer represents menacing avenues of approach for a prospective invader—it assumes instead the friendly aspect of a peaceful lake. Our line of defense is a natural one and can be maintained with a minimum of military effort and expense. It envisions no attack against anyone nor does it provide the bastions essential for offensive operations, but properly maintained would be an invincible defense against aggression. The holding of this littoral defense line in the Western Pacific is entirely dependent upon holding all segments thereof, for any major breach of that line by an unfriendly power would render vulnerable to determined attack every other major segment. This is a military estimate as to which I have yet to find a military leader who will take exception. For that reason I have strongly recommended in the past as a matter of military urgency that under no circumstances must Formosa fall under Communist control. Such an eventuality would at once threaten the freedom of the Philippines and the loss of Japan, and might well force our Western frontier back to the coast of California, Oregon and Washington. To understand the changes which now appear upon the Chinese mainland, one must understand the changes in Chinese character and culture over the past 50 years. China up to fifty years ago was completely non-homogeneous, being compartmented into groups divided against each other. The war-making tendency was almost non-existent, as they still followed the tenets of the Confucian ideal of pacifist culture. At the turn of the century, under the regime of Chan So Lin, efforts toward greater homogeneity produced the start of a nationalist urge. This was further and more successfully developed under the leadership of Chiang Kai Shek, but has been brought to its greatest fruition under the present regime, to the point that is has now taken on the character of a united nationalism of increasingly dominant aggressive tendencies. Through these past fifty years, the Chinese people have thus become militarized in their concepts and in their ideals. They now constitute excellent soldiers with competent staffs and commanders. This has produced a new and dominant power in Asia which for its own purposes is allied with Soviet Russia, but which in its own concepts and methods has become aggressively imperialistic with a lust for expansion and increased power normal to this type of imperialism. There is little of the ideological concept either one way or another in the Chinese makeup. The standard of living is so low and the capital accumulation has been so thoroughly dissipated by war that the masses are desperate and avid to follow any leadership which seems to promise the alleviation of local stringencies. I have from the beginning believed that the Chinese Communists' support of the North Koreans was the dominant one. Their interests are at present parallel to those of the Soviet, but I believe that the aggressiveness recently displayed not only in Korea, but also in Indo-China and Tibet and pointing toward the South, reflects predominately the same lust for the expansion of power which has animated every would-be conqueror since the beginning of time. The Japanese people since the war have undergone the greatest reformation recorded in modern history. With a commendable will, eagerness to learn and marked capacity to understand, they have, from the ashes left in war's wake, erected in Japan an edifice dedicated to the primacy of individual liberty and personal dignity, and in the ensuing process there has been created a truly representative government committed to the advance of political morality, freedom of economic enterprise, and social justice. Politically, economically and socially, Japan is now abreast of many free nations of the earth and will not again fail the universal trust. That it may be counted upon to wield a profoundly beneficial influence of the course of events in Asia is attested by the magnificent manner in which the Japanese people have met the recent challenges of war, unrest and confusion surrounding them from the outside, and checked Communism within their own frontiers without the slightest slackening in their forward progress. I sent all four of our occupation divisions to the Korean battlefront with the slightest qualms as to the effect of the resulting power vacuum in Japan. The results fully justified my faith. I know of no nation more serene, orderly and industrious—nor in which higher hopes can be entertained for future constructive service in the advance of the human race. Of our former ward, the Philippines, we can look forward in confidence that the existing unrest will be corrected and a strong and healthy nation will grow in the longer aftermath of war's terrible destructiveness. We must be patient and understanding and never fail them, as in our hour of need they did not fail us. A Christian nation, the Philippines stand as a mighty bulwark of Christianity in the Far East, and its capacity for high moral leadership in Asia is unlimited. On Formosa, the government of the Republic of China has had the opportunity to refute by action much of the salacious gossip which so undermined the strength of its leadership on the Chinese mainland. The Formosan people are receiving a just and enlightened administration with majority representation on the organs of government, and politically, economically and socially they appear to be advancing along sound and constructive lines. With this brief insight into the surrounding areas, I now turn to the Korean conflict. While I was not consulted prior to the President's decision to intervene in support of the Republic of Korea, that decision, from a military standpoint, proved a sound one as we hurled back the invader and decimated his forces. Our victory was complete and our objectives within reach when Red China intervened with numerically superior ground forces. This created a new war and an entirely new situation-a situation not contemplated when our forces were committed against the North Korean invaders—a situation which called for new decisions in the diplomatic sphere to permit the realistic adjustment of military strategy. Such decisions have not been forthcoming. While no man in his right kind would advocate sending our ground forces into continental China and such was never given a thought, the new situation did urgently demand a drastic revision of strategic planning if our political aim was to defeat this new enemy as we had defeated the old. Apart from the military need as I saw it, to neutralize the sanctuary protection given the enemy north of the Yalu, I felt that military necessity in the conduct of war made mandatory: First; the intensification of our economic blockade against China. Second; the imposition of a naval blockade against the China coast. Third; removal of restriction on air reconnaissance of China's coastal areas and of Manchuria. And, fourth; removal of restriction on the forces of the Republic of China on Formosa with logistical support to contribute to their effective operations against the common enemy. For entertaining these views, all professionally designed to support our forces committed to Korea and bring hostilities to an end with the least possible delay and at a saving of countless American and Allied lives, I have been severely criticized in lay circles, principally abroad, despite my understanding that from a military standpoint the above views have been fully shared in the past by practically every military leader concerned with the Korean campaign, including our own Joint Chiefs on Staff. I called for reinforcements, but was informed that reinforcements were not available. I made clear that if not permitted to destroy the enemy built-up bases north of the Yalu; if not permitted to utilize the friendly Chinese force of some six hundred thousand men on Formosa; if not permitted to blockade the China coast to prevent the Chinese Reds from getting succor from without; and if there were to be no hope of major reinforcements, the position of the command from the military standpoint forbade victory. We could hold in Korea by constant maneuver and at an approximate area where our support line advantages were in balance with the supply line disadvantages of the enemy, but we could hope at best for only an indecisive campaign, with its terrible and constant attrition upon our forces if the enemy utilized his full military potential. I have constantly called for the new political decisions essential to a solution. Efforts have been made to distort my position. It has been said that I was in effect a warmonger. Nothing could be further from the truth. I know war as few other men now living know it, and nothing to me is more revolting. I have long advocated its complete abolition as its very destructiveness on both friend and foe has rendered it useless as means of settling international disputes. Indeed, on the 2nd of September

1945, just following the surrender of the Japanese nation on the battle-ship Missouri, I formally cautioned as follows:

Men since the beginning of time have sought peace. Various meth-ods through the ages have been attempted to devise an international process to prevent or settle disputes between nations. From the very start, workable methods were found insofar as individual citizens were concerned, but the mechanics of instrumentality of larger international scope have never been successful. Military alliances, balances of power, Leagues of Nations, all in turn failed, leaving the only path to be by way of the old crucible of war. The utter destructiveness of war now blots out this alternative. We have had our last chance. If we will not devise some greater and more equitable system, Armageddon will be at our door. The problem basically is theological and involves a spiritual recrudes-cence and improvement of human character that will synchronize with our almost matchless advances in science, art, literature and all material cultural developments of the past two thousand years. It must be of the spirit if we are to save the flesh.

But once war is forced upon us, there is no other alternative than to apply every available means to bring it to a swift end. War's very object is victory—not prolonged indecision. In war, indeed, there can be no substitute for victory. There are some who for varying reasons would appease Red China. They are blind to history's clear lesson. For history teaches with unmistakable emphasis, that appeasement but begets new and bloodier war. It points to no single instance where the end has jus-tified that means—where appeasement has led to more than a sham peace. Like blackmail, it lays the basis for new and successively greater demands, until, as in blackmail, violence becomes the only other alter-native. Why, my soldiers asked of me, surrender military advantages to an enemy in the field? I could not answer. Some may say to avoid spread of the conflict into an all-out war with China; others, to avoid Soviet intervention. Neither explanation seems valid. For China is already engaging with the maximum power it can commit and the Soviet will not necessarily mesh its actions with our moves. Like a cobra, any new enemy will more likely strike whenever it feels that the relativity in mil-itary or other potential is in its favor on a worldwide basis. The tragedy of Korea is further heightened by the fact that as military action is confined to its territorial limits, it condemns that nation, which it is our purpose to save, to suffer the devastating impact of fully protected from such attack and devastation. Of the nations of the world, Korea alone, up to now, is the sole one which has risked its all against Communism. The magnificence of the courage and fortitude of the Korean people defies description. They have chosen to risk death rather than slavery. Their last words to me were 'Don't scuttle the Pacific.'

I have just left your fighting sons in Korea. They have met all tests there and I can report to you without reservation they are splendid in every way. It was my constant effort to preserve them and end this savage conflict honorably and with the least loss of time and a minimum sacrifice of life. Its growing bloodshed has caused me the deepest anguish and anxiety. These gallant men will remain often in my thoughts and in my prayers always. I am closing my fifty-two years of military service. When I joined the Army even before the turn of the century, it was the fulfillment of all my boyish hopes and dreams. The world has turned over many times since I took the oath on the plain at West Point and the hopes and dreams have long since vanished. But I still remember the refrain of one of the most popular barrack ballads of that day which proclaimed most proudly that:

'Old soldiers never die—they just fade away.' And like the old soldier of that ballad, I now close my military career and just fade away—an old soldier who tried to do his duty as God gave him the light to see that duty. Good-bye.

General Douglas MacArthur passed away in 1964

SUNDAY, JANUARY 23 • 2000

★ STAR TRIBUNE • A9

Jean MacArthur, shown in 1942, once was hailed as "a shining example, a woman of substance and character."

Gen. Douglas MacArthur's widow, Jean, dies at 101

Associated Press

NEW YORK — Jean MacArthur, wife of the late Gen. Douglas MacArthur, died Saturday at age 101.

MacArthur, whose vibrancy and charm won her admirers around the world, died at Lenox Hills Hospital in New York, said Col. William Davis, director of the MacArthur Foundation in Norfolk, Va.

Jean MacArthur's obituary

She was at the general's side in war and peace. She accompanied him aboard a PT boat when he was ordered out of the Philippines to escape a Japanese siege at the outset of the war in the Pacific. She represented him at official and social functions and mingled with throngs of Japanese on her trips around Japan during the postwar occupation. She shared his homecoming when he was relieved of command during the Korean War.

Near his death in 1964, MacArthur described her as "my constant friend, sweetheart and devoted supporter."

She had remained active in theater, opera, civic and philanthropic pursuits and served as honorary chairman of the Norfolk foundation created as a memorial to her husband.

"Jean MacArthur has witnessed the great cataclysms of our time, survived war and peace, conquered tragedy and known triumph," President Ronald Reagan said in awarding her the Presidential Medal of Freedom in 1988.

The citation for the medal, the nation's highest civilian award, called her "a shining example, a woman of substance and character, a loyal wife and mother, and like her general, a patriot."

Jean Marie Faircloth was born in Nashville on Dec. 28, 1898. Her parents divorced when she was young, and her mother took her children to live in their grandfather's home in Murfreesboro, Tenn.

She traveled widely after college and was on her way to China when she met MacArthur aboard ship in 1935. He was headed for Manila to become military adviser to the government of the Philippines.

MacArthur and Faircloth were seated together at dinner. He sent flowers the next day. "That was that," she said later. She got off in Manila and remained for 1½ years as their romance flowered.

They were married in New York on April 30, 1937. It was his second marriage, her first. Their son, Arthur, was born in Manila in 1938.

She is to be buried with her husband at the MacArthur Memorial in Virginia, a domed building dating from 1850 that once served as Norfolk's City Hall. It is now part of a complex that includes the Jean MacArthur Research Center, which houses her husband's archives.

The graduate

1954 Tent Buildings

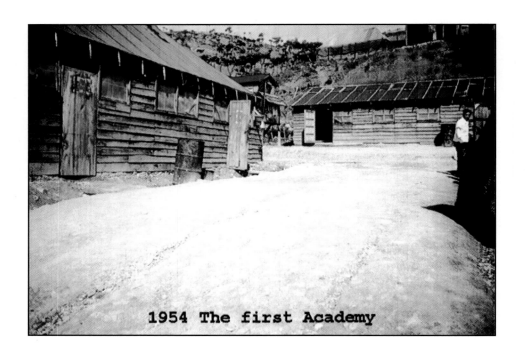

1954 The first Academy

1954 Parade Grounds

1954 Military Training Exercises

Road
Construction

Road taking shape

The school takes shape

Continued Progress

Main Building

Liberty Ship Instructions

Radar Instructions

Azimuth instruction
on the Bando

Gyrocompass
instructions

Cadets plotting in the Bando
Chartroom

In the wheelhouse of
the Bando

The New Merchant Marine Academy.
Photo courtesy of Korea Maritime University

About the Author

The author, born in Minnesota in 1928, left school at age 15 to accept employment at the U.S. Navy Shipyard in Bremerton, Washington. As an Electrician's Helper, he wired gun turrets on ships returning from the Pacific for repairs. He met a young girl from Minnesota at the government housing recreation center and they dated frequently. Her parents were also employed by the Navy Yard. Ray's occasional ferry trips into Seattle lured him into the U.S. Maritime Service recruiting office in 1944.

He completed boot training on Catalina Island off the California coast. After qualifying he attended the Radio Training School in Boston Harbor, Massachusetts for six months and graduated as a Warrant Officer in the U.S. Maritime Service.

His first ship assignment was a Liberty Ship, the S.S. *David Lubin*, out of Seattle and destined for the invasion of Okinawa. They steamed independently to Johnston Island, Eniwetok Atoll and joined a convoy at Ulithi in the Carolines. At Hugishi anchorage near Naha, Okinawa they discharged their cargo of Red Cross supplies and airfield strips. Anchored for a few weeks they escaped damage from frequent Kamikaze attacks. Ray and the captain of the Lubin were pinned down by sniper fire while crossing the island en route to their convoy conference at Buckner Bay. Only one occupant of the vehicle convoy was wounded and not seriously.

Subsequent ship assignments took him to Alaska and the Philippines. He then spent six months in 1946 with Pan American Airways on Wake Island followed by a short assignment with Northwest Orient Airlines in Minneapolis, Minnesota and Grand Forks, North Dakota. In an effort to break from the sea, he spent January through September of 1948 with the Western Union Telegraph Company in St. Paul, Minnesota as a cable clerk. During this period he married Marion Carlson, the young girl he had met at Bremerton, Washington. They made their first home in New York and he went back to sea. He was called to the Korean job within a year.

Chronology–Korea

By Francis J. Winslow *U S. Army Signal Corps officer in Korea 1948-1951*

Date   Event

Date	Event
2333 BC	First year of Korean Calendar. Tang-gun was mysterious and mythical father of Korea which he named Chosen.
681-935 AD	Palhae—Unified Shilla or Silla Period. Animism/ Shamanism.
918-1392	Koryu Dynasty. Capital at Kaesong/Songdo. Buddhism is center of culture.
1392—1910	Chosun/Yi Dynasty. Capital at Seoul. General Yi built Kwan Bok Palace at Seoul. Southern boundary of Chosun was the Han and the northern boundary extended to include Mukden, Manchuria. Confucianism replaced Buddhism.
1853	Admiral Perry opens door for US trade with Japan
1871 May /June	US Navy/Marine attack at Kangwha Island at mouth of Han River failed to cause Korea to open up to world trade. 243 Koreans, 3 US killed.
1876	Japan forces Korea to open up to world trade.
1894,—1895	Sino-Japanese war. China recognizes Korea's independence.
1904,—1905	Russo-Japanese War. Japan attacks and defeats Russians at Port Arthur (Lushun). In less than 50 years Japan became a world class power.
1905 Sept 5	Treaty of Portsmouth ends Russo–Japanese War. Japan's interest in Korea is recognized as is her annexation of the Liaotung Peninsula. US President Theodore Roosevelt mediates.

1905—1910 Sep 2	Japan declares protectorate over Korea.
1908	Root–Takahira agreement. US recognized primacy of Japan in southern Manchuria and Korea.
1910	Empire of Japan annexes Korea.
1922 Dec 30	Union of Soviet Socialist Republics (USSR) is established.
1921	Mao Zedong is one of founders of Chinese Communist Party
1927—1928	National Kuomintang government established in China by Chiang Kai-shek.
1931 Sep 18	Japanese troops in Manchuria, occupy Mukden (Shen-Yang) and strategic areas.
1932 Feb18	Japan establishes puppet state of Manchukuo in southern Manchuria.
1933 Nov 17	US recognizes USSR as government of Russia.
1935	Mao takes control of China Communist Party. Attacks Chinese Nationalists.
1937,—1939	Undeclared war between China and Japan
1938 Oct,—Dec	Canton, Hankow, Nanking fall to Japan.
1941 Dec 8	USA declares war on Japan
1943 Nov 22,—26	Cairo Declaration of FDR, Churchill, Chiang Kai-shek
1943 Dec 1	Cairo communiqué signed by US, China, Britain. It stated "Korea to be free and independent in due course"
1943 Sep 13	Chiang Kai-shek becomes President of China.
1945 Feb 4,—11	Yalta Declaration. FDR, Churchill, Chiang and Stalin. USSR agrees to enter war against Japan when hostilities in Europe cease. FDR tells Stalin that Korea requires long time to be ready for independence.

1945 May 8	Surrender of Germany (V-E Day). USSR takes ninety days to make good on its promise at Yalta to enter war against Japan when war ends in Europe.
1945 May 28	Stalin formally agrees to international trusteeship for Korea
1945 July	War Department told MacArthur to prepare for occupation of Korea as well as Japan
1945 July 17,-Aug 2	Potsdam conference. Truman, Stalin, Churchill. Reaffirms Cairo's Free & Independent Korea, in due course.
1945 Aug 6	Atomic bomb on Hiroshima.
1945 Aug 8	USSR declares war on Japan and subscribes to Potsdam Declaration
1945 Aug 9	Atomic bomb on Nagasaki.
1945 Aug 10	USSR invades Manchuria. Ousts Japanese forces, ships war booty to USSR, Continues to North Korea to act as USSR Army of Occupation.
1945 Aug 14	Japan unconditional surrender by Emperor. Korean Liberation Day.
1945 Aug 16	US Government decides unilaterally to use as 38th Parallel as division between US and Soviet zones. Two Army colonels, one being Dean Rusk (later Secretary of State) drew the line.
1945 Sep 2	Formal surrender of Japan on Battleship Missouri.
1945 Sep 7	Arrival of advance party of US Army of occupation and US Military Government government at Inchon.

1945 Sep 8 LT. Gen. Hodge and his XXIV Corps arrives in Korea with 6th and 7th, and 40th, Divisions. Hodge also commands US Army Forces In Korea (USFIK). Hodge appoints, sequentially, division commanders as head of US Army Military Government in Korea (USAMGIK).

1945 Sep 9 Japanese officials surrender their colonial authority in Seoul.

1946 Jan 14 South Korean Bureaus of Constabulary and Coast Guard established.

1946—1949 Civil war in China: Nationalist under Chiang and Communists under Mao.

1946 Sep 11 Military Governor directs his Military Government to act as advisors to their Korean counterparts.

1947 June 5 Marshall plan for Europe. Goes into effect under Foreign Assistance Act of 14 March 1948. Assume that some if not all aid foreign assistance was issued

1948 Apr 3 Congress passed the Economic Cooperation Act of 1948, the basis for aid program for the Republic of Korea. administered by the US Embassy.

1948 May 10 South Koreans vote for first time for nominees for members of ROK National Assembly who, in turn, vote for a President.

1948 May 20 Brig. Gen. Roberts assigned to Military Government as Director, Internal Security Department.

1948 Aug 15 Republic of Korea (ROK) established. US Military Government of Korea ends. All military advisors assigned to USAFIK's Provisional Military Advisory Group (PMAG) whose Chief is Brig. Gen. Roberts.

1948 Aug 27	Lt. Gen. Hodge replaced by Maj. Gen. Coulter as CG USAFIK and XXIV Corps
1948 Sep 9	Democratic People's Republic of Korea (DPRK) established.
1948 Oct 19	Yosu Rebellion by 14th Regt of ROK Constabulary
1948 Dec 15	Republic of Korea Army (ROKA) established. Constabulary terminated.
1949 Jan 15	XXIV Corps deactivated. 5th Regimental Combat Team activated Maj. Gen. Coulter departs. Brig. Gen. Roberts acts as both CG, USAFIK and Chief, PMAG
1949 Mar 23	Truman approves an advisory group for ROK.
1949 Apr 2	PMAG request to extend advisors to battalion level in Army, to district level in National Police, and to any level in Coast Guard
1949 Jun 29	Last of four increments of 5th Regimental Combat Team departs Inchon for Hawaii.
1949 Jun 30	USAFIK and PMAG terminated. US Army of Occupation in Republic of Korea ends.
1949 July 1	American Mission in Korea (AMIK) established under US Ambassador Muccio to administer Economic Cooperation Administration (ECA) programs and exercise operational control of newly established United States Advisory Group to the Republic of Korea (KMAG). Brig Gen. Roberts continues as group's Chief.
1949 Dec 9	Chiang, his Chinese Nationalist government, and armed forces escape to Formosa leaving China mainland to Mao.
1950 Jan 5	President Truman announces that US would take no military action to help Nationalist on Formosa in event of attack by Chinese Communists.

1950 Jan 12	Secretary of State amplifies the President's 5 January statement to declare that the US would only fight to defend Japan, Okinawa or Philippines. Korea and other unnamed Asian states would have to fight the Communists on their own.
1950 Jan 14	Five 2500 ton freighters arrive in Pusan from Yokohama shipyards with 17 Maritime Advisors to train Koreans in operation of the ships.
1950 Jun 25	The Democratic Peoples's Republic of Korea attacks the Republic of Korea at 0400 hours
1950 Jun 26	At 1600 hours Norwegian freighter Reinholt departs Inchon for Japan with 670 women and children dependents of American Mission in Korea.
1950 Jun 26	In Seoul mid morning AMIK male and female employees depart for Kimpo airport by bus from Banto for C-54 flights to Japan.
Jun 27	In Seoul at noon time military vehicles transport KMAG personnel departed for Suwon airstrip for evacuation by C-47s to Japan.
1950 Jun 27	Truman reverses its "no US support policy of Korea" by authorizing use of US air and naval forces.
1950 Jun 27	Brig Gen Church arrives Suwon to represent CINC Far East Command and to transfer control of KMAG from Department of State to Far East Command.
1950 Jun 27	A blacked-out convoy of vehicles leaves Hialeah Compound at midnight with all the women and children dependents of AMIK employees and the Maryknoll Sisters. They are unloaded ship-side and board the S.S. *Pioneer Dale* for evacuation to Japan.

1950 Jun 28 | ROKA authorities ordered a span of Han River highway bridge to be dropped at 0215 hours while loaded with people of all description and trapping a major portion of ROKA north of Han River.

1950 Jun 28 | Some 235 men, women and children of AMIK departed Pusan on The *Letitia Lykes* for Japan.

1950 Jun 29—30 | Suwon airfield busy with C-47s arriving with supplies for ROKA. USAF fighters provide cover from Japan protected transports from Yaks and IL-10s circling to north.

1950 Jun 30 | Truman commits US ground forces into action in Korea. MacArthur mid-day arrives at Suwon by C-54 for visit to forward area

1950 Jul 1 | KMAG convoy arrived in Taejon very early in morning. Maj. Gen. Dean and his 24th Div are first troops to arrive in Korea.

1950 Jul 2 | C-54 from Japan carrying radio station equipment for Pusan crashes into mountain north of Pusan killing all 18 officers and enlisted men on board.

1950 Jul 7 | United Nations Command established with Gen MacArthur in command.

1950 Jul—Aug | ROK Army with KMAG arrives in Taegu to defend Pusan Perimeter

1950 Sep 15 –18 | Inchon invasion and breakout of Pusan Perimeter

1950 Oct 1 | ROKA I Corps 3rd Inf and Capital divisions on east coast cross 38th parallel

1950 Oct 25 | Chinese troops enter war in support of communist North Korea.

1950 Dec 31 | Last of Department of State's Economic Cooperation Administration personnel (AMIK) hired in June 1949 depart Korea.

1951 Jul 14 | Truce talks initiated at Kaesong

Bibliography

Key to holder: "M" for Maurstad "W" for Winslow

Bristol, H. *Korea—A photographic report*, (Tokyo, June 1948).W

Chief of Military History, *Korea—1950* Department of the Army (Washington 1952). 281 pages. W
Bennett, D., Korea- As we Saw It *Baltimore and Ohio Magazine* (June 1951) W

de Chetelat, E. *Roaming Korea South of the Iron Curtain.* National Geographic (June, 1950). W

Del Rey of Maryknoll, Sister Maria, *Her Name Is Mercy,* (New York, 1957) M

Dorn, N "Daughter, Family Safe in Korea" The Columbus (Ohio) Dispatch. 27 June 1950 W

Encyclopedia Americana, 1960 Edition Vol.16, Korea, p.522-529 M

Encyclopedia Americana, 1960 Edition Vol. 18, MacArthur, Douglas, p.9-9a. Maryknoll, p.352 M

Fischer, Edward, *Light In The Far East,* Harold Henry's 42 years in Korea, (New York, 1976) M

Futrell, R. *The United States Air Force in KOREA 1950-1953* Center for Air Force History, (Washington, 1961). W

Gibney, F, Korea Progress Report, Foreign News, *Time, The Weekly Newsmagazine* (June 5 1950). W

Guttman, A. (ed.) *Korea: Cold War and Limited War,* 2d Edition D.C. Heath & Co., (Lexington Massachusetts 1972). W

Higgins, M. *War in Korea: the report of a woman combat correspondent* (Garden City, NY, 1951). W

History of Christianity in Korea. http://www.kimsoft.com/1997/xhist.htm (Internet August 2001). W

History of Korea from pre-918 to post 1953, **http:// www.violet.berkley.edu/~korea/history.html** (Internet August 2001). W

Hodge, Lt. Gen. John R., *With the U.S. Army in Korea* (National Geographic June, 1947) M

Hodge, Lt. Gen. John R., Korea—*Our Mission in Korea*, Troop Information and Education Section HQ XXIV Corps, Printed by TI&E Section GHQ Far East Command APO 500. Undated est. May 1947. 220 pages W

Kim, H. Edward, Seoul: Korean Showcase. *National Geographic* (Dec. 1979). W

Leckie, R. *CONFLICT: The History of the Korean War* (New York, 1962). W

Lowry, E.M., *KOREAN IDYL:then came WAR*, self-published 2001 Bandon, Oregon W/M

MacDonald, Callum A., *Korea, the War before Viet Nam* (New York, 1987) M

Mosier, Robert H., The *GI and the Kids of Korea* (National Geographic May, 1953) M

Paige, Glenn D. *The Korean Decision June 24-30, 1950* (New York, 1968) M

Pleshakov, Constantine, the *Tsar's Last Amada* (Basic 2002) W

Ryo, Emily, North *Korea*, Arms Control, Disarmament and International Security www.acdis.uiuc.edu

Sandler, S. *The Korean War: No Victors, No Vanquished* (Lexington, Kentucky 1999). W

Sauer, C. A., *Methodist Work in the Republic of Korea* 23 page Missions of Methodist Church, 7820 Reading Rd. Cincinnati OH 45237 1964 W

Sawyer, R. *Military Advisors in Korea: KMAG in Peace and War* Office of the Chief of Military History, Department of the Army, (Washington, 1962). W

Stone, I. *The Hidden History of the Korean War* (New York, 1952). W

Toland, J. *In Mortal Combat: Korea*, 1950-1953 (New York, 1991). W

White, Peter T., *South Korea: What Next?* (National Geographic Sept. 1975) M

Zellers, Larry, *In Enemy Hands, A Prisoner in North Korea* (Lexington, Kentucky 1991) M

Index

Index